r before

Minority Stress and Lesbian Women

Minority Stress and Lesbian Women

Virginia R. Brooks
University of Houston

LexingtonBooks
D.C. Heath and Company
Lexington, Massachusetts
Toronto

Library of Congress Cataloging in Publication Data

Brooks, Virginia R.
  Minority stress and lesbian women.

  Bibliography: p.
  Includes index.
  1. Lesbians—Psychology. 2. Discrimination against women.
3. Lesbianism—United States. 4. Power (Social sciences) I. Title.
HQ75.5.B76   306.7'6   80-8116
ISBN 0-669-03953-5   AACR2

13

6.   219p.
8.   index.

11

Copyright © 1981 by D.C. Heath and Company

Published simultaneously in Canada

Printed in the United States of America

International Standard Book Number: 0-669-03953-5

Library of Congress Catalog Card Number: 80-8116

*To the memory of my father,
Major John S. Brooks (1918-1970), a brave
soldier, an understanding father, a strong
and gentle man.*

Contents

List of Figures

List of Tables

Foreword

The questions asked by Virginia Brooks in the many pages that follow are all serious ones, and they are all important. They are important not only for the specific topic Brooks addresses, minority stress and lesbian women, but also for our understanding of the general phenomenon of stress in our society, the psychological and economic sources of stress, and how stress affects all minorities, including all women. In this cogent, scholarly, and carefully researched book, Brooks has supplied what will likely become a classic text for graduate and advanced undergraduate students. It is also a welcome addition to the material on stress available to the general reader acquainted with the language of the social sciences. And although that language is too often tied to conservative traditions and conservative perceptions of the world (and of the possibilities of the world), Brooks manages to use it to make radical analyses and to pose radical alternatives. I know the task was not a simple one; Brooks deserves our congratulations and our gratitude for her successful effort.

The book consists of three parts and the titles of each immediately and intelligently set a tone for what follows. In the first, Redefining the Problem, Brooks does exactly that. Her choice of words here deserves comment, for in her insistent and persuasive view it is critical to redefine problems—and not to accept what others have defined for us. Reviewing an enormous amount of material on the causes of lesbianism, for example, Brooks plays the role of a skilled surgeon, dissecting theories, discovering and rejecting false assumptions, thoroughly examining data, and creating new ways to understand the behavior complex labeled lesbian.

Chapter 2, The Etiological Question, is nothing less than a solid debunking of the many myths surrounding the causes of homosexuality, whether such myths are rooted in the biological/genetic, psychoanalytic, or social-learning approaches. Brooks uses her own research and the reanalysis of other data to support her argument that important factors in lesbianism are ". . . the power differential between men and women as well as the rejection of conventional female sex roles." Other theories of individual deficiency or pathology pale compared with her view.

Sex Roles, Androgyny, and Mental Health, chapter 3, all but indicts the mental-health profession for its attitudes toward and treatment of lesbian women and of all women. Calmly, rationally, and with precision, Brooks demonstrates that the description of the "mentally healthy female is incongruous with the description of a mentally healthy adult." She asks the essential question: What are the psychological costs of conformity associated with the traditional female role? She amasses data from a variety of sources and reports findings on the characteristics of married women as follows:

High femininity is associated with high anxiety and poor psychological adjustment.

Married women have higher rates of mental illness than single women.

Married women suffer greater stress than married men.

Happily married women are docile, indecisive, cautious.

Married women are more passive, more phobic, more depressed, and more neurotic and have more mental impairment than single women.

Housewives have higher attempted and completed suicide rates than any other occupational category.

In short, Brooks convinces the reader that being born female has considerable risks and that accepting a traditional female role in a society that does not value that role is decidedly dangerous to women's mental health. (One wonders why the Surgeon General has not apprised U.S. women of this fact.) The comparative mental-health data for nontraditional females are encouraging; we can take some heart in the findings that the benefits of autonomy, self-identity, and self-esteem can compensate for the stresses experienced by androgynous women in a sexist society.

Although Brooks's conclusions in previous chapters are in some ways revolutionary, the most radical chapters, to my mind, are Stratification and Exclusion (chapter 4), which fittingly ends part I, and The Theory of Minority Stress (chapter 5). In these chapters Brooks openly challenges psychoanalytic theory on its "double standard of mental health for women and men" and on its declaration of lesbian women and homosexual men as "pathological." She argues that psychoanalytic theory thus provides an accounting system that leads all too easily to the possibilities for prejudice, exclusion, and downright oppression. In a parallel way, she argues that sociological theories, in labeling nonconforming groups as "deviant subcultures," have provided another accounting system that leads to victimization. Brooks continually reminds us that the "defining of deviance is a prerogative of power" and that "the lexicon of human groups is not a benign classificatory system but *an instrument of communication and control*." She asserts clearly that the problems are problems of the system, not of the individual. In the remainder of the book, Brooks builds progressively and thoughtfully toward a new model of stress and stress management, using an impressive, comprehensive bibliography that is itself a wonder.

Finally, then, *Minority Stress and Lesbian Women* is the work of a talented scholar and writer who has dedicated her enormous energies and skills to a topic long deserving of serious attention. She has done so not only with the objective tools of her trade but with a sincere commitment to equality and human justice. Quietly and judiciously, this book asks us to join together toward the achievement of those goals.

Frances T. Farenthold

Preface

Much like Saint-Exupery's Little Prince, I am not able to let go of a question
once I have asked it. My questions about the role and status of lesbian women
in our society began to form soon after I entered the School of Social Welfare
at the University of California (Berkeley) in 1972. Now, nearly a decade later,
this book reflects the results of pursuing those questions.

During that time, as my own feminist consciousness grew—a process
that I now believe to be unending—I took heart from learning more about
women who had succeeded in leaving an indelible imprint on our culture
and its way of thinking, and I came to have an enormous respect for today's
academic feminists who are truly the vanguard of the revolt against sexism.
Academic work is often tedious and laborious and requires excessive isolation. When the work is done, there is no assurance that it will ever be read.

Fortunately for me, the hard-working professional staff at Lexington
Books took care of the latter problem, and I am very grateful to them for
publishing this work as I wrote it. I am hoping that some compensation for
the long periods of isolation will follow the book's publication through opportunities to meet with various groups regarding some of the book's topics
and through organizational activity that leads to a revitalization of one's
energies.

There are few people to thank for contributing to the actual work this
project has required, because I did it all myself. That is, there is no patient
and loyal spouse or secretary to thank for letting me exploit him or her. I
had only myself to exploit. Nonetheless, as the reader will discover, coping
abilities often have their roots in the past. It has always seemed unjust that
military wives and their children are not awarded Bronze Stars and Purple
Hearts for living a life of constant change. My mother, an iron woman, provided a wondrous model of feminine strength through our twenty moves,
and she successfully ingrained in her daughters an imperial can-do approach
to life, for which I am eternally grateful.

I was fortunate to find this kind of strength and discipline once again
when I began work on this book at Berkeley. I would like to express my
gratitude to Eileen Gambrill for her expert guidance, her dedication to em-
piricism, and her unwillingness to settle for less than my best. Her high standards will continue to influence my own aspirations.

Finally, my sincere gratitude to the women who took the time to
thoughtfully respond to a lengthy questionnaire, several of whom were
especially helpful in achieving the widespread distribution that makes this
study unique. One in particular deserves special recognition for being
everything that is meant by sisterhood, for her love and caring are extended
to everyone who is in need. Thank you, Pal, for being my friend.

Part I
Redefining the Problem

1 Introduction

Theories that purport to explain human behavior tend to reflect a particular culture in a given period. In historical perspective, theories which gain currency in a society at a given time generally reflect the social organization of that society and support the prevailing ideology underpinning the institutions of that society.

The lack of definitive and absolute laws in human behavior is clearly evidenced in fluctuating perspectives on "mental illness," "deviance," and sex roles across time and culture. For example, during periods when religious institutions have dominated various societies, demonic possession was the common explanation of most forms of mental dysfunction. Supernatural causes required supernatural cures, such as exorcism or more drastic measures. In the Colonial United States, for instance, the "possessed" were accused of witchcraft, and the stake or the gallows were common methods of "treatment." Thus, the ascribed causes of dysfunction in any age have also determined the methods of "cure."

Cultural variations in ascriptions of "deviance" to various patterns of sexual activity further underscore the lability of theories of human behavior. For example, in a study of seventy-six societies it was found that 64 percent considered homosexuality an acceptable means of sexual expression (Ford and Beach 1951). Similarly, cultural variations in sex-role prescriptions were illuminated in Mead's (1963) classic work describing three New Guinea tribes. Among the Tchambuli, for instance, Mead found that the accepted sex roles were the reverse of our cultural types.

Historical perspective or cultural comparison should enable social scientists to revise ill-founded theories of human behavior, such as those which categorize appropriate adult behavior by sex, and to discard ascriptions of "psychopathology" and "deviance" which are shown to be erroneous. However, theories that provide the rationale for restricting social and economic resources to specified groups seem impervious to standard forms of knowledge revision. One's perspective on these issues could be expected to vary according to one's claim on or access to social and economic resources. Resistance to social change, then, is seen as contingent on one's investment in the status quo.

Maintenance of the status quo nonetheless requires a supportive and credible ideology. The currently prevailing ideology finds its justification for social and economic discrimination in the "individual deficiency"

3

model. In this view, dysfunction results from some defect in the individual, and remedies are sought through individual adjustment. The formula for action for proponents of this view, which Ryan (1971) has termed *blaming the victim*, is: First, identify a social problem. Second, study those affected by the problem and discover in what ways they differ from others. Third, define the differences as the cause of the social problem itself. Fourth, change the individual.

A counterideology is the "institutional deficiency" model. This perspective holds that the root causes of social dysfunction lie within the institutional structure itself. It assumes that institutions operate in such a way as to sustain the malignant conditions of social and economic inequality, which in turn precipitate and perpetuate individual dysfunction. Advocates of this view would define environmental constraints as a political problem, and interventions would focus on changing institutions. The formula for action, then, is: First, identify a political problem and determine how institutions perpetuate that problem. Second, define the institutional changes that would be necessary to correct the problem. Third, design a strategy to effect institutional change.

The impetus required to effect institutional change must also derive from a specific cultural and temporal context. The reemergence of feminism and the development of the gay-rights movement in the 1970s followed three important trends toward social change that rose to prominence in the 1960s: the ecological revolution, the human-rights revolution, and the sexual revolution. All three may be viewed as changes in human consciousness toward aspects of human relationships, both to each other and to the environment.

The ecological revolution may be described as a response to greater public awareness of the crisis potential of overpopulation, depletion of natural resources, and pollution. Awareness has grown that the earth is a closed system having a finite life-support capacity and that nations are interdependent in seeking ways of meeting these potential crises. This reality requires that people "learn to work cooperatively in smaller expanses of space with persons of many tempos, styles, and values if Spaceship Earth is to survive" (Pearl and Pearl 1971, p. 38). As an example, awareness of the ecological crisis requires a different perspective on alternative lifestyles that do not glorify biological reproduction.

If the ecological revolution is a mandate which states, "We must learn to live together," the human-rights revolution may be considered a mandate which states, "We must live together in greater parity." The human-rights revolution, based on principles of individual freedom and of equality under the law, succeeded in mobilizing groups without these guarantees to take action on their own behalf.

The sexual revolution has resulted in the lifting of taboos against public discussion of human sexuality as well as examination of its complexity and

diversity. This process ideally leads to recognition and abandonment of obsolete myths that have perpetuated discrimination based on sex and
sociosexual orientation. These three important areas of social change provide a climate for the reemergence of feminism and the development of the
gay-rights movement.

The women's movement is examining the cultural constraints and role
prescriptions which limit women's options and opportunities. The gay-rights
movement similarly contests cultural prescriptions for "normative" sexual
behavior and the consequent denial of civil rights to those who do not conform. Both social movements are impacting the lives of lesbian women.
Yet, ironically, the bulk of current literature regarding women's changing
roles or homosexual issues largely ignores the role and status of lesbian
women.

This book attempts to correct this negligence. Although the number of
women in society who would define themselves as lesbian remains an
estimate, this estimate is reportedly at least 10 percent of the adult female
population. My research is based on a sample size (675) that greatly exceeds
that of any prior research on lesbian women and includes a much broader
and more varied representation. Respondents completed a seven-page questionnaire that was distributed to women's centers, women's restaurants,
and women's coffeehouses, as well as to gay centers and lesbian bars in the
San Francisco Bay area, Los Angeles area, and San Diego. This distribution
apparently attracted out-of-state visitors, for about one-third of the returns
came from locations outside California. (The appendixes contain a description of the sample, the methodology, and the questionnaire.)

This book describes the minority condition of lesbian women. One purpose of this analysis is to provide a foundation for promoting change in current social policies and laws which impinge on this minority group. In the
absence of such change, both participation in and contributions to societal
institutions are limited and frequently prohibited for lesbian women.
Clearly, the attainment of social justice in its broadest parameters is the
most important goal for lesbian women, particularly in the context of rising
aspirations of women everywhere to take their rightful place of coleadership
in the cultural institutions that shape and mold the future of civilization.

However, the marks of historical oppression are seldom (if ever)
dissolved by legislation alone. Thus, even if institutional discrimination
were eliminated, negative beliefs and attitudes persist which must be
changed through altered patterns of social interaction and new information.
The processes of restructuring perceptions of lesbianism must occur in both
majority (heterosexual/male) groups and in minority (lesbian/female)
groups since culturally pervasive stereotypes affect all sectors of society. Interactional patterns based on categorically ascribed statuses perpetuate
social stress for minority-group members, but most often these surfeit
stresses are inaccurately perceived or inadequately attended by the helping

professions who largely represent majority groups. Too often traditional therapeutic practice with lesbian women has focused on the assumed "psychopathology" of their sociosexual orientation rather than on the coping abilities needed by members of stigmatized or stereotyped groups (see Brooks 1981 for further discussion of therapists' biases). Thus, changing the beliefs and attitudes of those who offer psychotherapy is as important a goal in the amelioration of minority stress as is the elimination of other forms of institutional discrimination.

Individuals belonging to groups to which inferiority is categorically ascribed and which therefore experience reduced social status typically progress through four stages in reference to majority stereotypes and cultural constraints. The first, *redefinition of self*, becomes the first step for those who have internalized negative cultural stereotypes and faulty premises. This reorganization of self-concept permits the integration of new or changed behaviors and attitudes in social interaction, which can lead to enhanced social relatedness. Since self-acceptance generally promotes greater acceptance of others like oneself, a more *positive group identity* is likely to be achieved. Beyond self-redefinition and the achievement of positive group identity, minority members may *collectively mobilize efforts* toward gaining civil rights and equality under law. Considerably more time and effort are necessary to fully attain equality of lifestyle in the broader culture. Nonetheless, the final goal must be achieved for democratic societies to fulfill their promise of *cultural pluralism*.

In this context, the first two stages require new knowledge concerning the cultural mythology that has defined lesbianism. Similarly, better information regarding factors which contribute to positive and negative outcomes of minority stress may enhance the social functioning of lesbian women and maximize their ability to collectively pursue institutional change. Finally, a greater recognition of the common condition of minority groups—that is, exclusion from the benefits of culture as a consequence of social, economic, and political discrimination—may contribute to more concerted efforts of all minorities toward the goals of equality and cultural pluralism.

Overview

Restructuring concepts of lesbianism begins with a critical examination of "causal" theories in chapter 2. Some of the underlying assumptions of "etiological" theories are reassessed in the light of current knowledge, such as the assumption that adult sociosexual orientation is primarily determined by early childhood experience and the assumption of a uniform consistency of what are considered "masculine" and "feminine" characteristics.

Proponents of the various causal theories of lesbianism have generally espoused the view that lesbianism is a negative outcome of the socialization process. Chapter 3, while not arguing the pros or cons of sociosexual preference per se, does review evidence that supports a different view, evidence indicating that nonconformity to female sex-role prescriptions is associated with positive outcomes, and that these outcomes appear to be currently more prevalent among lesbian women than nonlesbian women. This latter finding is related to the high level of androgyny found in lesbian women, who as a group have been more resistant to male reward systems that encourage sex-typed behavior.

Given that typically "explanatory" theories are not substantiated by the evidence and that characteristics found to be prevalent among lesbian women are characteristics generally valued by others, what, then, is the rationale for culturally enforced negative sanctions toward lesbianism? Chapter 4 presents the rationale for defining women as a minority group and lesbian women as occupying two minority statuses. Based on data I obtained, the effects of social and economic stratification on lesbian women are discussed. These findings reveal that, irrespective of high aspirational and educational levels among lesbian women, sexual stratification restricts their economic rewards, and, irrespective of antifamily sentiment that is often attributed to lesbian women, about one-half hold traditional values in spite of the fact that legal sanctions are denied to them.

Chapter 5 examines the theoretical and empirical underpinnings of the concept of minority stress. Problems associated with measurement are considered, particularly in relation to structural stressors such as minority status that are the product of stratification. Chapter 6 explains the stress index utilized in my study and presents its major hypotheses. Also in chapter 6, the variables found to be related to positive and negative outcomes of stress among lesbian women are identified. Chapter 7 discusses the "coping" process and stress-mediating resources. A framework for assessing the impact of stressors on individuals is presented in chapter 5, and chapter 7 contains a systems model for the analysis of minority-stress variables which includes antecedents and a component view of coping resources.

The major stress-mediating resources identified—positive group identity, socioeconomic status, and social disclosure of one's sociosexual orientation—are the focus of chapters 8, 9, and 10, respectively. Faulty assumptions that may underlie identity conflicts and which may obstruct a lesbian woman's sense of self-esteem are examined in chapter 8. Variations in socioeconomic status which also influence self and group perceptions are discussed in chapter 9, and chapter 10 explores the variable of social disclosure as a life decision which has both costs and benefits in relation to minority-stress management.

Terms and Definitions

Necessary to the individual-deficiency model is a labeling system which distinguishes the "different" group from "normative" groups. One way in which this is accomplished is by using the words *homosexual* and *lesbian* as nouns, connoting a classification of individuals, rather than as adjectives (that is, words which modify a noun or pronoun so as to describe a behavioral characteristic). Identifying the total person as *a* lesbian or *a* homosexual appears to distinguish a type of species rather than a behavioral characteristic. Allport (1954) cites Margaret Mead's suggestion that labels of primary potency lose some of their force when they are changed from nouns into adjectives (p. 181) and suggests that this change in designation is particularly important in minority-group references.

Psycholinguistic theory holds that language causes a particular cognitive structure; that is, the way people think is in large part determined by the words they use (Whorf 1956). If it is true that we think as we speak, it follows that the correction of speech habits may be instrumental in revising false concepts. It may be argued that it is redundant to refer to a lesbian woman rather than a lesbian, but cognitively it is important to shift the classification of the individual to *woman* and the descriptive modifier to *lesbian*.

Similarly, linguistic separation of *lesbian women* from *homosexual men* seems necessary to reflect the realities of common use in which *homosexual* refers to men almost exclusively. The inclusion of women under this rubric is usually an afterthought, and assumptions relating to men are simply transposed to women. Results of this habit are factual distortions which serve to perpetuate the subordination of issues unique to lesbian women. Cognitively, then, formerly used designations have served as negative influences on perceptions of individuals identified with these groups and are in need of revision. The term *gay* generally has been used generically to refer to both homosexual men and lesbian women, and it is utilized in this way in this book.

Ultimately, these designations may be considered wholly obsolete, as the question of definition—that is, who is homosexual or heterosexual—seems equally cumbersome and misleading. The seven-point heterosexual-homosexual rating scale developed by Kinsey, Pomeroy, and Martin (1948) and their subsequent research clarified that sociosexual orientation is not the all-or-nothing phenomenon it was generally believed to be. Among the women in the Kinsey group's large sample, 28 percent, or more than one in four, reported same-sex attraction or experience (Kinsey et al. 1953). Among men this figure reached 50 percent (Kinsey, Pomeroy, and Martin 1948). From the other direction, research indicates that typically about three-fourths of the lesbian population have heterosexual histories.

Definition of the relevant population, then, remains arbitrary and must ultimately rely on self-definition.

Sexual behavior has become an overt cultural preoccupation in recent times, displayed both in the trend to oversexualize the human experience and in the trend to retreat to puritanical sexual mores. Lesbian women may be oppressed by either trend, and conflicts may result from the focus on only the sexual component of that identity. Interestingly, I found that sex-role ideology contributes much more importantly to opting out of the male-dominant heterosexual milieu than does heterosexuality per se. To the extent that this finding reflects a preference among lesbian women for a gynocentric (female-centered) social milieu rather than an androcentric (male-centered) one—that is, a milieu in which the effects of sexual stratification are removed—the phrase *sexual orientation* inadequately represents this preference. To include the cultural aspect and to balance the sexual aspect, the term *sociosexual* is employed in this book, with the exception of references to other literature for which the term would be inappropriate.

The problems in defining who is and who is not in one or the other sexual-preference categories have never diminished the enthusiasm of etiological theorists who, largely without the benefit of empirical data or adequate samples, have described "causes" of homosexuality and lesbianism and recommended "cures." These theories are the topic of the next chapter.

References

Allport, G.W. *The Nature of Prejudice*. Reading, Mass.: Addison-Wesley, 1954.

Brooks, V.R. "Sex and sexual orientation as variables in therapists' biases and therapy outcomes." *Clinical Social Work Journal*, 1981.

Ford, C.S. and Beach, F.A. "Homosexual behavior." In C.S. Ford and F.A. Beach, *Patterns of Sexual Behavior*. New York: Harper, 1951.

Kinsey, A.C.; Pomeroy, W.B.; and Martin, C.E. *Sexual Behavior in the Human Male*. Philadelphia: Saunders, 1948.

Kinsey, A.C.; Pomeroy, W.B.; Martin, C.E.; and Gebhard, P.H. *Sexual Behavior in the Humane Female*. Philadelphia: Saunders, 1953.

Mead, M. *Sex and Temperament in Three Primitive Societies*. New York: William Morrow, 1963.

Pearl, A., and Pearl, S. "Toward an ecological theory of value." *Social Policy* 2 (1971):30-38.

Ryan, W. *Blaming the Victim*. New York: Vintage, 1971.

Whorf, B.L. "Linguistic relativity and the relation of linguistic processes to perception and cognition." In *Language, Thought, and Reality*, edited by J. Carroll. Cambridge, Mass.: The M.I.T. Press and John Wiley & Sons, 1956.

2 The Etiological Question

The various factors which have been purported to cause or contribute to homosexuality and lesbianism can be categorized as biophysical, psychological, and sociological. The first group, of course, falls within the "nature" side of the nature-nurture controversy since the biophysical argument points to constitutional, congenital, or inherited traits or tendencies (Ellis 1915; Kallman 1952; Krafft-Ebing 1922). The "nurture" arguments consist of psychological and sociological theories which give precedence to environmental determinants of sexual orientation. These theories subscribe to the basic assumption that adult sexual behavior is largely determined in early childhood. Psychological theories of etiology are largely psychoanalytic in orientation, and sociological theories are founded on premises about early-childhood socialization processes.

The Biological Argument

The six components of biophysical maleness and femaleness are chromosomes, gonads (reproductive glands), fetal hormones, internal sex organs, external sex organs, and hormones at puberty (Money and Ehrhardt 1972).

Chromosomes

In the mechanism of inheritance, the human race has twenty-three pairs of chromosomes. Only one pair carries genes that determine characteristics in which men and women differ. The other twenty-two pairs determine non-sex-related characteristics. If the ovum is fertilized by a sperm bearing a Y chromosome, the resulting infant has one X and one Y chromosome (XY) in each pair and is chromosomally male. If the ovum is fertilized by an X-bearing sperm, the resulting infant has two X chromosomes (XX) in each pair and is chromosomally female.

Until recently, these two chromosome combinations, XX and XY, were believed to be the only possible outcomes of human fertilization. Thanks to the discovery of new chromosome-visualization techniques in 1956, it is now known that some female infants are born with three X chromosomes (XXX), other females are born with an X chromosome missing (XO), some male infants are born with one or two extra X chromosomes (XXY or XXXY), and some males are born with an extra Y chromosome (XYY). Rare cases of XXXXY and XXYY have also been reported, and some individuals are "mosaics," so that some cells in their bodies are, for example, XY while others are XXXY (Brecher 1969).

There appears to be, then, an enormous diversity of chromosomal "sexes." The range of biophysical diversity increases when we look at further components of human sexuality.

Gonads

All human embryos look alike for the first six weeks, including the sex glands, and all look female. In about the seventh week, if two X chromosomes are present, the rind of the gonad begins to develop, and the gonad matures as an ovary. In the absence of two X chromosomes, the core develops instead, and the gonad matures as a testis.

Fetal Hormones

During the second or third month of gestation, androgens from the male fetus's own testes masculinize the rest of the fetal body. At this stage, the testes of a male fetus may not secrete sufficient androgens, or the fetus may be insensitive to them and fail to masculinize. Also, androgen may get into the bloodstream of a female fetus, through the umbilical cord or in some other way, and masculinize the female fetus.

Internal Sex Organs

Every human fetus is partially hermaphroditic during one stage in its development, possessing the rudiments of two separate systems of internal sex organs, the male or Wolffian system and the female or Mullerian system. When fetal androgens are present, the Wolffian system develops and the Mullerian system withers away, so that the infant is born with a prostate gland, seminal vesicles, and other male internal sex accessories. Without the presence of fetal androgens, the Mullerian system develops and the Wolffian system withers away: the infant is born with a uterus, a cervix, Fallopian tubes, and other female internal sex accessories.

External Sex Organs

External organ development is the basis of sex assignment at birth. However, ambiguities do occur in the development of external genitalia, and until the recent development of new diagnostic techniques, sex assignment in these cases was highly arbitrary.

Hormones at Puberty

The pubertal effects of ovaries beginning to secrete estrogens and of testes secreting androgens are well known. This stage of development contains its potential ambiguities as well: the boy at puberty may be feminized by estrogens, or the girl may be masculinized by androgens.

The common assumption, then, that there are only two clearly dichotomized sexes seems in need of some revision to accommodate the range of potential diversity in the six biophysical components of human sexuality.

Hormonal Variance and Sexual Orientation

The belief that homosexual men and lesbian women differ from heterosexual men and women, respectively, in the levels of various hormones still has considerable currency in medical research. Even when differences are found (for example, Gartrell, Loriaux, and Chase 1977; Loraine et al. 1971), the question of whether the difference can be considered a predisposing factor in becoming lesbian or homosexual or whether the difference is a result of homosexual or lesbian activity is not answered.

Research *has* shown that androgen determines the intensity but not the direction of the sex drive for both sexes (Ford and Beach 1951). For example, attempts to "cure" homosexual men by administering male hormones did not change the direction of their sex drive, but merely increased it (Gould 1974). Research has also indicated that androgen-excess women have not chosen lesbianism in any greater proportion than those in the general population (Money and Ehrhardt 1972).

Summary of the Evidence

Money's research group originally sought to discover whether sexual variance could be accounted for at one of the anatomic or physiological levels of sexual development. In the process, they found that homosexual, bisexual, and heterosexual men and women do not differ in the six biophysical components of human sexuality. The studies of Money, Hampson, and Hampson (1955) and of Stoller (1968) have produced evidence that, irrespective of the maleness or femaleness of chromosomes, gonads, or hormones, these factors are very unreliable indicators of a person's gender identity—that is, one's awareness of being a boy or girl, man or woman; by contrast, assigned sex and rearing are highly reliable indicators.[1]

The most lucid statement "explaining" the homosexual response as a biophysical alternative is found in Kinsey et al. (1953). It bears quoting in full (Kinsey et al. 1953, pp. 446-447):

> The classification of sexual behavior as masturbatory, heterosexual, or homosexual is based upon the nature of the stimulus which initiates the behavior. . . . It cannot be too frequently emphasized that the behavior of any animal must depend upon the nature of stimulus which it meets . . . and its background of previous experience. Unless it has been conditioned by previous experience, an animal should respond identically to identical stimuli, whether they emanate from some part of its own body, from another individual of the same sex, or from an individual of the opposite sex. The classification of sexual behavior as masturbatory, heterosexual, or homosexual is, therefore, unfortunate if it suggests that only different types of persons seek out or accept each kind of sexual activity. There is nothing known in the anatomy or physiology of sexual response and orgasm which distinguishes masturbatory, heterosexual, or homosexual reactions. The terms are of value only because they describe the source of the sexual stimulation, and they should not be taken as descriptions of the individuals who respond to the various stimuli. It would clarify our thinking if the terms could be dropped completely out of our vocabulary, for then sociosexual behavior could be described as activity between a female and a male, or between two females, or between two males, and this would constitute a more objective record of the fact. For the present, however, we shall have to use the term homosexual in something of its standard meaning, except that we shall use it primarily to describe sexual relationships, and shall prefer not to use it to describe the individuals who were involved in those relationships. The inherent physiological capacity of an animal to respond to any sufficient stimulus seems, then, the basic explanation of the fact that some individuals respond to stimuli originating in other individuals of their own sex—and it appears to indicate that every individual could so respond if the opportunity offered and one were not conditioned against making such responses.

The conclusions of Kinsey and his associates focus on the physiological capacity of animals to respond sexually to any sufficient stimulus prior to experiential conditioning. Yet, it is widely believed that there is an inherent property of maleness or femaleness in animals which predisposes opposite-sex attraction. In fact, homosexuality has been found to occur in every type of animal that has been extensively studied, and in the vertebrates it increases as one ascends the taxonomic tree toward the mammal (Denniston 1965).

Thus, determinants of sexual orientation have not been explained by biophysical factors. In sum, the following evidence negates this argument: (1) Homosexuality occurs in every type of animal that has been extensively studied (Denniston 1965). (2) All animals have the inherent capacity to respond to any sufficient stimulus if they have not been conditioned against making such responses (Kinsey et al. 1953). (3) Sex hormones determine the intensity but not the direction of the sex drive (Ford and Beach 1951). (4) Of the six factors contributing to biophysical maleness or femaleness, none has been found to be related to homosexuality (Money, Hampson, and Hampson 1955; Stoller 1968).

Whereas the biophysical theories relate to both male homosexuality and lesbianism, the environmental theories to be considered here refer specifically to lesbianism, although environmental theories about male homosexuality and lesbianism are typically mirror images of each other. Prior to consideration of these specific theories and research findings, important methodological issues pertaining to the research itself are examined.

Methodological Considerations

The majority of studies of lesbian women share deficiencies of methodology which range from overgeneralization of findings from small and skewed samples to overt bias in the pursuit and interpretation of data (Brown 1975). This bias is most evident in studies whose theoretical formulations of female personality are based on psychoanalytic concepts and which utilize case reports of psychiatric patients as their source of data. Such studies generally share an etiological preoccupation and a belief in early-childhood determinacy of adult behavior. They are prescriptive rather than descriptive, emphasizing "normative" sexual behavior and "appropriate" sex-role behaviors.

Other deficiencies are common to most studies, including those without overt bias. These concern source of sample and sample size, disparity of control groups, and definitions of lesbian populations. Most studies of lesbian women that did not use psychiatric patients as the source of their samples employed members of homophile organizations such as the Daughters of Bilitis in the United States and the Minorities Research Group in England. Members of these organizations may, in fact, be representative of the lesbian population in general, but the nonrandomness of selection leaves the question of representation in doubt. In regard to sample size, it may be seen from table 2-1 that only two studies have had a sample size exceeding 100 (Gundlach and Riess 1968; Kenyon 1968a, 1968b), and these two samples consisted of members of homophile organizations.

In many studies, control groups were not matched according to important variables which may have affected results. For example, many compared the psychological adjustment of married housewives to that of lesbian women who are, by and large, "single" career women. In general, these studies reported better psychological adjustment among lesbian than among

Table 2-1
Summary of Empirical Studies of Lesbian Women: Sample Size and Source, 1957-1975

Study	Lesbian Sample Size	Source
Armon (1960)	30	Homophile organizations
Bene (1965)	37	Homophile organization
Brown (1975)	86	Volunteers responding to an open letter sent to lesbian organizations and periodicals
Freedman (1967)	62	Homophile organization
Gundlach and Riess (1968)	226	Homophile organization
Hedblom (1972)	65	70% friendship pyramids; 30% bars
Hopkins (1969)	24	Homophile organization
Kaye et al. (1967)	24	Psychiatric patients
Kenyon (1968a, 1968b)	123	Homophile organization
Liddicoat (1957)	50	Not institutionalized, not seeking psychotherapy
Oberstone (1974)	25	Friendship pyramids
Poole (1972)	50	Los Angeles bars
Raphael (1974)	41	Rap-group participants
Saghir and Robins (1969); Saghir et al. (1970)	57	60% homophile organization; 30% "word of mouth"; 10% bars
Siegelman (1972)	84	55% homophile organization; 45% bookstore
Swanson et al. (1972)	40	Psychiatric patients
Thompson, McCandless, and Strickland (1971)	84	"Network of friends"
Wilson and Greene (1971)	46	Obtained through a homosexual friend

Empirical studies other than those listed here published in the same period and located by the author either concerned adolescents (for example, Kremer and Rifkin 1969) or were focused on the social and/or sexual aspects of lesbianism rather than on etiological issues or psychological adjustment (for example, Chafetz 1974).

heterosexual women (Freedman 1967; Hopkins 1969, Siegelman 1972; Thompson, McCandless, and Strickland 1971; Wilson and Greene 1971). However, these differences may reflect factors associated with economic dependence and independence more than factors associated with sexual orientation per se. Given that the majority of married women are to some degree economically dependent on their husbands, economic dependency may be the primary variable in results showing that married women have poorer psychological adjustment than single women (Bem 1972; Cannon and Redick 1973; Farberow and Schneidman 1965; Gove 1972; Gurin, Veroff, and Feld 1960; Johnson and Terman 1935; Knupfer, Clark, and Room 1966; U.S. Department of Health, Education, and Welfare 1970).

Finally, very few studies have attempted to assess the balance between heterosexual and lesbian aspects of an individual's history, for example, by utilizing the heterosexual-homosexual rating scale (Kinsey, Pomeroy, and Martin 1948) which subsequently will be referred to as the Kinsey scale. Without such assessment, the classification of subjects as heterosexual or lesbian for comparative purposes is somewhat arbitrary. Heterosexuality was frequently assumed if subjects were married; lesbianism was assumed if a subject reported any lesbian behavior. This type of classification coupled with small sample sizes, as in Bene's (1965) study, could affect outcomes reported on such samples.

A study that illustrates many of these methodological deficiencies, by Kaye et al. (1967), was based on reports from psychoanalysts concerning twenty-four psychiatric patients considered to be lesbian. At the onset of treatment 53 percent of the sample were bisexual, and 70 percent were having heterosexual experiences at the time the analysts completed the questionnaires. Nonetheless, the authors concluded that "homosexuality in women, rather than being a conscious volitional preference, is a massive adaptational response to a crippling inhibition of normal heterosexual development" (p. 633) and that "50% of them can be significantly helped by psychoanalytic treatment" (p. 633). The following review and analysis of the literature pertaining to lesbian women attempt to assess the findings of these studies apart from their unwarranted and overgeneralized conclusions.

The Psychoanalytic Argument

Psychoanalytic formulations that have been advanced as causes of lesbianism tend to cluster around two themes: negative parental relations in childhood and heterosexual aversion. Theories relating to the first theme emphasize the early family environment, generally indicting a defective or deficient parent or parents and resulting "arrested" development. Theories relating to the second theme elaborate the basic Freudian premise that lesbianism is based on an irrational fear of the opposite sex.

Theories relating to the theme of negative parental relations and some of their proponents are mother fixation, or hatred, rejection, or fear of the father (Bergler 1951; Caprio 1954; Deutsch 1944; Fenichel 1945; Freud 1933; Socarides 1963); father fixation, or hatred, rejection, or fear of the mother (Bergler 1943; Wilbur 1965); continuation of a childhood "bisexual" phase, or fixation at or regression to an early stage of psychosexual development (Deutsch 1944; Freud 1933; London and Caprio 1950; Socarides 1963); defense against or flight from incestuous desires (Farnham 1951); and penis envy and castration complex (Deutsch 1944; Fenichel 1945; Freud 1950; Wilbur 1965).

Numerous authors (Brown 1973; Firestone 1970; Friedan 1963; Greer 1972; Millett 1970; Sherfey 1966; Weisstein 1971) have offered succinct analyses and criticisms of Freud's basic contentions regarding female sexuality, several of which relate to lesbianism ("penis envy," "vaginal orgasm," "masculinity complex"). My task here is to review the empirical testing of these contentions in relation to lesbianism.

The first two theories—fixation, hatred, rejection, or fear of the mother or father—imply that disturbed parent-child relations are causative factors in lesbianism. In comparing the mother-daughter relations of lesbian and nonlesbian women, no significant differences were found (Armon 1960; Bene 1965; Kaye et al. 1967). In comparing father-daughter relations, results were contradictory. Two studies found no evidence of disturbed father-daughter relations in lesbian women (Armon 1960; Kremer and Rifkin 1969); one reported a relation between lesbianism and a weak, incompetent father (Bene 1965), and another reported a relation between lesbianism and a close-binding, intimate father (Kaye et al. 1967).

The Kenyon study (1968b) found poorer relations between lesbian women and both parents than in the nonlesbian group. Of these two groups, however, the lesbian sample's previous psychiatric history was three times greater than that of the nonlesbian sample. Swanson et al. (1972), on the basis of a comparative study of lesbian and nonlesbian outpatients in a psychiatric clinic, concluded that disturbed parental relations were a factor relating to psychiatric disorder in general, not specifically to lesbianism.

Of the three remaining theories in this group (adolescent regression, flight from incest, "penis envy"), no differences were found between lesbian and nonlesbian subjects (Armon 1960; Kaye et al. 1967). Thus the psychoanalytic contention that lesbianism is associated with negative family relations is not substantiated by the evidence.

The second group of psychoanalytic theories attributes lesbianism to irrational fear of or aversion to the opposite sex. These theories and some of their proponents are fear of pregnancy or venereal disease (Cory 1964; Rado 1933), heterosexual trauma or disappointment (Ellis 1915; Socarides 1963), satiation with males (Krafft-Ebing 1922), society's heterosexual taboos (Henry 1941), seeing parents in coitus (Farnham 1951), seduction by older females (Ellis 1915; Wilbur 1965), and masturbation (Ellis 1915; Krafft-Ebing 1922).

The first causal theory in this group, fear of pregnancy or venereal disease, would seem to imply that nonlesbian women would be enthusiastic about pregnancy and venereal disease. It seems reasonable to assume, given the present availability of birth-control methods and legal abortions, that concern over the possibility of pregnancy would at least not "cause" a sociosexual orientation toward women.

A logical case could be made for fear of venereal disease if one believes that people in general consider the possibility of venereal disease before engaging in sexual relations. This is unlikely in view of the fact that venereal disease has assumed epidemic proportions across the country. For example, syphillis rates have more than tripled for males and more than doubled for females in the past twenty years, and male rates continue to be nearly three times higher than female rates (U.S. Department of Health, Education, and Welfare 1976).

A causative theory of this genre could be more realistically proposed in reference to gynecological difficulties and cancer. In regard to the first, Kenyon (1968a), with a sample of 123 lesbian women and a control group of 123 married women, found that the lesbian women had had fewer gynecological operations and significantly less premenstrual tension. In regard to the latter, experiments have confirmed the possibility that sperm can trigger cervical cancer by invading the nonsexual (somatic) cells of the cervix (Nelson 1975).

The second causal theory in this group is referred to as "heterosexual trauma or disappointment." In reference to heterosexual trauma, Swanson et al. (1972), with a U.S. sample of forty lesbian women and forty nonlesbian women, found that prior to 16 years of age, six of the lesbian women and four of the nonlesbian women were seduced or raped by adult males (uncle, three; father, two; stepfather, two; stranger, two; and family friend, one). Thus one-seventh and one-tenth of both groups, respectively, may be said to have experienced heterosexual trauma at an early age, but the difference between the two groups was not significant.

There could be various interpretations of the meaning of *heterosexual disappointment*, but if the term is taken literally to indicate sexual disappointment, two studies provide data on this question. Gundlach and Riess (1968), with a sample of 226 lesbian women and 234 nonlesbian women, report in a table captioned "You Can't Say the Girls Don't Try" that although 75 percent of the lesbian sample had had intercourse with a male, 42 percent of these women did not experience orgasm. In the control group, 94 percent had had intercourse with a male, and only 9 percent reported not having orgasm. In the second study, Saghir and Robins (1969), with a sample of 56 lesbian and 43 nonlesbian women, report that 79 percent of the lesbian sample had had intercourse with a male and 62 percent of them did not experience orgasm. No comparative data on the control group were reported.

While this evidence would appear to support the causal theory of "heterosexual disappointment," the psychoanalytic implication is that such a response is based on irrational fear of or aversion to the opposite sex. The notion of irrational fear could at best be applied to the 21 to 25 percent of these samples who had not experienced heterosexual intercourse, and would not suffice as a causal explanation. The notion of aversion, detached from the psychoanalytic inference of irrationality, cannot be totally discounted, although extinction of heterosexual behavior through lack of reinforcement would appear to describe the phenomenon more accurately. Further, the underlying assumption of the causal theory of "heterosexual disappointment" implies the superiority of female partners; that is, disappointment with a male partner drives the female to a female partner, whereupon she establishes a commitment to lesbian partners. This assumption is reminiscent of the white male's fear of or covert belief in the sexual superiority of the black male, and it is suggested that the historical treatment of black men and lesbian women in this society has not been unrelated to these beliefs.

The third causal theory, sexual satiation, seems intrinsically illogical in the face of current knowledge in respect to female sexuality. For instance, in confirming the multiple-orgasmic potential of women, Masters and Johnson (1961, p. 792) reported:

> If a female who is capable of having regular orgasms is properly stimulated within a short period after her first climax, she will in most instances be capable of having a second, third, fourth, and even a fifth and sixth orgasm before she is fully satiated. As contrasted with the male's usual inability to have more than one orgasm in a short period, many females, especially when clitorally stimulated, can regularly have five or six full orgasms within a matter of minutes.

Further, according to Sherfey (1966, p. 112)

> . . . the more orgasms a woman has, the stronger they become; the more orgasms she has, the more she *can* have. To all intents and purposes, the human female is sexually insatiable in the presence of the highest degrees of sexual stimulation.

If one is in search of a causal theory, then, the evidence suggests that lack of fulfillment is a more plausible one.

A factor which apparently contributes to the probability of lack of fulfillment has a physical basis. During heterosexual intercourse, the penis holds the vaginal walls apart, which decreases the intensity of vaginal contractions and thus decreases the intensity of the female orgasm. "The orgasm that occurs without the penis inside feels more distinct on a physical basis because it is physically more intense" (Kline-Graber and Graber 1975, p. 6; see also Masters and Johnson 1966, p. 133).

A fourth causal theory, society's heterosexual taboos (for example, against intercourse or pregnancy outside of wedlock), seems reasonable in reference to exclusive lesbianism if at the same time it is acknowledged that society's taboos against lesbianism are a causal factor in exclusive heterosexuality. Since previous studies have found that heterosexual experience among lesbian women has ranged from 62 (Daughters of Bilitis 1959) to 79 percent (Saghir and Robins 1969), the Gundlach and Riess (1968) conclusion that "the lesbian population has not had any universally strong prohibitions toward heterosexuality" seems valid. Moreover, it is increasingly difficult to locate heterosexual taboos in contemporary society, while taboos against lesbianism remain virulent.

The fifth causal theory, which contends that seeing parents in coitus results in lesbianism, inherently makes a judgment about the aesthetics of heterosexual intercourse.

The sixth causal theory, seduction by older females, hints at the lesbian-as-superior-partner theme again while at the same time invoking a predatory image. One could as reasonably wonder suspiciously if young women are seduced into heterosexuality by older males. Studies investigating this hypothesis have, nonetheless, found no evidence of youthful seduction (Kaye et al. 1967; Liddicoat 1957; Saghir and Robins 1969; Swanson et al. 1972).

The seventh and final causal theory in this group indicts masturbation as leading to lesbianism. It is not surprising that this factor was proposed no more recently than 1922, since we learned from Kinsey and his associates (1953, pp. 142-143) that 58 percent of his white female sample of 5,940 had reached orgasm through masturbation at some time in their lives. With the additional knowledge provided by subsequent sexologists such as Masters and Johnson, not only have the taboos against masturbation been lifted for many people, but also instructional materials and courses are offered to assist individuals who wish to better develop this means of sexual outlet. Since it does not appear that 58 percent or more of the female population are oriented toward their own sex, masturbation is apparently not the "cause" of lesbianism.

Kaye et al. (1967) found no significant differences in the masturbatory histories of lesbian and nonlesbian women; Kenyon (1968b) found that significantly more lesbian than nonlesbian women "admitted" to masturbation. However, lesbian women have been found to be more candid about themselves than nonlesbian women, as measured by the Eysenck and Eysenck (1963) personality inventory and the Crowne and Marlowe (1960) social desirability scale by Freedman (1967) and Siegelman (1972), respectively.

This group of theories, then, emphasizes an aversion to or avoidance of heterosexuality rather than a positive attraction to members of one's own sex. One or more of these factors could probably be found in the histories (herstories?) of all women, which tends to negate their explanatory value. In sum, psychoanalytic theories about the etiology of lesbianism, both those relating to negative family relations and those relating to heterosexual aversion, have not been supported by the evidence.

The Socialization Argument

In contrast to psychoanalytic theories, which regard sexual variance as a manifestation of underlying pathology, the socialization perspective views sexual behaviors that depart from accepted social norms as learned ways of coping with environmental and self-imposed demands (Bandura 1969). Homosexual or lesbian behavior per se is regarded as the result of unusual reinforcement and/or modeling influences that served to promote and maintain sexual-response patterns to culturally inappropriate sexual stimuli (Greenstein 1966; Poole 1972; Simon and Gagnon 1967). Specifically, it is believed that "sex-inappropriate" behaviors have been rewarded by socializing agents and/or that cross-sex modeling has occurred (Bandura 1969).

If differences do exist in the childhood socialization patterns of heterosexual and lesbian women, it would be worthwhile to investigate what factors are operative in the development of these patterns. Pursuing answers to this speculation requires an overview of childhood socialization theories and, in particular, of sex-role development theories and related research.

Sex-Role Development: An Overview

Socialization refers to patterns of antecedent variables which shape behavior and tie it to the social system in which an individual lives (Hess 1970). It assumes a relevant reference group whose norms are to be transmitted to the new member through an agent or agents acting for the group. Although the term *socialization* is most frequently used to refer to learning in children, the process it describes continues in various contexts throughout the life of the individual in a complex society (Hess 1970).

The term *sex role* is used to indicate learned responses to the socially or culturally defined expectations of being either male or female (Chafetz 1974). Since role definitions are subject to change over time and situations, sex-role socialization may be continuous from birth on.

There are varying theories of how sex-role development occurs. The major theoretical dichotomy is essentially a nature-nurture debate, or cognitive-developmental versus social-learning argument. The cognitive-developmental or self-socialization argument is that sex-role development occurs from inevitable maturational components of the biological process and that one's cognitive capacities are more crucial to sex-role attitudes than parental attitudes (Kohlberg 1966). The social-learning argument takes the reverse position—that environmental factors are more critical in sex-role development than biological factors and that sex-differentiated behaviors are learned through modeling and reinforcement in early childhood (Hartley 1964; Lynn 1959; Mischel 1970; Sears 1965). Social-learning theorists differ primarily in emphasis: some ascribe primacy to modeling influences; and others, to reinforcement.

In their monumental work on the psychology of sex differences, Maccoby and Jacklin (1974) survey and analyze the empirical evidence relating to postulated influences on sex-role development, which they classify into three main categories: modeling, reinforcement, and self-socialization. According to Maccoby and Jacklin, these three theories in brief are as follows: (1) modeling: children choose same-sex models (particularly the same-sex parent) and use these models more than opposite-sex models for patterning their own behavior; (2) reinforcement: through praise or discouragement, children receive positive reinforcement for what is considered sex-appropriate behavior and negative reinforcement for what is considered sex-inappropriate behavior; and (3) self-socialization: children first develop a concept of what it is to be male or female and then, once they have a clear understanding of their own gender identity, attempt to fit their behavior to their concept of what behavior is sex-appropriate. That is, once the child has achieved a fairly stable self-concept (including a stable gender identity), he or she will select models accordingly, and socialization will become a more and more autonomous process.

Maccoby and Jacklin (1974) have provided a systematic analysis and interpretation of research findings in relation to these three major theories. Their analysis shows that modeling plays a minor role in the development of sex-role behavior. The findings indicate that children do not choose with any consistency a same-sex model more than a cross-sex model. Further, same-sex parent-child similarities have not been demonstrated on any of the dimensions measured. In general, Maccoby and Jacklin suggest that modeling is crucial in the acquisition of a wide repertoire of potential behaviors, but that this repertoire is not sex-role restrictive to any important degree.

Their survey of the data concerning differential reinforcement reveals a remarkable degree of similarity in the socialization of the two sexes. That is, existing evidence has not revealed any consistent process of "shaping" behaviors that are normally part of sex stereotypes. For example, no consistent differences were found in the social shaping of boys and girls in relation to aggression, achievement motivation, sexual exploration, independence and dependence, or maternal interaction (Maccoby and Jacklin 1974). The evidence did indicate, however, that both mothers and fathers more strongly discourage "sex-inappropriate" activities in sons than in daughters (Fling and Manosevitz 1972; Lansky 1967) and that "sex-appropriate" activities for girls are less clearly defined and less firmly enforced (Maccoby and Jacklin 1974). In turn, this difference was accounted for in part by the differential status ascribed to "masculine" and "feminine" interests. Although these findings indicate some differential reinforcement of sex-typed behaviors between boys and girls, they do not appear to be as inclusive as had been generally believed.

Maccoby and Jacklin (1974, p. 366) conclude that modeling and reinforcement are necessary but insufficient to account for the acquisition of sex-typed behavior and argue that the explanation lies in the interaction of these two processes with cognitive-developmental processes:

> A child's sex-role concepts are limited in the same way the rest of his concepts are, by the level of cognitive skills he has developed. . . . Consequently, his actions in adopting sex-typed behavior, and in treating others according to sex-role stereotypes, also change in ways that parallel his conceptual growth.

Fallacies in Socialization Theories

Socialization theories which have viewed lesbianism as a result of cross-sex modeling or differential reinforcement of cross-sex behaviors in early childhood are dependent on two fallacious assumptions: (1) there is consistency in what are considered to be appropriate "masculine" and "feminine" characteristics or behaviors, and (2) adult social behavior is primarily determined by early-childhood socialization (Becker 1964; Brim 1966; Inkeles 1969; Kirsh 1974; Neugarten 1968). The first assumption allows for "sex-appropriate" behavioral prescriptions which are assumed to be equally applicable to all groups and social conditions in our society. It is worthwhile to examine the limitations this view has imposed on sex-role research.

The assumed consistency of "masculine" and "feminine" characteristics or behaviors affects the way in which they are measured. Sex-role inventories generally have treated masculinity and femininity as two ends of a single continuum, as if they were inversely correlated (Bem 1972). Thus, people who do not fit one category or the other may be systematically ignored. For example, in a study of the relation between the child's sex role and the sex of the dominant parent (Hetherington 1965), fully one-third of the families were discarded because neither parent was found to dominate the other; they were too equalitarian (Bem 1972).

The notion of uniform sex-appropriate behaviors has also resulted in in-attention to variables which may supersede in importance those typically studied. For instance, the status differential between male and female roles and its effect on "appropriate" sex-role acquisition have been largely neglected. As Ovesey (1956, p. 341) observed:

> The polarities of masculinity and femininity are identified respectively with positive and negative value judgments. Masculinity represents strength, dominance, superiority; femininity represents weakness, submissiveness, inferiority. The former is equated with success, the latter with failure.

As previously noted, this status differential is reflected in the fact that both mothers and fathers more strongly discourage sex-inappropriate behavior in sons than in daughters. Ovesey (1956, p. 350) argued that it is more difficult to cope with the possibility of homosexuality in males than lesbianism in females because for a male it connotes femininity, which has a low status value, while for a female it connotes masculinity, which has a high status value. That girls perceive this status differential is evidenced in a study of preadolescent girls which showed that no girl wanted to be con-sidered a *sissy*, a term generally reserved for undesirable feminine behaviors (Hartley 1964).

Other variables which have been largely ignored in sex-role research, and which would influence perceptions of "appropriate" sex-role behaviors, are social class, race, region, family structures other than intact nuclear families, and other subcultural categories (Chafetz 1974). For ex-ample, middle-class girls have been found to define their sex roles much more broadly and inclusively than working-class girls (Hartley 1964; Rabban 1950), and there are indications that lower-class males emphasize ag-gressiveness and dominance more than middle- or upper-class males (McKinley 1964). Most research describes white middle-class nuclear families; little attention has been given to nonwhite ethnic groups, lower- or upper-class families, regional differences, or family structures in which a child may have multiple models of both sexes or only one primary model (Hochschild 1973). In short, our culture does not conform to the single, white middle-class model presented in the literature, wherein each parent enacts a precise, sex-differentiated role in an ever-consistent manner.

The designation of specific characteristics or behaviors as "sex-appropriate" or "sex-inappropriate" appears to be a highly labile exercise of diminishing use. Such definitions remain subject to cultural and tem-poral relativity, and inevitably one must ask, Appropriate for whom and appropriate for what?

The second fallacy to be considered is the premise that adult social behavior is primarily determined by early-childhood socialization. This view relies in part on a single-cause, single-effect approach to explanation,

and in effect, it holds that childhood antecedents determine adult consequents. Proponents of this view acknowledge that social learning continues
at moderate rates throughout life, but primacy is assigned to socialization
which occurs in infancy and childhood (Becker 1964; Brim 1966; Inkeles
1969; Kirsh 1974; Neugarten 1968). Bloom (1964) recognizes that some
characteristics may be expected to change relatively rapidly, such as
political opinions, but holds the view that other characteristics (for example, aggressiveness in males, dependence in females, and general intelligence) appear to stabilize before age 5 and that "stable characteristics
appear to either be nonreversible or at least only partially reversible" (p.
207). A Skinnerian view, on the contrary, would argue that there is no
reason why external contingencies should not continue to shape and reshape
the individual and would not point to any developmental change in the
relevance of external socialization forces (Maccoby and Jacklin 1974). This
view would acknowledge the influence of socializing agents during early
childhood, but would not support the contention that these influences
primarily determine adult social behavior. The impact of external socialization forces is seen to remain consistent throughout the various life stages.

The question of continuity and change in human behavior is bridged by
the conclusions of Mischel's investigations. Mischel (1969) distinguishes
between cognitive and intellective dimensions of personality which appear
to be relatively consistent over time and across situations, and social
behavior, which, by comparison, is quite malleable. It seems reasonable to
assume, then, that while the socializing agents of an individual's early
childhood contribute importantly to the child's cognitive skills and intellectual development, their influence on social behavior through subsequent life
stages, including adult sociosexual behavior, is modified or altered according to the cumulative events of one's continuous socialization. Response
systems may be evoked and maintained by varying sets of regulating conditions, then, and the cognitive and intellective dimensions of personality
would influence the individual's perception of and response to these conditions.

Thus, the assumption that there is consistency in what are considered to
be appropriate "masculine" and "feminine" characteristics or behaviors
for all groups and social conditions, as well as the assumption that adult
social behavior is primarily determined by early-childhood socialization, is
not supported by the evidence. These assumptions, in turn, have under-
girded the socialization argument regarding lesbianism—that is, that it is
the result of reinforcement of "sex-inappropriate" behaviors and/or cross-
sex modeling.

The view that lesbian women have received greater reinforcement for
"sex-inappropriate" behaviors than heterosexual women is weakened by
the evidence which shows that "sex-inappropriate" activities for girls in

general are less clearly defined and less firmly enforced than are "sex-inappropriate" activities for boys (Maccoby and Jacklin 1974). In turn, this difference was accounted for by the differential status ascribed to masculine and feminine interests. It is perhaps more accurate to posit that girls are not punished for showing interest in "boys'" activities than that they are specifically rewarded for doing so.

Regarding cross-sex modeling, Maccoby and Jacklin's (1974) extensive analysis indicated that children in general show no consistency in selecting same-sex or other-sex models. Evidence does indicate, however, that a child's gender identity appears to stabilize roughly between the ages of 2 and 4 (Money, Hampson, and Hampson 1955; Sears 1951; Stoller 1968). In this regard, the gender identity of lesbian women has been found to be unequivocally feminine (Armon 1960; Freedman 1967; Gundlach and Riess 1968). The Gundlach and Riess study (1968, p. 226) concluded, "Homosexuality among women in our society seems unrelated to the establishment of feminine identity."

Childhood Activities of Lesbian and Nonlesbian Women

"Reasons" for some girls to evidence more interest in "boys'" activities than others could include, then, less rigidity on the part of parent figures in defining "sex-appropriate" behaviors and the girl's early perception of the status differential between "boys'" and "girls'" play activities. The former appears to be partially a function of socioeconomic status, and the latter may be associated with the Moss and Kagan (1958) finding that more intelligent girls preferred boys' games to girls' games.

The childhood activities of lesbian and heterosexual women have been found to differ. Poole (1972) found that heterosexual women more often than lesbian women preferred playing "house" with self as mother, "mother with dolls," "having a baby," "grown-up lady," and that they preferred playing with girls rather than boys. Two other studies found that lesbian women more often than heterosexual women preferred boys' games, played with guns, had physical fights, disliked dolls, were regarded as "tomboys," excelled in athletics, and played mostly with boys (Gundlach and Riess 1968; Kaye et al. 1967). These differences, however, seem to be a matter of degree. Gundlach and Riess (1968) reported that while three-quarters of their lesbian sample were "tomboys," so were nearly half of the comparison women. These findings suggest that girls who become lesbian as adults have chosen boys' activities more often than girls who become heterosexual as adults.

Using a list of childhood activities composed of items from these three studies (Gundlach and Riess 1968; Kaye et al. 1967; Poole 1972), I also found that over three-fourths of lesbian respondents reported participation in or preference for boys' activities as children. The results (table 2-2) are not directly comparable to those of the three previous studies which compared lesbian and nonlesbian samples, but they do support the premise that lesbian women in general have preferred boys' activities to girls' activities in childhood.

Childhood role play was found to be correlated with the Kinsey scale ($x^2 = 83.34$, $df = 24$, $p < .00001$). That is, "masculine" activity choices increased with more exclusively lesbian sexual histories. Additionally, subsample results indicated that the bisexual respondents (Kinsey scale: 0 to 3) reported greater interest in feminine childhood activities than the remainder of the sample (Kinsey scale: 4 to 6). These percentages are shown in table 2-3.

These findings suggest that preference for boys' activities in childhood increases along a continuum of adult female sociosexual orientations from heterosexual to bisexual to lesbian. While this evidence supports the premise that lesbian women have more frequently rejected "feminine" childhood activities, a number of factors may contribute to these choices, including socioeconomic status and intelligence. As noted previously, middle-class girls have been found to define their sex roles much more broadly and inclusively than working-class girls (Hartley 1964; Rabban 1950), and more intelligent girls have been found to prefer boys' games to girls' games (Moss and Kagan 1958). The Gundlach and Riess (1968) finding that significantly more lesbian women had excelled in athletics suggests that another relevant variable could be competence. That is, the discovery of competence in physical activities would be in itself rewarding and would serve to reinforce these preferences.

Finally, that any of these factors are related to adult sexual orientation is not supported by the evidence. The "cross-gender identity" explanation is refuted by the evidence which shows the gender identity of lesbian women to be unequivocally feminine (Armon 1960; Freedman 1967; Gundlach and Riess 1968). Further, prior studies (Gundlach and Riess 1968; Saghir and

Table 2-2
Childhood Role Play

Masculine/Feminine Activity[a]	Percentage
High feminine	5.1
Moderate feminine	11.6
Equally masculine-feminine	7.5
Moderate masculine	28.9
High masculine	46.9

[a]For interpretation see Appendix A.

Table 2-3

Childhood Role-Play Comparisons between Bisexual Subsample and Remainder of Sample

Masculine/Feminine Activity[a]	Percentage	
	Bisexual Subsample	Remainder of Sample
High feminine	12.9	4.0
Moderate feminine	21.2	10.2
Equally masculine-feminine	14.1	6.6
Moderate masculine	25.9	29.3
High masculine	25.9	50.0

[a]For interpretation see Appendix A.

Robins 1969) indicate that from 75 to 79 percent of lesbian women have heterosexual histories. (My study shows this figure to be 81 percent.) This evidence does not support the proposition that sexual orientation is irrevocably determined in childhood. On the contrary, it indicates that adult sociosexual orientation is considerably more malleable than is commonly believed and adds credence to the view that socialization is a continuous, life-long process.

The Sociocultural Response

According to social-learning theory, adult socialization is a reciprocal, interactive process which may be examined in terms of the rewards that reinforce adult activity and establish or change patterns of adult behavior (Albrecht and Gift 1975). Age, sex, previous experience, stage in life, reference groups, and major life events are viewed as exerting influence on the adult socialization of an individual (Albrecht and Gift 1975). This view conceptualizes socialization as a process which continues throughout the life span of an individual and rejects the notion that adult behavior is predetermined by childhood socialization. In this framework, adult experiences that reinforce and establish or change patterns of behavior can be examined in relation to adult sociosexual preferences.

In the realm of sexual behavior, Millett (1970) has argued that power-structured relationships are by definition political and that heterosexual intercourse is a "charged microcosm" of the sociopolitical relationship between men and women, representing a psychological pattern of dominance and submission. The role of dominance in human sexual behavior has been explored by a few male authors (Collins 1971; Gilder 1973; Maslow 1939; Wilson 1972), but remains largely theoretical in content rather than empirical. Maslow's investigation did include interviews with over a hundred women. On the basis of this study, Maslow concluded that highly dominant women (meaning women with a high level of self-esteem) were highly sexed and inclined to sexual experimentation, while low-dominance women had almost no sexual feeling.

Gundlach and Riess (1968) discuss this issue in terms of levels of maturation and sexual attitudes. They conclude that most men achieve only the maturity level of opportunism or conventionality and that many more women than men achieve the higher maturity levels necessary for complete relationships of some depth of feeling and mutuality. Additionally, these authors raise a highly relevant question, which unfortunately their research did not address: Is the choice of a love or sexual partner equivalent to the choice of the sociosexual role played by the person? If this question were rephrased as "Does the inequity of power between men and women influence sociosexual preference?" some theories and findings in my study would answer affirmatively. Prior to the review of these findings, varying perspectives on human sexual motivation as they relate to lesbianism are discussed.

These perspectives as they relate to lesbianism are interrelated, but for purposes of discussion they can be categorized as the "power" model, the social-script model, and the social-learning model. The power model argues that lesbianism is not only a sexual preference but also a political stance against male domination (Abbott and Love 1972; Cory 1964). This view does not appear to be invalid, but it requires some elaboration and extension. Among lesbian women today, this view has raised the issue of whether one is a "political lesbian" or a "real lesbian." The logical extension of this dichotomy would suggest that, for the "political lesbian," the cultural correction of power inequalities between men and women would allow her to redirect her sexual interests to heterosexual relations. The "real lesbian," it implies, is one who would be sociosexually attracted to women irrespective of the cultural power spectrum.

This appears to be a false dichotomy. Sexual preferences in adults are influenced by multiple and complex environmental factors which are not static, which may vary across time and situation, and which are not necessarily consciously determined. The power differential between men and women cannot monolithically "explain" same-sex attraction. Various options besides lesbianism are available for those who reject sexual politics, ranging from nontraditional heterosexual relationships to celibacy. The crux of this matter is the distinction betwen *reactive* male-negation, which the power model implies, and *active* female-affirmation. While these two processes may not be entirely independent of each other, the matter of emphasis seems important to distinguish.

The social-script model of human sexuality holds that "the social meaning given to the physical acts releases biological events" (Gagnon and Simon

1973, p. 22). In other words, the social and cultural meanings attributed to specific sexual activities provide the motivational elements that produce arousal. Combining this perspective with the power-differential view would suggest that the social meaning of heterosexual relationships in a male-dominated society (that is, submission or subordination) reduces the attractiveness of this option for some proportion of the female population.

Along the same vein, social-learning theory, divested of its past value judgments in relation to lesbianism, would "account" for lesbianism as follows: lesbian behavioral systems result for women who receive greater positive reinforcement sociosexually from members of their own sex than from the other sex. Or, more specifically, the physical and emotional characteristics and the behaviors and attitudes of women are more reinforcing to lesbian women than are those of men. This view is essentially the same as that proposed by Chafetz (1974), who pointed to the centrality of sex roles and role behaviors in influencing sexual preference. Removing the phenomenon of lesbianism from the "pathological" or "defective" categorization may permit more fruitful investigation of factors in interpersonal attraction between women. Such research could better define the physical and emotional characteristics and the behaviors and attitudes of women which are more reinforcing to lesbian women than are those of men.

My findings support the view that the power differential between men and women as well as rejection of conventional female sex roles may be highly relevant factors in same-sex selection. Respondents were asked to rank aspects of heterosexual relationships which were most unattractive (1) through least unattractive (6). Table 2-4 shows the percentage who rank the various items either first or second.

It can be seen that 78 and 62 percent, respectively, ranked male dominance and women's role expectations as the most undesirable aspects of heterosexual relationships. From the evidence reviewed in this chapter,

Table 2-4
Unattractive Aspects of Heterosexual Relationships

Aspect	Percentage		
	First	Second	Combined
Assumption of male dominance	55.2	22.3	77.5
Women's role expectations	26.1	36.3	62.4
Lack of emotional involvement	16.3	9.3	25.6
Intercourse	13.9	7.6	21.5
Birth control, abortion, pregnancy concerns	9.6	8.2	17.8
Lack of knowledge of female sexuality	7.8	8.3	16.1

it can be concluded that previously held "explanatory" theories of lesbianism are not supported by the evidence. Instead, it appears that constraints imposed by the culturally assigned female sex role are a salient factor in the lack of impetus toward heterosexual relationships. The next chapter examines various outcomes associated with the acceptance or rejection of these role constraints.

Note

1. The concepts and terms *gender identity, gender role,* and *sex role* have been defined by many authors (for example, Hampson 1965; Keller 1974; Money, Hampson, and Hampson 1955; Sears 1965; Stoller 1968), but their use in the literature is still inconsistent and lacking in agreement as to their meaning. In this context, *sex* indicates a biological category (male or female); *gender* indicates a psychological category (masculine or feminine).

References

Abbott, S., and Love, B. *Sappho Was a Right-on Woman: A Liberated View of Lesbianism.* New York: Stein and Day, 1972.

Albrecht, G.L., and Gift, H.C. "Adult socialization: Ambiguity and adult life crises." In *Life-Span Developmental Psychology: Normative Life Crisis,* edited by N. Datan and L. Ginsberg. New York: Academic Press, 1975.

Armon, V. "Some personality variables in overt female homosexuality." *Journal of Projective Techniques* 24 (1960):292-309.

Bandura, A. *Principles of Behavior Modification.* New York: Holt, Rinehart and Winston, 1969.

Becker, H. "Personal change in adult life." *Sociometry* 27 (1964):40-53.

Bem, S. "Psychology looks at sex-roles: Where have all the androgynous people gone?" Paper presented at U.C.L.A. Symposium on Women, May 1972.

Bene, E. "On the genesis of female homosexuality." *British Journal of Psychiatry* 111 (1965):815-821.

Bergler, E. "The respective importance of reality and phantasy in the genesis of female homosexuality." *Journal of Criminal Psychopathology* 5 (1943):27-48.

————. *Neurotic Counterfeit Sex.* New York: Grune & Stratton, 1951.

Bloom, B.S. *Stability and Change in Human Characteristics.* New York: Wiley, 1964.

Brecher, E.M. *The Sex Researchers.* Boston: Little, Brown, 1969.

Brim, O.G., Jr. "Socialization through the life cycle." In *Socialization after Childhood: Two Essays*, edited by O.G. Brim, Jr., and S. Wheeler. New York: Wiley, 1966.

Brown, L. "Investigating the stereotypic picture of lesbians in the clinical literature." Paper presented at the 83d Annual Convention of the American Psychological Association in Chicago, 1975.

Brown, P. "Male supremacy in Freud." In *Radical Psychology*, edited by P. Brown. New York: Harper & Row, 1973.

Cannon, M., and Redick, R. "Differential utilization of psychiatric facilities by men and women, United States." National Institute of Mental Health, Statistical Note 81. Washington: Survey and Reports Section, Biometry Branch, 1973.

Caprio, F.S. *Female Homosexuality: A Psychodynamic Study of Lesbianism*. New York: Grove Press, 1954.

Chafetz, J. *Masculine/Feminine or Human? An Overview of the Sociology of Sex Roles*. Itasca, Ill.: F.E. Peacock Publishers, 1974.

Collins, R. "A conflict theory of sexual stratification." *Social Problems* 19 (1971):3-21.

Cory, D. *The Lesbian in America*. New York: The Citadel Press, 1964.

Crowne, D.P., and Marlowe, D. "A new scale of social desirability independent of psychopathology." *Journal of Consulting Psychology* 14 (1960):349-354.

Daughters of Bilitis, Editorial Staff. "Some comparisons about lesbians." *The Ladder* 3 (September 1959):4-26.

Denniston, R.H. "Ambisexuality in animals." In *Sexual Inversion: The Multiple Roots of Homosexuality*, edited by J. Marmor. New York: Basic Books, 1965.

Deutsch, H. *The Psychology of Women*. Vol. 1. New York: Grune & Stratton, 1944.

Ellis, H. *Studies in the Psychology of Sex*. Vol. 2: *Sexual Inversion*. 3d ed. Philadelphia: F.A. Davis, 1915.

Eysenck, H., and Eysenck, S. *The Eysenck Personality Inventory*. San Diego: Educational and Industrial Testing Service, 1963.

Farberow, N., and Schneidman, E. "Statistical comparisons between attempted and committed suicides." In N. Farberow, *The Cry for Help*. New York: McGraw-Hill, 1965.

Farnham, M.F. *The Adolescent*. New York: Harper and Brothers, 1951.

Fenichel, O. *The Psychoanalytical Theory of Neurosis*. 2d ed. New York: W.W. Norton, 1945.

Firestone, S. "Freudianism: The misguided feminism." In S. Firestone, *The Dialectic of Sex*. New York: Bantam Books, 1970.

Fling, S., and Manosevitz, M. "Sex-typing in nursery school children's play interests." *Developmental Psychology* 7 (1972):146-152.

Ford, C.S., and Beach, F.A. "Homosexual Behavior." In C.S. Ford and F.A. Beach, *Patterns of Sexual Behavior*. New York: Harper and Brothers, 1951.

Freedman, M.J. "Homosexuality among women and psychological adjustment." Doctoral dissertation, Case Western Reserve University, 1967. *Dissertation Abstracts* 28/10-B (1967):4294 (University Microfilms No. 68-03308).

Freud, S. *New Introductory Lectures on Psychoanalysis*, translated by W. Sprott. New York: Norton, 1933.

──────. "Female homosexuality." In *Collected Papers*, vol. 5 (2d ed.), translated by J. Strachey. London: Hogarth Press and Institute of Psychoanalysis, 1950.

Friedan, B. "The sexual solipsism of Sigmund Freud." In B. Friedan, *The Feminine Mystique*. New York: Dell, 1963.

Gagnon, J.H., and Simon, W. *Sexual Conduct: The Social Sources of Human Sexuality*. Chicago: Aldine, 1973.

Gartrell, N.K.; Loriaux, D.L.; and Chase, T.N. "Plasma testosterone in homosexual and heterosexual women." *American Journal of Psychiatry* 134 (1977):1117-1119.

Gilder, F. *Sexual Suicide*. New York: Bantam Books, 1973.

Gould, R. "What we don't know about homosexuality." *The New York Times Magazine*, February 24, 1974.

Gove, W. "The relationship between sex-roles, marital status and mental illness." *Social Forces* 51 (1972):33-44.

Greenstein, J. "Father characteristics and sex-typing." *Journal of Personality and Social Psychology* 3 (1966):271-277.

Greer, G. *The Female Eunuch*. New York: Bantam Books, 1972.

Gundlach, R.H., and Riess, B.F. "Self and sexual identity in the female: A study of female homosexuals." In *New Directions in Mental Health*, vol. 1, edited by B.F. Riess. New York: Grune & Stratton, 1968.

Gurin, G.; Veroff, J.; and Feld, S. *Americans View Their Mental Health: A Nationwide Interview Survey*. New York: Basic Books, 1960.

Hampson, J.L. "Determinants of psychosexual orientation." In F. Beach, *Sex and Behavior*. New York: Wiley, 1965.

Hartley, R.E. "A developmental view of female sex-role definition and identification." *Merrill-Palmer Quarterly* 10 (1964):3-16.

Hedblom, J.H. "Social, sexual, and occupational lives of homosexual women." *Sexual Behavior* 2 (1972):33-37.

Henry, G. *Sex Variances: A Study of Homosexual Patterns*. New York: Paul Hoeber, 1941.

Hess, R.D. "Social class and ethnic influences on socialization." In *Carmichael's Manual of Child Psychology*, edited by Paul Mussen. Vol. 2, 3d ed. New York: Wiley, 1970.

Hetherington, E.M. "A developmental study of the effects of sex of the dominant parent on sex-role preference, identification, and imitation in children." *Journal of Personality and Social Psychology* 2 (1965):188-194.

Hochschild, A.R. "A review of sex role research." *American Journal of Sociology* 78 (1973):1011-1029.

Hopkins, J.H. "The lesbian personality." *British Journal of Psychiatry* 115 (1969):1433-1436.

Inkeles, A. "Social structure and socialization." In *Handbook of Socialization Theory and Research*, edited by D. Goslin. Chicago: Rand McNally, 1969.

Johnson, W.B., and Terman, L.M. "Personality characteristics of happily married, unhappily married, and divorced persons." *Character and Personality* 2 (June 1935):304-305.

Kallman, F. "Comparative twin study on the genetic aspects of male homosexuality." *Journal of Nervous and Mental Disorders* 115 (1952):283-298.

Kaye, H.; Berl, S.; Clare, J.; Eleston, M.; Gershwin, B.; Gershwin, P.; Kogan, L.; Torda, C.; and Wilbur, C. "Homosexuality in women." *Archives of General Psychiatry* 17 (1967):626-634.

Keller, S. "The female role: Constants and change." In *Women in Therapy*, edited by V. Franks and V. Burtle. New York: Brunner/Mazel, 1974.

Kenyon, F.E. "Physique and physical health of female homosexuals." *Journal of Neurology, Neurosurgery and Psychiatry* (London) 31 (1968a):487-489.

————. "Studies in female homosexuality—4 and 5." *British Journal of Psychiatry* 114 (1968b):1337-1350.

Kinsey, A.C.; Pomeroy, W.B.; and Martin, C.E. *Sexual Behavior in the Human Male*. Philadelphia: Saunders, 1948.

Kinsey, A.C.; Pomeroy, W.B.; Martin, C.E.; and Gebhard, P.H. *Sexual Behavior in the Human Female*. Philadelphia: Saunders, 1953.

Kirsh, B. "Consciousness-raising groups as therapy for women." In *Women in Therapy*, edited by V. Franks and V. Burtle. New York: Brunner/Mazel, 1974.

Kline-Graber, G., and Graber, B. *Woman's Orgasm: A Guide to Sexual Satisfaction*. New York: Bobbs-Merrill, 1975.

Knupfer, G.; Clark, W.; and Room, R. "The mental health of the unmarried." *American Journal of Psychiatry* 122 (1966):841-851.

Kohlberg, L. "A cognitive developmental analysis of children's sex-role concepts and attitudes." In *The Development of Sex Differences*, edited by E.E. Maccoby. Stanford, Calif.: Stanford University Press, 1966.

Krafft-Ebing, R. von. *Psychopathia Sexualis*, translated by F. Rebman. Brooklyn, N.Y.: Physicians & Surgeons Book Co., 1922.

Kremer, M.W., and Rifkin, A.H. "The early development of homosexuality: A study of adolescent lesbians." *American Journal of Psychiatry* 126 (1969):91-96.

Lansky, L.M. "The family structure also affects the model: Sex-role attitudes in parents of pre-school children." *Merrill-Palmer Quarterly* 13 (1967):139-150.

Liddicoat, R. Letter to the editor. *British Medical Journal* 2 (1957):1110-1111. (Summary of author's doctoral dissertation at the University of Witwatersrand, "Homosexuality: Results of a Survey as Related to Various Theories.")

London, L., and Caprio, F. *Sexual Deviations.* Washington: Linacre Press, 1950.

Loraine, J.; Adamopoulos, D.; Kirkham, K.; Ismail, A.; and Dove, G. "Patterns of hormone excretion in male and female homosexuals." *Nature* (London) 234 (1971):552-555.

Lynn, D.B. "A note on sex differences in the development of masculine and feminine identification." *Psychological Review* 66 (March 1959): 126-135.

Maccoby, E.E., and Jacklin, C.N. *Psychology of Sex Differences.* Stanford, Calif.: Stanford University Press, 1974.

Maslow, A.H. "Dominance, personality, and social behavior in women." Journal of Social Psychology 10 (1939):3-39.

Masters, W., and Johnson, V. "Orgasm, Anatomy of the female." In *Encyclopedia of Sexual Behavior*, vol. 2, edited by A. Ellis and A. Abarbanel. New York: Hawthorn, 1961.

————. *Human Sexual Response.* Boston: Little, Brown, 1966.

McKinley, D.G. *Social Class and Family Life.* Glencoe, Ill.: Free Press, 1964.

Millett, K. "Freud and the influence of psychoanalytical thought, and some post-Freudians." In K. Millett, *Sexual Politics.* New York: Doubleday, 1970.

Mischel, W. "Continuity and change in personality." *American Psychologist* 24 (1969):1012-1018.

————. "Sex-typing and socialization." In *Carmichael's Manual of Child Psychology*, vol. 2, edited by P.H. Mussen. New York: Wiley, 1970.

Money, J., and Ehrhardt, A. *Man and Woman, Boy and Girl: The Differentiation and Dimorphism of Gender Identity from Conception to Maturity.* Baltimore: Md.: The Johns Hopkins University Press, 1972.

Money, J.; Hampson, J.G.; and Hampson, J.L. "An examination of some basic concepts: The evidence of human hermaphroditism." *Bulletin Johns Hopkins Hospital* 107 (1955):301-319.

Moss, H., and Kagan, J. "Maternal influences on early I.Q. scores." *Psychological Reports* 4 (1958):655-661.

Nelson, H. "Experiments indicate sperm may trigger cancer." *Los Angeles Times*, March 23, 1975, pt. 1, p. 23.

Neugarten, B.L. "Adult personality: Toward a psychology of the life cycle." In *Middle Age and Aging*, edited by B.L. Neugarten. Chicago: University of Chicago Press, 1968.

Oberstone, A.K. "Dimensions of psychological adjustment and style of life in single lesbians and single heterosexual women." Doctoral dissertation, California School of Professional Psychology, 1974. *Dissertation Abstracts International* 35/10-B (1974):5088 (University Microfilms No. 75-8510).

Ovesey, L. "Masculine aspirations in women: An adaptational analysis." *Psychiatry* 19 (1956):341-351.

Poole, K. "The etiology of gender identity and the lesbian." *The Journal of Social Psychology* 87 (1972):51-57.

Rabban, M. "Sex-role identification in young children in two diverse social groups." *Genetic Psychological Moncgraph* 42 (1950):81-158.

Rado, S. "Fear of castration in women." *Psychoanalytic Quarterly* 2 (1933): 425-475.

Raphael, S.M. "'Coming out': The emergence of the movement Lesbian." Doctoral dissertation, Case Western Reserve University, 1974. *Dissertation Abstracts* 35/08-A (1974):5536 (University Microfilms No. 75-5084).

Saghir, M., and Robins, E. "Homosexuality. I. Sexual behavior of the female homosexual." *Archives of General Psychiatry* 20 (1969):192-201.

Saghir, M.; Robins, E.; Walbran, B.; and Gentry, K. "Homosexuality, IV. Psychiatric disorders and disability in the female homosexual." *American Journal of Psychiatry* 127 (1970):147-154.

Sears, P. "Doll play aggression in normal young children." *Psychological Monographs* 65 (1951):1-42.

Sears, R. "Development of gender role." In *Sex and Behavior*, edited by F. Beach. New York: Wiley, 1965.

Sherfey, M.J. *The Nature and Evolution of Female Sexuality*. New York: Random House, 1966.

Siegelman, M. "Adjustment of homosexual and heterosexual women." *British Journal of Psychiatry* 120 (1972):477-481.

Simon, W., and Gagnon, J. "Femininity in the lesbian community." *Social Problems* 15 (1967):212-221.

Socarides, C.W. "The historical development of theoretical and clinical concepts of overt female homosexuality." *Journal of American Psychoanalytical Association* 11 (1963):386-412.

Stoller, R.J. *Sex and Gender*. New York: Science House, 1968.

Swanson, D.; Loomis, S.; Lukesh, R.; Cronin, R.; and Smith, J. "Clinical features of the female homosexual patient: A comparison with the heterosexual patient." *Journal of Nervous and Mental Disease* 155 (1972):119-124.

Thompson, N.L.; McCandless, B.R.; and Strickland, B.R. "Personal adjustment of male and female homosexuals and heterosexuals." *Journal of Abnormal Psychology* 78 (1971):237-240.

U.S. Department of Health, Education, and Welfare. *Selected Symptoms of Psychological Distress, United States.* Washington: Public Health Service, Health Service and Mental Health Administration, August 1970.

_____ . Public Health Service, Center for Disease Control. *VD Statistical Letter*, May 1976, p. 124.

Weisstein, N. "Psychology constructs the female." In *Woman in Sexist Society*, edited by V. Gornick and B. Moran. New York: New American Library, 1971.

Wilbur, C.B. "Clinical aspects of female homosexuality." In *Sexual Inversion: The Multiple Roots of Homosexuality*, edited by J. Marmor. New York: Basic Books, 1965.

Wilson, C. "Dominance and sex." *Human Behavior* October, 1972, pp. 38-43.

Wilson, M.L., and Greene, R.L. "Personality characteristics of female homosexuals." *Psychological Reports* 28 (1971):407-412.

3

Sex Roles, Androgyny, and Mental Health

Chapter 2 reviewed various "causal" theories of lesbianism. The search for "causes" from any of these theoretical orientations has been based on the premise that lesbianism is a negative outcome and that by studying its "causes" it can be prevented or "cured." This chapter reviews evidence that supports a different view. The pros or cons of lesbianism, viewed as a sexual choice, are not presented here. Evidence is presented, however, which indicates that nonconformity to female sex-role prescriptions is associated with positive outcomes and that these outcomes have been found to be currently more prevalent among lesbian women than among heterosexual women, owing perhaps to the differential impact on these two groups of male reward systems which reinforce sex-typed behaviors.

Concepts and Linkages

As discussed in chapter 2, individual social behavior tends to vary over time and across situations in response to different regulating conditions. Bem and Allen (1974) add a further distinction regarding behavioral continuity and change. They state that an individual's behavior is likely to be stable with respect to those attributes that are central to his or her self-definition, but that those not central to self-definition are expected to vary according to the situation. It is believed that masculinity and femininity are central attributes for some people but not for others (Maccoby and Jacklin 1974).

Men for whom "masculinity" and women for whom "femininity" are central self-definitions are considered to be highly sex-typed. Sex-typed individuals have been found to have more restricted self-concepts and greater rigidity in behavior than "androgynous" individuals (Bem and Lewis 1975). Psychological androgyny is defined as having high levels of masculinity *and* femininity. Persons with an androgynous orientation have been found to have greater sex-role adaptability, which allows them to engage in situationally appropriate behavior regardless of its connotations as masculine or feminine (Orlofsky 1977).

There is evidence to support the view that adaptability in response patterns, which may equate with having a broader repertoire of response options, is more socially desirable than the less flexible, traitlike consistency of those with sex-typed images to maintain. For example, "masculinity" in girls and "femininity" in boys have been correlated consistently with higher overall intelligence, higher creativity, higher analytic thinking, and higher spatial ability (Barron 1957; Bieri 1960; MacKinnon 1962; Moss and Kagan 1958; Oetzel 1961; Roe 1959). This evidence suggests that conformity to stereotypic sex roles restricts an individual's intellectual growth and development. The apparent consequences of this conformity for the individual's psychological adjustment is another important area which bears examination and requires an overview of what is considered "good" psychological adjustment.

The value dilemma inherent in describing or measuring "good" psychological adjustment or "positive" mental health greatly restricts the credibility of any attempt to define mental-health criteria. As with sex-role prescriptions, one must ask, Good for whom and good for what? A second dilemma in establishing widely accepted criteria of mental health is the existence of conflicting theoretical orientations. As Jahoda (1958, 1970) has noted, mental health can be defined in at least two ways: as a relatively constant and enduring function of personality and as a momentary function of personality and situation. The first view will lead to a classification of *individuals* as more or less healthy; the second view will lead to a classification of *actions* as more or less healthy. The first view relies on the assumption of broad consensus in regard to what constitutes mental health and lacks operationally defined concepts or specific behavioral referents. However, it has been the most commonly used basis for measuring psychological adjustment, and as such, it requires a brief description.

Six major categories of concepts have been utilized as criteria for mental health: attitudes and perceptions toward self; perception of reality; growth, development, and self-actualization; environmental mastery; autonomy; and integration (Jahoda 1958, 1970; French 1968). These categories are not wholly dissimilar to basic dimensions of psychological functioning referred to as outcome criteria in the empirical investigation of mental health: self-adjustment, environmental adjustment, and mental functioning (Bednar and Lawlis 1971).

The conceptualization of mental health, in addition to the valuation of "good" and "bad" that it generally incurs and the amorphous concepts that it frequently employs, is made more difficult by a third dilemma: the standards of mental health are differentially applied to men and women. As demonstrated by the Broverman group's study, the profile of the mentally healthy adult and that of the mentally healthy male are essentially the same, while the mentally healthy female, as defined by mental-health professionals, is more submissive, more easily influenced, more susceptible to having hurt feelings, more excitable in a minor crisis, more conceited about her appearance, more emotional, less aggressive, less independent, less adventurous, less competitive, less objective, and aversive to math and science (Broverman et al. 1970).

This description of the mentally healthy female, which is incongruous with the description of a mentally healthy adult, raises questions about the psychological cost of conformity to the traditional female sex role. To ascertain what constitutes conformity or nonconformity to the female sex role, a definition of the core elements of the female role is required. According to Keller (1974), these are a concentration on marriage, home, and children as the primary focus; reliance on a male provider for sustenance and status; an emphasis on nurturance and life-preserving activities (sympathy, care, love, compassion); an injunction that women live through and for others rather than for the self; a stress on beauty, personal adornment, and eroticism; and a ban on the expression of direct assertion, aggression, and power strivings, as well as on taking direct sexual initiative.

Keller offers a cost/benefit analysis of accepting the ascribed female sex role. The benefits are supposed to include economic security; emotional security; socially sanctioned narcissism; the pleasure of being nurturant, warm, and sympathetic; and the lack of pressure to achieve. The costs are supposed to include lesser autonomy, lack of formal training and know-how, and categorical subordination to men. In essence, she concludes, it seems the female role exchanges autonomy for security.

The two major departures from the conventional female role are described as challenging women's economic dependence and challenging their sexual dependence on men. As Keller notes, lesbian women have neither economic nor sexual dependence on men and thus by both criteria represent a nonconforming group in relation to the conventional female role. On the basis of Keller's argument, differences in psychological adjustment between lesbian women and heterosexual and/or married women, if any, would reflect consequences of conformity or nonconformity to the conventional female sex role. That is, a continuum of conformity may be hypothesized based on the following expectations: married women would be economically and sexually dependent more frequently; single heterosexual women more frequently would be sexually dependent, but not economically dependent; and lesbian women more frequently would be neither economically nor sexually dependent. This classification obscures individual variations,[1] but the continuum can be utilized as a rough guideline in assessing the psychological consequences of conforming to the conventional female sex role.

Sex-Role Conformity versus Nonconformity:
Comparative Outcomes

The nonconformity of lesbian women to the traditional female sex role apparently yields not "masculinity" but androgyny. According to Bem (1972), the behavioral correlates of an androgynous orientation are asserttiveness, perseverance, self-confidence, independence, *and* tenderness, nurturance, sensitivity, and the ability to express emotions. Comparative studies of lesbian and nonlesbian women on measures of assertiveness (Hopkins 1969), dominance (Hopkins 1969; Siegelman 1972; Wilson and Greene 1971), perseverance (Wilson and Greene 1971), self-confidence (Thompson, McCandless, and Strickland 1971), independence (Hopkins 1969), tenderness (Siegelman 1972), and capacity for intimate contact and feeling reactivity (Freedman 1967) have found lesbian women to rate significantly higher on these characteristics than nonlesbian women. Studies which compare the psychological adjustment of lesbian and nonlesbian women, then, may also be viewed as measuring differences between women who are more androgynous and women who are more highly sex-typed.

In general, available evidence shows no important differences between lesbian and nonlesbian women on measures of "psychopathology" (Armon 1960; Brown 1975; Freedman 1967; Hopkins 1969; Oberstone 1974; Siegelman 1972; Thompson, McCandless, and Strickland 1971; Wilson and Greene 1971). Where differences in personality characteristics do obtain, the profile of lesbian women (table 3-1) can be seen to more closely parallel the socially desirable characteristics of the mentally healthy adult derived from the Broverman group's study (table 3-2) (Broverman et al. 1970).

Most of the studies which have compared lesbian and nonlesbian women fail to specify the marital status of the nonlesbian samples. The exceptions are that Armon's (1960) and Hopkins's (1969) comparison groups were married

Table 3-1
Personality Characteristics of Lesbian Women in Comparison to Heterosexual Women

Study	Characteristics
Freedman (1967)	Lesbian women higher on inner direction, self-actualization, existentiality, feeling reactivity, acceptance of one's own aggressiveness, capacity for intimate contact
Hopkins (1969)	Lesbian women more independent, composed, reserved, dominant, assertive, progressive, bohemian, self-sufficient, resilient
Siegelman (1972)	Lesbian women higher on goal-directedness, self-acceptance, tendermindedness, dominance
Thompson, McCandless, and Strickland (1971)	Lesbian women more self-confident
Wilson and Greene (1971)	Lesbian women higher on dominance, capacity for status, good impression, intellectual efficiency, endurance

Table 3-2
Stereotypic Questionnaire: Socially Desirable Characteristics

Male-valued items:	Aggressive, independent, not emotional, objective, not easily influenced, dominant, likes math and science, not excitable in a minor crisis, active, competitive, logical, worldly, skilled in business, direct, feelings not easily hurt, adventurous, makes decisions easily, does not cry, acts as a leader, self-confident, comfortable about being aggressive, ambitious, able to separate feelings from ideas, not conceited about appearance
Female-valued items:	Talkative, tactful, gentle, aware of feelings of others, religious, interested in own appearance, neat in habits, quiet, need for security, enjoys art and literature, expresses tender feelings

Derived from I.K. Broverman, D.M. Broverman, F.E. Clarkson, P.S. Rosenkrantz, and S.R. Vogel, "Sex-Role Stereotypes and Clinical Judgments of Mental Health," *Journal of Consulting and Clinical Psychology* 34 (1970):1-7.

and Oberstone's (1974) was single. Thus, the relevance of sexual orientation to positive personality characteristics is inconclusive, since the effects of a heterosexual orientation may be compounded with those of economic dependence. It is useful, then, to consider the evidence of studies which have compared the psychological adjustment of married and single women.

Bem (1972) reported that high femininity has been found to be associated with high anxiety and low social acceptance (Cosentino and Heilbrun 1964; Gray 1957; Webb 1963) and concluded on the basis of her extensive survey of the literature that high femininity seems to be associated with poorer psychological adjustment. Bernard (1971) observed that conforming to the standards of femininity fits women for marriage, but that these standards, however suitable they may have been in the past, may now be dysfunctional. "They are not standards of good mental health; in fact, adjustment to the demands of marriage may greatly impair mental health" (Bernard 1971, p. 157).

Johnson and Terman (1935) noted that "happily married women" were docile rather than aggressive, indecisive and cautious rather than daring, and not very self-sufficient. A more recent study (Knupfer, Clark, and Room 1966) found that more married women than single women were bothered by feelings of depression, disliked their present jobs, sometimes felt they were about to go to pieces, were afraid of death, worried about catching diseases and were bothered by pains and ailments. Overall, more married than single women were reported to be passive, phobic, and depressed, with at least half of the married women falling into one or another of these three categories. A much larger study (U.S. Department of Health, Education, and Welfare 1970) surveyed a probability sample of 7,710 people between the ages of 18 and 79. They found that white women who were never married reported fewer symptoms of psychological distress than white married or separated women.

Gove (1972) found that the relatively high rates of mental illness in married women account for the higher rates of mental illness among women. Other studies substantiate the differential effect of marriage on women and men. Gurin, Veroff, and Feld (1960) found that wives report greater stress and more problems in marriage than do husbands. Cannon and Redick (1973) found that among women, those who are married are more likely to have some mental dysfunction, whereas among men, those who are *un*married are more likely to have such problems. Finally, Farberow and Schneidman (1965) found that housewives comprised the largest single occupational category of both attempted and completed suicides.

Table 3-3 lists findings regarding the characteristics of married women as found in the above-mentioned studies.

Seen in juxtaposition to the socially desirable characteristics of the mentally healthy adult (table 3-2) and to characteristics of lesbian women (table 3-1), the premise that conformity to the conventional female sex role is inversely correlated with positive psychological adjustment seems strongly substantiated.

More recent investigations relating to psychological outcomes of androgyny versus nonandrogyny add further support to this thesis, particularly investigations that have measured degree of self-actualization and level

Table 3-3
Characteristics of Married Women

Reported by	Findings
Bem (1972)	High femininity associated with high anxiety, low social acceptance, poor psychological adjustment
Cannon and Redick (1973)	Married women had higher rates of mental illness than single women
Farberow and Schneidman (1965)	Housewives had higher attempted and completed suicide rates than any other occupational category
Gove (1972)	Married women had higher rates of mental illness than single women
Gurin, Veroff, and Feld (1960)	Married women had greater stress than husbands
Johnson and Terman (1935)	Happily married women were docile, indecisive, cautious, not self-sufficient
Knupfer, Clark, and Room (1966)	Married women were more passive, more phobic, more depressed, and more neurotic and had more mental impairment than single women
U.S. Department of Health, Education, and Welfare (1970)	Married women had more psychological distress than never-married women

of self-esteem. A *self-actualized person* has been described as one who is efficient in self-expression in interpersonal relations (Rogers 1951), and *self-esteem* has been defined as evaluative attitudes toward the self or personal judgment of worthiness (Coopersmith 1967). Androgynous individuals were found to be more highly self-actualized (Cristall and Dean 1976) and to have higher levels of self-esteem than more sex-typed individuals (Orlofsky 1977; Spence, Helmreich, and Stapp 1975; Wetter 1975). Both Orlofsky (1977) and Wetter (1975) found that high femininity was most often associated with low self-esteem in females.

An inverse relationship has also been found between occupational advancement and femininity (Block, Von Der Lippe, and Block 1973). This study is particularly significant because its sample was drawn from two ongoing longitudinal studies being conducted at the University of California at Berkeley; thus information was available on each subject from childhood to 30 or 40 years of age. They found that, of those employed, 75 percent of the low-feminine women had a pattern of upward occupational mobility, while the comparable figure for the high-feminine women was around 30 percent. These authors concluded that sex-role typing for men appears to expand the personal options available to them, while for women, sex-role typing seems to restrict the alternatives of action and expression. As the Broverman group's study (1970, p. 7) concluded, "The cause of mental health may be better served if both men and women are encouraged toward maximum realization of individual potential, rather than to an adjustment to existing restrictive sex roles."

In sum, conformity to the conventional female sex role has been shown to be inversely related to positive psychological adjustment (Bem 1972; Cannon and Redick 1973; Farberow and Schneidman 1965; Gove 1972; Gurin, Veroff, and Feld 1960; Johnson and Terman 1935; Knupfer, Clark, and Room 1966; U.S. Department of Health, Education, and Welfare 1970), self-esteem (Orlofsky 1977; Spence, Helmreich, and Stapp 1975; Wetter 1975), and upward occupational mobility (Block, Von Der Lippe, and Block 1973). Using the Keller (1974) criteria of the female sex role, lesbian women, who are neither economically nor sexually dependent on men, may be described as the least conforming category of women and thus may be expected to evidence higher levels of psychological adjustment, self-esteem, and occupational achievement than nonlesbian women. These expectations appear to be partially supported by the evidence indicating that personality characteristics of lesbian women more closely parallel the socially desirable characteristics of the mentally healthy adult in the Broverman group's study (1970) than do those of nonlesbian women (Freedman 1967; Hopkins 1969; Siegelman 1972; Thompson, McCandless, and Strickland 1971; Wilson and Greene 1971) and that lesbian women in general have achieved higher educational levels than nonlesbian women (Kenyon 1968, Wilson and Greene 1971).

Androgyny and Lesbian Women

Indexes of sex-role behaviors and preferences were obtained in my study pertaining to adult role functions, self-assessment, and partner preference in relation to "masculinity" and "femininity," and preference for "masculinity" or "femininity" in men. In contrast to measures of psychological androgyny (for example, Bem's sex role inventory 1974; the Berzins, Welling, and Wetter PRF ANDRO scale 1978), the indexes utilized in this research focus more on specific sex-typed behaviors and functions to ascertain levels of sex-role flexibility among lesbian women, as well as self-perception and desirability in others of sex-typed behaviors.

Using a list of fourteen adult role functions, half of which would be considered traditionally "masculine" and traditionally "feminine," respondents indicated the person whom they would prefer to take responsibility for each function in a couple relationship of their own—self, partner, or "both equally." The percentages of "both equally" responses were summed and divided by 14 to yield the overall respondents' androgyny score, which was 80.7 percent. Results per item are shown in table 3-4.

Similarly, a separate question ascertained preference in relation to who takes the initiative in love-making; 6.5 percent preferred to take the initiative, 9.3 percent preferred their partner to do so, and 82.5 percent indicated it made no difference. Respondents were also asked to indicate whether they considered themselves to be more masculine, more feminine, or equally masculine and feminine and to indicate which of these three patterns they would prefer in a partner. On the self-rating, 10.5 percent considered them-

Table 3-4
Preferences in Adult Role Functions

| Role Function | Percentage | | |
	Myself	Partner	Both Equally
Deciding where we lived	3.4	1.6	95.0
Cooking	9.9	12.8	77.3
Mowing yard, gardening, etc.	9.9	8.4	81.7
Housecleaning	6.1	7.2	86.6
Handling the finances	9.9	8.0	82.0
Laundry	7.7	6.4	85.9
Car repairs	12.7	15.6	71.7
Arranging social activities	4.4	3.1	92.5
Driving the car	10.2	9.4	80.3
Caring for pets or children	5.3	7.1	87.6
Household repairs	9.3	7.7	83.0
Buying groceries	8.0	6.4	85.6
Earning the income	2.7	3.1	94.2
Choosing friends	1.9	1.2	96.9

selves more masculine, 18.8 percent considered themselves more feminine, and 67.3 percent considered themselves equally masculine and feminine. On partner preference, 4.3 percent preferred their partner to be more masculine, 18.5 percent preferred their partner to be more feminine, and 72.7 percent preferred their partner to be equally masculine and feminine.

This androgynous orientation apparently carries over into lesbian appraisals of men. Respondents were asked whether they were ever attracted to men, and if so, to indicate whether they preferred a man to be more masculine or more feminine in comparison to other men. Separate evaluations were made for psychological and physical characteristics. Although about 28 percent of respondents indicated that they were never attracted to men, of those who at one time or another found men attractive nearly one-half (47.2 percent) preferred them to be more "feminine" psychologically, while only 7.1 percent preferred them to be more "masculine." (The remainder made no distinction.) Responses regarding physical characteristics were more divergent: about 23 percent preferred more-masculine men and about 19 percent preferred more-feminine men. (Again, the remainder made no distinction.) These findings further underscore the relevance of sex roles to lesbian sexual choices and their general preference for androgynous behavior.

Thus, in addition to the androgynous personality profile of lesbian women presented in table 3-1, my findings provide further evidence of a high level of androgyny among lesbian women. The prevalence of role flexibility is evidenced by the findings that 81 percent of the sample viewed adult role functions as interchangeable between partners and that 83 percent indicated interchangeability in relation to initiating love-making as well. Further, 67 percent assessed themselves as equally masculine and feminine, and 73 percent preferred a partner who was equally masculine and feminine. The high level of androgyny evidenced in lesbian women and the association of androgyny in women with characteristics of positive mental health and upward occupational mobility indicate that viewing lesbianism as a negative outcome of socialization has no basis in fact.

The evidence (summarized in table 3-1) indicating greater androgyny among lesbian women than among nonlesbian women suggests that lesbian women, as a group, have been more resistant to male reward systems that reinforce sex-typed behavior. This lack of conformity to the rules of sexual stratification, then, may provide the key to understanding culturally enforced negative sanctions against lesbianism. Notions of inherent or learned personal defect are not sustained by empirical findings, and outcomes associated with lesbianism, as discussed in this chapter, are in accord with culturally sanctioned goals and values (upward occupational mobility and positive mental health). The rationale for negative sanctions against lesbianism, then, must derive from other sources. To explore this rationale requires an overview of the ascribed status of women in our society which, in turn, illuminates reasons for negating lesbianism.

Note

1. In reference to individual variation, 45 percent of married women living with husbands are employed (Van Dusen and Sheldon 1976). Too, most working women, lesbian and nonlesbian, are economically dependent on male approval to some extent; thus, economic dependence is in this sense a matter of degree. Additionally, some lesbian women also are married, some women are bisexual, and so forth.

References

Armon, V. "Some personality variables in overt female homosexuality." *Journal of Projective Techniques* 24 (1960):292-309.

Barron, F. "Originality in relation to personality and intellect." *Journal of Personality* 25 (1957):730-742.

Bednar, R., and Lawlis, G. "Empirical research in group psychotherapy." In *Handbook of Psychotherapy and Behavior Change: An Empirical Analysis*, edited by A. Bergin and S. Garfield. New York: Wiley, 1971.

Bem, D. and Allen, A. "On predicting some of the people some of the time: The search for cross-situational consistencies in behavior." *Psychological Review* 81 (1974):506-520.

Bem, S. "Psychology looks at sex-roles: Where have all the androgynous people gone?" Paper presented at U.C.L.A. Symposium on Women, May 1972.

Bem, S., and Lewis, S. "Sex role adaptability: One consequence of psychological androgyny." *Journal of Personality and Social Psychology* 31 (1975):634-643.

Bernard, J. "The paradox of the happy marriage." In *Women in Sexist Society*, edited by V. Gornick and B. Moran. New York: Basic Books, 1971.

Bieri, J. "Parental identification, acceptance of authority, and within-sex differences in cognitive behavior." *Journal of Abnormal and Social Psychology* 60 (1960):76-79.

Block, J.H.; Von Der Lippe, A.; and Block, J. "Sex-role and socialization patterns: Some personality concomitants and environmental antecedents." *Journal of Consulting and Clinical Psychology* 41 (1973): 321-341.

Broverman, I.K.; Broverman, D.M.; Clarkson, F.E.; Rosenkrantz, P.S.; and Vogel, S.R. "Sex-role stereotypes and clinical judgments of mental health." *Journal of Consulting and Clinical Psychology* 34 (1970):1-7.

Brown, L. "Investigating the stereotypic picture of lesbians in the clinical literature." Paper presented at the 83d Annual Convention of the American Psychological Association in Chicago, 1975.

Cannon, M., and Redick, R. "Differential utilization of psychiatric facilities by men and women, United States." National Institute of Mental Health, Statistical Note 81. Washington: Survey and Reports Section, Biometry Branch, 1973.

Coopersmith, S. *The Antecedents of Self-Esteem.* San Francisco: W.H. Freeman, 1967.

Cosentino, F., and Heilbrun, A. "Anxiety correlates of sex-role identity in college students." *Psychological Reports* 14 (1964):729-730.

Cristall, L., and Dean, R. "Relationship of sex-role stereotypes and self-actualization." *Psychological Reports* 39 (1976):842.

Farberow, N., and Schneidman, E. "Statistical comparisons between attempted and committed suicides." In N. Farberow, *The Cry for Help.* New York: McGraw-Hill, 1965.

Freedman, M.J. "Homosexuality among women and psychological adjustment." Doctoral dissertation, Case Western Reserve University, 1967. *Dissertation Abstracts* 28/10-B (1967):4294 (University Microfilms No. 68-03308).

French, J., Jr. "The conceptualization and measurement of mental health in terms of self-identity theory." In *The Definition and Measurement of Mental Health.* Washington: U.S. Department of Health, Education, and Welfare, Public Health Service, Health Services and Mental Health Administration, National Center for Health Statistics, 1968.

Gove, W. "The relationship between sex-roles, marital status and mental illness." *Social Forces* 51 (1972):33-44.

Gray, S.W. "Masculinity-Femininity in relation to anxiety and social acceptance." *Child Development* 28 (1957):203-214.

Gurin, G.; Veroff, J.; and Feld, S. *Americans View Their Mental Health: A Nationwide Interview Survey.* New York: Basic Books, 1960.

Hopkins, J.H. "The lesbian personality." *British Journal of Psychiatry* 115 (1969):1433-1436.

Jahoda, M. *Current Concepts of Positive Mental Health.* New York: Basic Books, 1958.

————. "Criteria for positive mental health." In *Psychopathology Today*, edited by W.S. Sahakian. Itasca, Ill.: F.E. Peacock, 1970.

Johnson, W.B., and Terman, L.M. "Personality characteristics of happily married, unhappily married, and divorced persons." *Character and Personality* 2 (June 1935):304-305.

Keller, S. "The female role: Constants and change." In *Women in Therapy*, edited by V. Franks and V. Burtle. New York: Brunner/ Mazel, 1974.

Kenyon, F.E. "Studies in female homosexuality, 4 and 5." *British Journal of Psychiatry* 114 (1968):1337-1350.

Knupfer, G.; Clark, W.; and Room, R. "The mental health of the unmarried." *American Journal of Psychiatry* 122 (1966):841-851.

Maccoby, E.E., and Jacklin, C.N. *Psychology of Sex Differences*. Stanford, Calif.: Stanford University Press, 1974.

MacKinnon, D.W. "The nature and nurture of creative talent." *American Psychologist* 17 (1962):484-495.

Moss, H., and Kagan, J. "Maternal influences on early I.Q. scores." *Psychological Reports* 4 (1958):655-661.

Oberstone, A.K. "Dimensions of psychological adjustment and style of life in single lesbians and single heterosexual women." Doctoral dissertation, California School of Professional Psychology, 1974. *Dissertation Abstracts* 35/10-B (1974):5088 (University Microfilms No. 75-8510).

Oetzel, R. "The relationship between sex-role acceptance and cognitive abilities." Master's thesis, Stanford University, 1961.

Orlofsky, J.L. "Sex-role orientation, identity formation, and self-esteem in college men and women." *Sex Roles* 3 (1977):561-575.

Roe, A. "Personal problems and science." In *The Third (1959) University of Utah Research Conference on the Identification of Creative Scientific Talent*, edited by C.W. Taylor. Salt Lake City: University of Utah Press, 1959.

Rogers, C. *Client-Centered Therapy*. Boston: Houghton Mifflin, 1951.

Siegelman, M. "Adjustment of homosexual and heterosexual women." *British Journal of Psychiatry* 120 (1972):477-481.

Spence, J.T.; Helmreich, R.; and Stapp, J. "Ratings of self-peers on sex-role attributes and their relation to self-esteem and conceptions of masculinity and femininity." *Journal of Personality and Social Psychology* 32 (1975):29-39.

Thompson, N.L.; McCandless, B.R.; and Strickland, B.R. "Personal adjustment of male and female homosexuals and heterosexuals." *Journal of Abnormal Psychology* 78 (1971):237-240.

U.S. Department of Health, Education, and Welfare. *Selected Symptoms of Psychological Distress, United States*. Washington: U.S. Department of Health, Education, and Welfare, Public Health Service, Health Service and Mental Health Administration, August 1970.

Van Dusen, R., and Sheldon, E. "The changing status of American women: A life cycle perspective." *American Psychologist* 31 (1976):106-116.

Webb, A.P. "Sex-role preferences and adjustment in early adolescents." *Child Development* 34 (1963):609-618.

Wetter, R. "Levels of self-esteem associated with four sex role categories." Paper presented at the 83d Annual Convention of the American Psychological Association, Chicago, 1975.

Wilson, M.L., and Greene, R.L. "Personality characteristics of female homosexuals." *Psychological Reports* 28 (1971):407-412.

4 Stratification and Exclusion

Power has been defined as control over resources, and *institutions* have been defined as concentrations of power in the service of some value (Stinchcombe 1968). Historically, the institutions[1] that have largely determined the status of women are the family (sex and reproduction, socialization of children) and the economic system (production, distribution, and consumption) (Mitchell 1966). In patriarchal systems, the primary value served by institutions is male supremacy. In the family structure, male supremacy supports the view of women as the property of man and ensures paternity through monogamous marriage (Davis 1971; Mitchell 1966). In the economic system, sexual stratification has ensured male control over economic resources.

The defining of deviance is also a prerogative of power (Dieppa 1972). In tracing the history of legal and social control over voluntary sexual conduct, May (1930) identified the cornerstone of prohibitions as the patriarchal view of woman as the property of man. This view predicated the concept of monogamous marriage as the only acceptable form of sexual union, and criminal laws were enacted prohibiting other forms of sexual union. Thus, laws controlling voluntary nonmarital sexual expression enforced the concept of family organization necessary to ensure paternity and patriarchal rights. Economically, stratification by sexual orientation has served to reduce competition for resources.

Lesbianism and male homosexuality have been perceived as countervailing forces in patriarchal systems, for they represent nonreproductive sexual alternatives. The cultural negation of lesbianism has served to maintain the link between sex and reproduction and to preserve women's economic dependence on men. More recently, the rationale for stigmatizing lesbianism has been provided by the individual-deficiency model, which serves the vested interests of men who both perpetuate the ideology and are served by it. The employment of this model to negate lesbianism has diverted attention from the cultural and institutional forces which originally mandated this negation and justifies the ongoing restriction of lesbian women from equal access to social and economic opportunities.

Minority Status of Women

The unequal status of women in our society has been analyzed at various levels. Hochschild (1973) classified the various perspectives by their

53

primary unit of analysis: sex differences, sex roles, women as a minority group, and women as a caste. She states (p. 1013):

> Each puts a different construction on the behavior of the two sexes; what is to type 1 a feminine trait such as passivity is to type 2 a role element, to type 3 is a minority characteristic, and to type 4 is a response to powerlessness.

These units of analysis are roughly analogous to the four major explanatory theories of human behavior, that is, the biological, psychological, sociological, and cultural explanations.

Data are available to support the view that the outcome of women's ascribed status has characteristics of both a caste and a minority. A *caste* society is one in which groups of people are assigned superior or inferior positions in the stratification hierarchy on the basis of some common ascribed characteristic (Chafetz 1974). Patriarchy has been described as a sexual caste system (Andreas 1971; Chafetz 1974; Hacker 1951) which perpetuates male dominance of major institutions and thus male control over economic and social resources. That is, patriarchy, by assigning subordinate roles to women, effectively reduces competition for scarce and prized resources. The status of women in major societal institutions supports the caste view and quantifies exclusion.

Women's position in the U.S. economy has been detailed by numerous authors (Amundsen 1971; Bernard 1971; Bird 1968; Chafetz 1974; Epstein 1970; Knudsen 1969; Mead and Kaplan 1965). The statistics presented here are illustrative of their findings. Women comprise a growing share of the workforce (49 percent in 1975), but receive a declining percentage of men's pay (63 percent in 1956, 57 percent in 1974), earning less in every category of occupation. In business, fewer than 12 percent of the directors of the 1,300 largest companies are women. Among top-level management in the federal Civil Services, only 4 percent are women. Women comprise 7 percent of all lawyers and 9 percent of all physicians. In academia, women are only 21 percent of all college and university professors, 8.6 percent of the full professors, and 13 percent of those receiving doctorates. Women comprise 4.3 percent of the Armed Forces and are a fractional number in the ministry. In politics, although women comprise 53 percent of registered voters, they hold only 5 percent of elective positions. In 1974, median earnings of full-time workers were white men, $12,343; minority men, $9,082; white women, $7,025; minority women, $6,611 ("Special Section: The American Woman" 1975).

These figures indicate that sexual stratification is the most salient factor in maintaining patterns of inequitable resource allocation, followed closely by racial stratification. That there is no singular stratification hierarchy in our society, as the caste concept implies, suggests that the minority concept is more accurate both in describing women's status and in defining the common conditions of excluded groups.

In broad terms, some psychological consequences of internalizing the cultural negation of one's minority group have been identified as group self-hatred, self-castigation, identification with the dominant group, and the creation of self-fulfilling prophecies with always adverse outcomes (for example, Allport 1954; Hacker 1951; Lewin 1948). Some of the behavioral consequences as expressed toward majority-group members may be excessive accommodation behaviors such as smiling and laughing (protective clowning), appearing helpless or ignorant, a deferential posture and manner, and concealment of real feelings (Allport 1954). Minority characteristics of women have been described more specifically as including dislike for their own sex, negative self-image, insecurity, self-blame, a submissive attitude, identification with males, and low aspirations (Allport 1954; Freeman 1971; Hacker 1951; Myrdal 1944). Some research has shown that women are prejudiced toward their own sex (Goldberg 1972) and have a more negative self-concept than men (Broverman et al, 1972). [*Prejudice* is defined as a stereotyped negative set of attitudes; *discrimination*, as a stereotyped negative set of behaviors (Kirsch 1974).]

In the literature, the common reference for a definition of minority group was that coined by Wirth (1945), p. 347:

> A minority group is any group of people who, because of their physical or cultural characteristics, are singled out from the others in the society in which they live for differential and unequal treatment, and who therefore regard themselves as objects of collective discrimination.

This definition is not sufficiently inclusive on the objective criterion, that is, "physical or cultural characteristics." And its employment of a subjective criterion (that is, "regard themselves as objects of collective discrimination") is a blame-the-victim distortion.

Concerning the objective criterion, Allport (1954) listed the types of groups against which prejudice was known to exist througout the world. This list includes groups based on race, sex, age level, ethnicity, linguistic characteristics, caste, region, ideology, nation, religion, social class, occupation and educational level. It includes many groups which experience prejudice for reasons not covered by Wirth's "physical or cultural" criterion.

In regard to the subjective criterion—the awareness of discrimination—Hacker (1951) has suggested that there are two types who would not fit this specification: those who do not know that they are being discriminated against on a group basis and, those who acknowledge the propriety of differential treatment on a group basis. She adds, "Although the term 'minority group' is inapplicable to both types, the term 'minority group status' may be substituted" (p. 61). Although individuals in the former category lack awareness of their status and individuals in the latter category accept it, members of a minority group nonetheless share the same status and are subject to the same discrimination.

Since there is currently disagreement about what constitutes a minority group, criteria are proposed here which are based on *outcome*. Members of a society possess an infinite number of differing characteristics, but the outcome of possessing a "different" characteristic is not standardized. In general, minority status exists if, on the basis of a group characteristic, an individual's legal rights, economic opportunities, or social benefits are restricted. In this context, "minority" equates with marginality and relative powerlessness, contains no quantitative referent in terms of number of people occupying the category, and refers to groups which are interchangeable over time. The criteria suggested are as follows: (1) A *minority group* may be defined as any group of people who, on the basis of one characteristic, are categorically ascribed inferior status, denied equal access to legitimate socioeconomic opportunities, and denied equal participation and fair representation in major societal institutions. (2) This condition as defined here has persisted over time, is systemically embedded in the culture, and requires institutional change as opposed to individual change for alleviation and prevention.

Rationale for Minority Exclusion

Categorical ascription of inferior status on the basis of sex, sexual orientation, race, ethnicity, or any other group characteristic reduces social, sexual, and economic competition and thus protects the vested interests of those who control resources. Effective exclusion requires a supportive ideology, however, for exclusion must be justified according to whatever doctrine governs the prevailing belief system in any given society at any given time. The current U.S. belief system derives from both religion and science. If one basis for justification loses credibility, the other is generally invoked.

The secular basis has been largely the product of social science. We noted earlier Ryan's (1971) description of the method by which social science has implemented the individual-deficiency doctrine: (1) identify a social problem; (2) study those affected by the problem and discover in what ways they are different from the rest of us; (3) define the differences as the cause of the social problem itself; and (4) change the victim. He makes the following inference about the utility of this blaming-the-victim ideology (Ryan 1971, p. 29):

. . . if unsatisfactory resolution of one's Oedipus complex accounts for all emotional distress and mental disorder, then by all means let us attend to that and postpone worrying about the pounding day-to-day stresses of life on the bottom rungs that drive so many to drink, dope, and madness.

One function of the individual-deficiency approach is, of course, to divert attention from the systemic necessity to reduce social, sexual, and economic competition. Psychoanalytic theory, by declaring a double standard of mental health for women and men and by declaring lesbianism and homosexuality to be pathological, provided an accounting system for individual difference. Sociological theory, by labeling nonconforming groups as "deviant subcultures," provided an accounting system for group differences which, not incidentally, failed to discriminate among symptoms of victimization, victims, and victimizers. (Throughout the literature of deviancy one finds homosexuality grouped with drug addiction, alcoholism, prostitution, and criminality).

The lexicon of human groups is not a benign classificatory system, but an instrument of communication and control used to define the identity, status, and destiny of target groups (Baird 1970). Duster (1970) identified the overall condition necessary for exclusion as denial of the humanity of the victims. This is achieved in part by name calling; by implying that if contact is unavoidable, it is unequal; and by ensuring that the values and culture of target populations are seen as useless or ridiculous. Szasz (1970, p. 244) noted similarly, "As the man with the Jewish religion was considered not fully human because he was not Christian—so the homosexual is considered not fully human because he is not heterosexual."

These exclusionary tactics serve the vested interests of those empowered to exercise them. Chesler (1972) has estimated that no more than 12 percent of the United States' two most powerful clinical professions, psychiatry and psychology, are women. And Chesler (1972, pp. 63-65) concluded, "It is obvious that a predominately female psychiatric population in America has been diagnosed, psychoanalyzed, researched, and hospitalized by a predominantly male professional population." Similarly, about 98 per cent of sociologists are white males from middle- and upper-middle-class backgrounds (Glenn and Weiner 1969). It is not surprising, then, that this industry's "official version of social reality" services an ideology which justifies the exclusion of nonwhite, nonmale groups.

Some members of minority groups within the social sciences are contributing to a reconstruction of social reality. This endeavor begins by rejecting the notion of value-free social science: "Science is inevitably a handservant of ideology, a tool for people to shape, if not create reality" (McWorter 1973). Reconstruction continues with a redefinition of "social problems" from the viewpoint of those who purportedly have or are the problem.

Social and Economic Exclusion of Lesbian Women

The individual-deficiency model allows for ascribing nonconformity to cultural norms and social mores to some psychological defect in the non-conforming individual, as opposed to taking into account the impact of economic and social exclusion on the behavior of members of marginal groups. According to Allport (1954), two functions of stratification are the division of labor and the defining of social prerogatives. Consequences of sexual stratification and stratification by sociosexual preference, then, should be most apparent through the examination of economic barriers and social restrictions. This section reports the findings of my study in relation to these two areas, beginning with social restrictions.

Social Exclusion

The right to marry and form a family are social prerogatives of opposite-sex pairs, and thus no institutional means are available to same-sex pairs to share in these cultural goals. Paradoxically, lesbian women are frequently characterized as having rejected the social institutions of marriage and family, although attitudes toward these institutions have never been empirically examined. To ascertain attitudes toward marriage and family formation per se, divested of the contingency requiring an opposite-sex partner, I gathered data regarding these institutions and related values in terms of same-sex relations.

Attitudes toward legally sanctioned same-sex marriages, child rearing, and monogamy were found to be quite polarized among respondents. Those for whom sufficient data were available were found to be nearly equally divided on most of these issues. Table 4-1 shows these results.

A composite measure of these three items was formulated, the *value index,* to provide an overall score reflecting either a traditional or a nontraditional value constellation. The traditional classification represents two or three of the following choices: expects sexual fidelity in a couple relationship, probably would get married, and may want to raise a child. The nontraditional classification represents two or three of the following choices: prefers to be free to have affairs, would never want to be married, and has no desire to raise a child. The value index indicated that 41.8 percent of the total sample held nontraditional values, 33.5 percent held traditional values, and insufficient data were available for 24.7 percent. Upon analysis, certain variables were found to partially account for these differences in attitudes.

Attitudes toward monogamy were found to vary with age and political orientation (results on "political orientation" are presented in the following

Table 4-1
Attitudes toward Monogamy, Marriage, and Children

	View	*Percentage*
Monogamy	Expect sexual fidelity	50.8
	Free to have other relationships	49.2
Same-sex marriage	Would never marry	48.4
	No longer would marry	13.8
	Probably would marry	37.8
Child rearing	Interested in child rearing	49.2
	Not interested in child rearing	50.7

section). Preference for monogamy, defined here as sexual fidelity, increased with age ($x^2 = 22.47$, $df = 6$, $p < .001$) and procapitalist orientation ($x^2 = 30.21$, $df = 4$, $p < .00001$). Profidelity did not relate to socioeconomic status of respondents or economic status of family of origin. Further, there was no relationship between age and political orientation, even though both were related to attitudes toward monogamy.

The overall picture of lesbian attitudes toward monogamy (51 percent in favor, 49 percent not in favor) may be compared with the results of a recent study which surveyed views on masculinity (Tavris 1977) and tapped 28,000 respondents who were readers of *Psychology Today*. Men in general felt sexual fidelity was less important for men than for women (42 percent important for a man, 56 percent important for a woman). About 67 percent of the women felt it was important for both men and women. The lesbian-profidelity figure in my study, then, is closer to the male than the female percentage, although the lesbian sample was not asked to differentiate attitudes by sex.

Both political orientation and economic status of family of origin were found to correlate significantly with attitudes toward legally sanctioned same-sex marriage ($x^2 = 26.10$, $df = 4$, $p < .00001$ and $x^2 = 8.40$, $df = 3$, $p < .04$, respectively). The percentage of respondents who favored legal marriage increased as political orientation became more procapitalism and as the economic status of the family of origin became higher. Attitudes toward legally sanctioned same-sex marriages were not related to age or socioeconomic status of respondents.

Attitudes toward child rearing, however, were related to age and socioeconomic status, as well as to political orientation. There was less interest in child rearing as age increased ($x^2 = 127.33$, $df = 48$, $p < .00001$), as socioeconomic status rose ($x^2 = 59.04$, $df = 40$, $p < .002$), and as political orientation became more procapitalism ($x^2 = 9.96$, $df = 4$, $p < .04$). Economic status of family of origin was not related to views toward child rearing.

In sum, respondents in this study who favored legal marriage were more often procapitalism and from upper-middle- or upper-class families. Respondents who favored monogamy were more often over 30 and procapitalism. On the other hand, those interested in raising children were more often under 30, of lower-class status, and more politically radical. In regard to this last finding, it is speculated that few aspects of discrimination could be more potentially alienating than the treatment of lesbian mothers in this society.

The age factor demarcated values for both child rearing and monogamy at age 30. Those under 30 were more likely to favor raising children, but less likely to want sexual fidelity. Those over 30 were more likely to be disinterested in raising children, but more likely to want sexual fidelity. The age of 30 has been found to relate to the stabilization of a lesbian sociosexual orientation as well (Saghir and Robins 1969). It was, by and large, the age at which heterosexual experimentation ceased.

These findings as a whole seem compatible with adult development and constraints affecting a lesbian orientation. Adolescence and young adulthood are the stages of development in which most young people begin to date, "court," and generally begin to form ideas through tentative relationships about what they consider to be desirable characteristics in a potential partner. This activity is more often delayed for same-sex-oriented young women until they are emancipated from their families and are of age to enter the lesbian subculture. Hence, a monogamous relationship at this stage may seem less desirable than having the freedom to explore.

Culturally enforced negative sanctions against lesbian women create stress and conflict during this emergent and exploratory stage which would account in part for continued attempts to adapt to heterosexual conventions. The possibility of raising children is more feasible in young adulthood, for one's future seems less determined and multiple options appear to be available.

If and when this period of exploration confirms for the individual her love-object choice and this choice is for a member of her own sex, the desire for a stable relationship appears to gain priority. At the same time, the precariousness of being a lesbian mother in a society which continues to deny lesbian mothers custody of their own children would discourage most from considering parenthood. Those interested in being a partner to a lesbian mother may invest emotionally and financially in child rearing while having no legal status as parent, whether in custody prerogatives, for tax purposes, educational benefits, or any situation in which legal status is pertinent. Thus, by age 30, more lesbian women favor monogamy, and fewer are interested in childrearing.

The extent to which these attitudes were formed before or after an awareness of one's sociosexual orientation is inconclusive. That is, whether a woman's disinclination toward more or less permanent relational commitments (partner, child) is a factor in love-object choices or is an attitudinal adaptation to the actual constraints of lesbian status cannot be stated on the basis of these data. The data show, however, that 24 percent of the sample had been or were still legally married, while 72 percent of the sample had never married, and that 16 percent of the sample had children. Additionally, in response to the question which ascertained whether one would, given the option, legally marry a same-sex partner, only 36 percent stated that they probably would, while 59 percent indicated that they would not. Thus, a favorable disposition toward legal marriage appears to have improved only slightly, from about one-fourth to a little over one-third of the sample, in relation to sex of partner. While only about one out of six actually had children, more than two out of five indicated an interest in raising children. In this area, then, a marked change seems to occur in relation to sex of partner.

It is also apparent that a lack of enthusiasm for legal marriage does not equate with a lack of desire for a stable relationship. Respondents ranked various life goals according to their importance to them, and more of the sample ranked a stable relationship first or second (59 percent) than any other life goal. Life goals in rank of importance are shown in table 4-2.

In combination with the results indicating that 51 percent of the sample were promonogamy and 49 percent were not and that 51 percent were currently coupled while 47 percent were not, a roughly equal division seems apparent in relational expectations. These percentages suggest that characterizations of lesbian women as conventional and conservative (for example, Cotton 1975; Hedblom 1972; Simon and Gagnon 1967) may have been considerably overstated.

Collectively, however, these results do not suport the antifamily

Table 4-2
Life-Goal Priorities of Respondents

Goals	Percentage		
	First	*Second*	*Combined*
A stable love relationship	33.8	25.6	59.4
Notable achievement in work	30.2	20.4	50.6
Spiritual growth	22.4	9.6	32.0
Trustworthy friends	12.0	24.5	36.5
Financial security	8.8	12.2	21.0
Good sexual relations	2.6	7.2	9.8

stereotype sometimes presumed of lesbian women, and they suggest that differences, if any, between lesbian women and women in general may be only a matter of degree. The Census Bureau reported in 1975 that marriages are declining, divorce rates are increasing, and more women are remaining single longer and having fewer children (if any) when they do marry ("Women of the Year" 1976). Further, the number of never-married women over the age of 24 has doubled in the past few years ("Special Section: The American Woman" 1975).

These figures indicate that an increasing number of women are choosing careers and economic independence over marriage and children, a choice, of course, that men do not have to make. Lesbian women, in contrast, seldom have the option not to work. As shown in table 4-2, the second most consistent goal of respondents was "notable achievement in work," ranked first or second in priority by 51 percent. (Paradoxically, only 21 percent ranked "financial security" first or second.) These findings suggest, then, that more than economic necessity is motivating occupational endeavors. The desire for self-fulfillment through attainment seems to be also a factor. The pathways toward high achievement for lesbian women, however, present a disproportionate number of obstacles.

Economic Barriers

The commitment to career among lesbian women is further emphasized by the demographic data, which show that more than three out of five respondents had or were working toward a college degree (63 percent). Of the sample 19 percent, or almost one in five, reported their current occupation as student; 44 percent had completed at least one college degree, compared to 10 percent of the general adult female population (Bureau of the Census 1975). This finding is similar to that reported by Henry (1955) who, in reference to homosexual men, found that there were nearly four times as many college graduates among this group as in the general census group (42 percent versus 11.7 percent). The number of respondents with advanced education or professional degrees was nine times greater than in the general adult female population (28.3 percent versus 3.0 percent) (Bureau of the Census 1975). Other studies (Kenyon 1968; Wilson and Greene 1971) have also found lesbian women to have higher educational levels than nonlesbian women.

Chafetz (1974) discussed some of the myths which have provided the rationale for discrimination against women in employment. She repudiates these myths as they apply to all women, but two of them are particularly inapplicable to lesbian women: "females are only working for 'pin money,' " and "women aren't worth hiring where any training or investment is involved, since they just get married or pregnant and quit'' (Chafetz 1974, pp. 124-125). Clearly, lesbian women are not working for "pin money" since few would have the option to not work. Further, the probability of marriage and/or pregnancy is relatively nonexistent. The "Catch 22" provided by the sociocultural environment is, of course, that stating their lesbian orientation to an employer may jeopardize their existing or potential position.

Information was obtained on the issue of disclosure in the work environment. Respondents were asked, "Would your job or business be in jeopardy if your lesbianism were known?" Of the four possible responses, 12 percent of the sample answered "yes," 20.2 percent answered "probably," 29.2 percent answered "don't know," and 38.6 percent were able to state unequivocally "no." Thus, nearly two-thirds of respondents could not state with any certainty that they would not lose their jobs if their sociosexual orientation were known. The discordance of these findings with the fact that half of the respondents stated that achievement or satisfaction in their work was either their first or second priority in life is apparent.

Considerable variability on this issue was found among regions. The total sample of 675 was divided into subsamples for data analysis, showing that 44.5 percent were from southern California, 36.1 percent were from northern California, and 19.4 percent were from other geographical areas. Regional differences can be seen in table 4-3. (Subsamples are further described in Appendix A.)

It can be seen that only 21 percent from northern California indicated that their jobs might be jeopardized if their orientation were known to their employer; by comparison, this figure for the other two geographical regions (38.9 percent, southern California; 40.3 percent, other regions) was about twice as high. These regional differences suggest that the psychological environment in which lesbian women pursue their careers varies greatly according to place of residence and may well be a major determinant in overall career satisfaction.

Overall, irrespective of the high level of aspiration and education

Table 4-3
Job Jeopardy among Respondents, by Region

Job Would Be in Jeopardy	Percentage		
	Northern California	Southern California	Other Regions
Yes	8.1	13.1	16.9
Probably	12.9	25.8	23.4
Don't know	26.7	30.1	35.0
No	52.4	30.9	31.5

among respondents, nearly two out of three felt that their jobs might be jeopardized if their orientation were known. Moreover, although graduate education was nine times more prevalent among respondents than among the general adult female population (28.3 percent versus 3.0 percent), the mean income of the sample was $4,739, which is slightly above the comparable figure for all white females ($4,328) and considerably below the mean income of white males who have a seventh-grade education or less ($5,874) (Bureau of the Census 1975).

Irrespective of educational or aspirational level, then, lesbian women have neither a sense of security in their jobs nor equitable economic rewards. The latter fact, of course, is attributed to the economic effects of sexual stratification in general, since sociosexual orientation is not typically known by employers. The awareness that one's sex is a greater obstacle to economic security than is one's sociosexual orientation was reflected by respondents in their assessment of stress areas in their lives. Respondents ranked aspects of their identities which they felt caused the most stress in their lives, and more than twice as many attributed greater stress to being female than to being lesbian (58.3 percent versus 28.6 percent).

This finding is not surprising in that the majority of lesbian women are not "visible" as such, nor are they "disclosed," but all are visibly female. Discrimination on the basis of lesbian status, then, is variable; discrimination on the basis of female status is consistent, and being female in a patriarchal system results in reduced socioeconomic opportunities and rewards.

Alienation from the present socioeconomic system was clearly indicated in the political orientations of respondents, shown in table 4-4.

Thus, about one-third of the total sample ascribed in some degree to capitalism, while about two-thirds did not. These results do not appear to differ widely from those obtained in a poll conducted for the Peoples Bicentennial Commission by Hart Research Associates, who interviewed 1,209 people in all regions and on all income levels. In reference to the economy, 41 percent favored "making a major adjustment to try things

Table 4-4
Political Orientation of Respondents

View	Percentage
Procapitalism	18.8
Capitalism with power- structure change	16.2
Radical change in means of production and distribution	55.8
Anarchy	9.2

which have not been tried before," while 37 percent favored minor economic changes and only 17 percent felt the economic system should be kept as it is (*San Francisco Sunday Examiner and Chronicle* 1975).

In relation to the areas discussed in this chapter, then, the attitudes and values of lesbian women do not appear to diverge importantly from those found in the general population. As is the case with other minority groups, a fair proportion of lesbian women appear to share the traditional cultural goals of our society, but they are in many ways denied the institutional means to attain these goals. Exclusion from or unequal access to the social and economic rewards of a society results in increased stress for members of excluded groups. Thus the conceptualization of minority stress within the context of relevant stress research is the subject of the next chapter.

Note

1. Institutions may be concrete organizational forms or customs, attitudes, and beliefs common enough to be considered typical or prevailing (*Manas* 1972).

References

Allport, G.W. *The Nature of Prejudice*. Reading, Mass.: Addison-Wesley, 1954.

Amundsen, K. *The Silenced Majority*. Englewood Cliffs, N.J.: Prentice-Hall, 1971.

Andreas, C. *Sex and Caste in America*. Englewood Cliffs, N.J.: Prentice-Hall, 1971.

Baird, K.E. "Semantics and Afro-American liberation." *Social Casework* 51 (1970):265-269.

Bernard, J. "The paradox of the happy marriage." In *Women in Sexist Society,* edited by V. Gornick and B. Moran. New York: Basic Books, 1971.

Bird, C. *Born Female: The High Cost of Keeping Women Down*. New York: David McKay, 1968.

Broverman, I.K.; Vogel, S.R.; Broverman, D.M.; Clarkson, F.E.; and Rosenkrantz, P.S. "Sex-role sterotypes: A current appraisal." *Journal of Social Issues* 28 (1972):59-78.

Bureau of the Census. In *The World Almanac*. New York: Newspaper Enterprise Association, 1975.

Chafetz, J. *Masculine/Feminine or Human? An Overview of the Sociology of Sex Roles*. Itasca, Ill.: F.E. Peacock, 1974.

Chesler, P. *Women and Madness.* Garden City, N.Y.: Doubleday, 1972.

Cotton, W.L. "Social and sexual relationships of lesbians." *The Journal of Sex Research* 11 (1975):139-148.

Davis, E.G. *The First Sex.* Baltimore, Md.: Penguin Books, 1971.

Dieppa, I. "Ethnic minority content in the social work curriculum." Paper presented in Workshop Series on Minority Group Content and the Enrichment of Social Work Curriculum for the Consortium of Texas Schools of Social Work, Austin, Tex., April 24-25, 1972.

Duster, T. "Conditions for a guilt-free massacre." Paper presented at Wright Institute's Conference on the Legitimation of Evil, February 21-22, 1970, San Francisco.

Epstein, C.F. *Woman's Place.* Berkeley: University of California Press, 1970.

Freeman, J. "The building of the gilded cage." In *Notes from the Third Year,* edited by A. Koedt and S. Firestone. New York: Notes From the Second Year, 1971.

Glenn, N., and Weiner, D. "Some trends in the social origins of American sociologists." *The American Sociologist* 4 (1969):291-302.

Goldberg, P. "Are women prejudiced against women?" In *Toward a Sociology of Women,* edited by C. Safilios-Rothschild. Lexington, Mass.: Xerox, 1972.

Hacker, H.M. "Women as a minority group." *Social Forces* 30 (1951): 60-69.

Hedblom, J.H. "Social, sexual, and occupational lives of homosexual women." *Sexual Behavior* 2 (1972):33-37.

Henry, G. *All the Sexes: A Study of Masculinity and Feminity.* New York: Rinehart, 1955.

Hochschild, A.R. "A review of sex role research." *American Journal of Sociology* 78 (1973):1011-1029.

Kenyon, F.E. "Studies in female homosexuality 4 and 5." *British Journal of Psychiatry* 114 (1968):1337-1350.

Kirsh, B. "Consciousness-raising groups as therapy for women." In *Women in Therapy,* edited by V. Franks and V. Burtle. New York: Brunner/Mazel, 1974.

Knudsen, D. "The declining status of women: Popular myths and the failure of functionalist thought." *Social Forces* 48 (December 1969): 183-193.

Lewin, K. *Resolving Social Conflicts.* New York: Harper, 1948.

Manas 25, no. 47 (November 22, 1972):1.

May, G. *Social Control of Sex Expression.* New York: William Morrow, 1930.

McWorter, G.A. "The ideology of black social science." In *The Death of White Sociology,* edited by J.A. Ladner. New York: Vintage, 1973.

Mead, M., and Kaplan, F., eds. *American Women: The Report of the President's Commission on the Status of Women.* New York: Scribner, 1965.

Mitchell, J. "Women: The longest revolution." *New Left Review* 40 (1966):11-37.

Myrdal, G. *An American Dilemma.* New York: Harper, 1944.

Ryan, W. *Blaming the Victim.* New York: Vintage, 1971.

Saghir, M., and Robins, E. "Homesexuality. I. Sexual behavior of the female homosexual." *Archives of General Psychiatry* 20 (1969): 192-201.

San Francisco Sunday Examiner and Chronicle 1975, no. 35 (August 31, 1975):1, 4A, col. 6.

Simon, W., and Gagnon, J. "Femininity in the lesbian community." *Social Problems* 15 (1967):212-221.

"Special Section: The American Woman." *U.S. News and World Report,* December 8, 1975, pp. 54-74.

Stinchcombe, A.L. *Constructing Social Theories.* New York: Harcourt Brace and World, 1968.

Szasz, T. *The Manufacture of Madness.* New York: Dell, 1970.

Tavris, C. "The new masculinity." *Psychology Today,* January 1977.

Wilson, M.L., and Greene, R.L. "Personality characteristics of female homosexuals." *Psychological Reports* 28 (1971):407-412.

Wirth, L. "The problem of minority groups." In *The Science of Man in the World Crisis,* edited by R. Linton. New York: Columbia University Press, 1945.

"Women of the Year—Great Changes, New Chances, Tough Choices." *Time,* January 5, 1976, pp. 6-16.

Part II
Minority Stress:
Theoretical and
Empirical Model

5 The Theory of Minority Stress

The initial cause of minority stress is the cultural ascription of inferior status to particular groups. This ascription of defectiveness to various categories of people, particularly categories based on sex, race, and sociosexual preference, often precipitates negative life events for the minority member over which the individual has little control. The repetitive occurrence of these negative events can induce a sense of powerlessness which, in turn, may lead to maladaptive responses. Responses to these negative events can be expected to vary according to the mediating resources available to the individual, both internal and external. To the extent that these mediating resources can be identified, efforts toward the alleviation of minority stress can become more effective. This chapter begins with an examination of the general field of stress theory and research to ascertain information which may contribute to understanding minority stress.

Overview of Stress Theory

Stressors may be defined as any antecedent agent or situation that requires a system to readjust or adapt. They may originate from multiple sources, including the natural environment, the man-made environment, culture, social milieus, psychological events, and biophysical phenomena. In this context, the focus is on sociocultural events which result in psychological and sometimes biophysical stress. *Stress* in a system may be defined as the state intervening between an antecedent stressor and consequent readjustment or adaptation (Dohrenwend 1961; Holmes and Rahe 1967; Selye 1974). This book is primarily concerned with stress in the individual system, but systems concepts generally apply to any size of system, such as groups, communities, or nations. Adaptation generally connotes a positive resolution, and maladaptation generally refers to a negative resolution of stress; however, these classifications require a value judgment and in some instances may be arbitrary. For example, a woman may be offered an important job promotion that requires her to move to another city, and at the same time, she may be reluctant to leave her present location in which her affiliative needs are well met. This example illustrates that although accepting the new position may be adaptive (functional) in relation to career advancement, it may be maladaptive (dysfunctional) in relation to her social ties. Adaptation, then, must be considered contextually and from the perspective of adaptive for whom and for how long. The designation of responses to stressors as adaptive or maladaptive is, at best, contingent on a value-based equation between the primacy of individual needs and the prevailing norms of a society at a given time. The general paradigm for viewing the stress process is presented in figure 5-1, with the circle representing any open system.

The investigation of variables that appear to critically affect responses to stress has, in general, pursued two avenues: one has focused on properties or conditions of the stressor itself, and the other has focused on characteristics of the person(s) exposed to the stressor. The first approach, focusing on properties or conditions of the stressor, has led to the theory that the frequency, duration, and intensity of a stressor are the most critical determinants of responses. The second approach, examining characteristics of the individual exposed to the stressor, has led various investigators to identify three major factors as most critical in determining responses to stressors: the meaning of the event to the individual, the degree of threat to the gratification of needs, and the amount of change required. Most investigators of stress outcomes acknowledge that these four influences are interrelated and that each aspect contributes to stress responses. However, they differ considerably in regard to which factor receives major emphasis.

These differences in emphasis are reflected in the conclusions of several stress investigators. For example, Selye (1974, pp. 28-29) concludes, "From the point of view of its stress-producing or stressor activity, it is immaterial whether the agent or situation we face is pleasant or unpleasant; all that counts is the intensity of the demand for readjustment or adaptation." A different conclusion was reached by Brown (1974), who examined causal links between life events and schizophrenia and depression. His findings

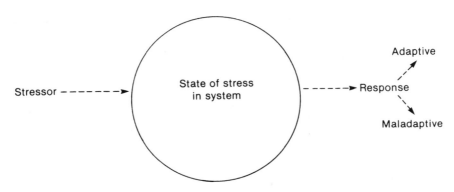

Figure 5-1. Stress Paradigm

indicate that dysfunction is associated with severe long-term threat events, but not with short-term threat events. Further, the experience of loss was the most important component of long-term threat events. Brown (1974, p. 236) concludes, "There is little doubt that the existence of a causal link between life events and illness makes theoretical sense only when considered in terms of the meaning of life events for particular individuals." In contrast, Lieberman (1974, p. 152), on the basis of his investigation of stress among the elderly, concludes, "The central element in defining crisis is the degree of change and not the meaning a person attaches to the particular event, or even the amount of loss involved."

Other research findings contradict Selye's (1974) view that the desirability or undesirability of the event is immaterial and, similarly, Lieberman's (1975) conclusion that the degree of change required is the critical factor in stress as opposed to the meaning of the event. [It should be noted that Lieberman's (1975) research was conducted with an elderly nursing home population, and it could be that change per se has a much more critical impact as age increases.] Vinokur and Selzer (1975) found that the linkage between stressful events and "mental distress" did not hold for desirable life events, but was present for undesirable events. They conclude that the quality of the events, that is, their desirability or undesirability, is the crucial determinant of outcomes of stress. Myers, Lindenthal, and Pepper (1974) also found that "psychiatric symptoms" were related to undesirable events more than to desirable events. Together, these findings support Brown's (1974) thesis that the meaning of an event to an individual must be considered the critical factor in the overall impact of a stressor.

The different conclusions of stress investigators at this stage of social-science efforts to unravel stress phenomena are not surprising, and each makes an important contribution to a fuller knowledge of individual responses to stressful life events. Cumulatively, each contribution allows successive efforts to incorporate additional knowledge and expand the framework of inquiry. From this perspective, a framework is employed here that leads toward a synthesis of the factors found to be most salient in individual responses to stress.

In agreement with Brown (1974), the central thesis of this framework is that the meaning of an event to a specific person in a specific situation is the crucible of a stressor's impact. Components of the "meaning of the event" which may lend themselves to greater specificity are the degree of threat to need fulfillment (for example, self-esteem, esteem from others, sexual satisfaction, economic maintenance) and the amount of change required by the event. These components obviously would be importantly affected by the frequency, duration, and intensity of the stressor. Although the study of the interrelatedness of these components is of vital interest to investigators of general stress phenomena, the relevance of these factors to conceptualizing minority stress is the primary purpose here.

Characteristics of Stressors

The duration of a stressor is generally categorized as short- versus long-term or brief versus prolonged, but this division is based on a somewhat arbitrary demarcation point along a continuum. The duration of the stressor itself can be differentiated from the duration of the *effect* of the stressor on an individual, but the latter would be expected to vary according to characteristics of the individual. Irrespective of whether the duration of the stressor or the duration of the effect of the stressor is being considered, the experience of prolonged stress has been found to be more damaging and requires a longer time for recovery than brief stress (Davis 1956).

Pearlin (1975) has suggested a more fruitful conceptualization which distinguishes crises and ephemeral threats from durable, structured experiences that people have as they engage in their various social roles. The organization of experience around sex roles is cited as an example (Pearlin 1975, pp. 192-193):

> . . . research into the social origins of stress must eventually take sex into account. Sex, of course, is one of the pivotal ascribed statuses around which a variety of critical and potentially stressful experiences are organized through the entire span of life. Because of the very structure of society itself, many experiences having the potential for arousing stress differentially impinge on men and women. . . . In attempting to account for sex differences in psychological disturbance, it seems a very good bet to pay special attention to those social role areas in which women are exposed to stress-provoking experiences but from which men are relatively insulated.

Pearlin's description of structural stress incorporates the key factor of minority stress; that is, it derives from a categorically ascribed inferior status around which critical and potentially stressful experiences are organized throughout the life span. In regard to duration of a stressor, then, minority status as a potential stressor exists throughout the life span of an individual if the minority status is based on a biological characteristic such as race or sex. A minority status based on a nonbiological characteristic such as sociosexual preference or religion is a potential stressor for that portion of the life span during which the status is applicable. Given the durational aspect of minority stress, the cumulative frequency of stressful life events relating to that minority status could be expected to affect, one way or another, the intensity of each subsequent event relating to that minority status. Thus, the meaning of a single event may be

influenced more by its structural implications than by its ephemeral characteristics, and the intensity of a stressor may be affected more by the event's
relation to ongoing structural constraints than by its more immediate and
apparent antecedents.

As an example, the stress event of not getting a job promotion for which
one is fully qualified might produce a moderate amount of stress for any individual. If, however, the person not receiving the promotion is a woman
and the person receiving the promotion is a man, the meaning of the event
to the woman may be affected by its structural implications. If she has experienced previous incidents of denied opportunities in her career on the
basis of sex, the current denial of opportunity may have a different meaning
for her than for an individual who had not previously experienced sex-based
job discrimination. The structural implications of an event, then, can alter
the meaning of the event by linking it to a series of events which have occurred over a long time, although the event itself may be of short duration.
The effect of the stressor, if perceived as relating to ongoing structural constraints, may elicit responses associated with prolonged stress.

Although this example illustrates the relation of characteristics of the
stressor—that is, duration, frequency, and intensity—to minority stress,
this knowledge of stressor characteristics would not be sufficient to predict
responses to a stressor. To understand potential responses to any stressor,
attention must be focused on characteristics of the person(s) exposed to the
stressor.

Characteristics of Individuals in Stress Situations

It has been stated that the meaning of an event to an individual is the critical
factor in its impact as a stressor and, further, that two major determinants
of the meaning of an event are the degree of threat to need fulfillment which
the event poses and the amount of change required by the event. Even if exposed to the same stressor, then, these two components of the meaning of
an event would be expected to differ from individual to individual. This
premise has been supported in a number of studies.

For example, in an attempt to identify characteristics of individuals that
seem to allay the effects of stressful life events, some researchers have
studied populations who have experienced the same or a very similar crisis
and have attempted to differentiate characteristics of those who do and do
not experience negative effects as a consequence of the event. Hinkle (1974)
reports results of cumulative research that began in 1952 and reflects col-
laborative efforts of various disciplines. These studies focus on the effects
that may be produced by rapid culture change, social dislocation, and
changes in interpersonal relations, and they examine these variables in

relation to subsequent frequency and severity of physical illness. Populations investigated included Chinese immigrants who came to the United States during the Communist accession to power between 1946 and 1949, refugees from the Hungarian Revolution of 1956, and people from the United States who had been prisoners of war in North Korea. The people who remained free from illness in the face of these major life changes which caused profound reactions in other members of the groups were described as appearing to have psychological characteristics that provided "emotional insulation."

The Hungarians who seemed most adaptive *perceived* the events as less threatening than their less adaptive counterparts, which suggests a greater reliance on internal sources of self-esteem as opposed to dependence on external sources of self-esteem. This assumption would concur with Coopersmith's (1967) conclusion that the degree of threat perceived by an individual in a stressful situation is largely determined by its implications for the person's self-esteem. Thus, for the person whose self-esteem is based more on inner qualities (for instance, a sense of self as competent and persevering) than on status-conferring external roles or material possessions, the stressful experience of culture change or social dislocation is less threatening to need fulfillment because the inner qualities remain stable and act as a buffer to the outer changes.

Among the prisoners of war, those who had previous familiarity with social isolation and interrogation displayed the highest adaptive capacities, pointing to the importance of previously learned behaviors that were accessible at the onset of the crisis event. That is, prior experience with the stressful events and the prelearning of adaptive behaviors reduced the amount of change required in the subsequent encounter with similar events. The prior experience with similar events and prelearning of adaptive behaviors also may be linked to self-esteem, particularly self-esteem based on knowledge of one's abilities. A person with low self-esteem has been found to be less capable of resisting pressures to conform (Janis 1954); thus, the knowledge that one has an effective behavioral repertoire for resisting pressures to conform can be, in itself, a source of self-esteem. In sum, both an individual's prevailing level of self-esteem *and* its principal sources at the onset of a stressful life event would greatly influence the stressor's ultimate impact.

The findings of these studies contribute to the conceptualization of minority stress in two important ways. First, they indicate that although members of a minority group may be exposed to the same structural stressor of categorically reduced status, individuals belonging to that minority group will differ widely in their responses. Second, they point to the important role of cognitive factors in interpreting the meaning of that or any related stressor, which, in turn, will affect an individual's response to that stressor.

The role of cognitive factors in influencing the impact of a stressor on an individual can be entered in a schema which illustrates their relation to the other factors known to affect the impact of a stressor. Figure 7-2 presents the second part of this schema, and chapter 7 provides an analysis of individual stress-mediating resources. Self-esteem as a central stress-mediating resource has been indicated in this discussion, and its role and meaning also are elaborated in chapter 7. Figure 5-2 presents the first part of this schema.

Minority Status as Stressor

Returning to the example of the woman who did not receive a job promotion, the meaning of the event to her could be examined in relation to both its degree of threat to her need fulfillment and the amount of change required of her. The degree of threat would be expected to vary according to

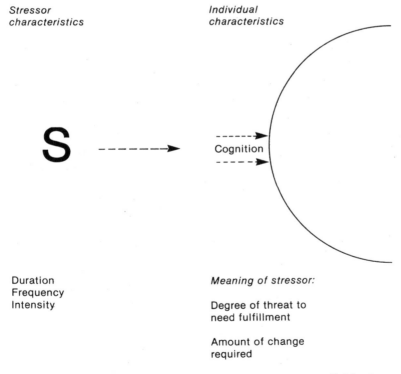

Figure 5-2. Variables in Impact of Stressor on Individual

the extent that her career advancement provided various types of need satisfaction. In relation to self-esteem, the degree of threat would be expected to vary according to whether she attributed the lack of advancement to her own deficiencies or to an employer's sex bias in making the promotion. The former carries negative implications for her self-esteem, whereas the latter would not. Further, the level of self-esteem and its principal sources at the time the event occurs would greatly influence the amount of change required by the event. Change could involve psychological processes (for example, cognitive restructuring of the meaning of the event), behavioral adjustments (for example, being more assertive regarding one's qualifications and career goals to the employer), or environmental alterations (for example, accepting a better position with a new employer). Previous experience with a similar event could be expected to influence the type and amount of change required by these response options.

This example focuses on a single event, that is, not getting a job promotion for which one is qualified, and illustrates the interrelatedness of stressor characteristics and the meaning of the event to the individual. It is intended also to illustrate that the structural implications of a stressful event—one, in this instance, that may occur in the experience of any person in the labor force—may greatly impact the meaning and outcome of that event. For the minority person, categorically ascribed inferior status and blocked access to legitimate social and economic opportunities are conditions which may prevail throughout the life span. Stress in a system, as noted earlier, has been defined as the state intervening between an antecedent stressor and consequent readjustment or adaptation (Dohrenwend 1961; Holmes and Rahe 1967; Selye 1974). Since the source of minority stress is woven into the cultural fabric and persists over time, thus ensuring that multiple antecedent stressors will recur in the sociobehavioral environment, "readjustment" becomes, in a sense, adaptation to a perpetual state of stress. Although the structural basis of minority stress all but precludes the possibility of its total resolution until the sustaining structures change, it does not preclude the individual learning of more effective coping responses that can greatly reduce levels of stress.

However, a critical impediment to learning more effective coping responses may be the cumulative effect of minority status as a stressor, which is an integral part of its duration. Given the potential frequency and intensity of stressful life events relating to minority status, the *cumulative effect* may be defined as a subjective preoccupation with that status and with the potential consequences of occupying that status, which is, nonetheless, based on objective events. As Allport (1954, p. 145) pointed out, "A minority group member has to make many times as many adjustments to his status as does the majority group member. . . . the awareness, the strain, the accommodation all fall more heavily and more frequently on the minority group members.'' Thus, the objective reality of more frequent events relating to one's minority status could be expected to form a cognitive expectancy in the minority individual.

This cognitive expectancy has been described in various ways by those who have investigated the minority condition. In their work on the black experience, Kardiner and Ovesey (1951, pp. 302-303) provide a description of the consequences of belonging to a stigmatized minority in relation to social interactions with dominant groups:

> . . . his self-esteem suffers . . . because he is constantly receiving an unpleasant image of himself from the behavior of others to him. This is the subjective impact of social discrimination, and it sounds as though its effects ought to be localized and limited in influence. This is not the case. It seems to be an ever-present and unrelieved irritant. Its influence is not alone due to the fact that it is painful in its intensity, but also because the individual, in order to maintain internal balance and to protect himself from being overwhelmed by it, must initiate restitutive maneuvers in order to keep functioning. In addition to maintaining an internal balance, the individual must continue to maintain a social facade and some kind of adaptation to the offending stimuli so that he can preserve some social effectiveness.

Similarly, Allport (1954, p. 144) illustrated this cognitive expectancy with statements made by three Jewish students:

> I wait in fear for an anti-Jewish remark; there is a definite physiological disturbance: a feeling of helplessness at all times, an anxiety, a dread.

> Anti-Semitism is a constant force in the Jew's life. . . .

> I have encountered at first hand very few overt expressions of anti-Semitism. Nevertheless, I am always aware of its presence off-stage, as it were, ready to come into the act, and I never know what will be the cue for its entrance. I am never quite free of this foreboding of a dim sense of some vaguely impending doom.

It would appear, then, that interactions with dominant-group members often require minority-group members to maintain a degree of vigilance in regard to the minority component of their identity, and these interactions increase the frequency of events that require adaptation. Minority status as a stressor is predicated on the cultural ascription of inferiority to selected groups by dominant members of that society. To the extent that events and interactions reflect this cultural ascription of lesser status to a minority person, these events and interactions require adjustment for the minority person.

The importance of identifying components of minority stress lies in their relation to outcomes, particularly the outcome of individual dysfunction.

The major distinction between minority status as a stressor and more ephemeral events that can produce stress for any individual is its structural dimension. As a part of the existing social structure, the duration and cumulative frequency of stressful events require a minority person to maintain a cognitive expectancy in relation to these recurrent events and, over time, to make successive adaptations to these events. Behavior resulting from a stressor may be adaptive or maladaptive, but the probability of maladaptive responses varies directly with the intensity and duration of stress (Davis 1956; Dohrenwend 1961; Torrance 1965). On the basis of these findings, then, it would be reasonable to assume that minority-group members would evidence higher rates of dysfunction than majority-group members.

Minority Stress and Problems in Measurement

The theory that social and economic stratification are major antecedents of individual stress, and that this consequent state of stress increases the probability of individual dysfunction, has not met with easy acceptance. This line of thought challenges biophysical theories of causation that attribute mental dysfunction to biophysical deficiencies or defects, and it equally challenges intrapsychic theories which attribute psychological and psychosomatic disorders to conflict between biopsychological instincts. These two theoretical orientations represent the individual-deficiency model, more commonly referred to as the *medical* model, and presuppose that interventions must focus on "curing" the individual.

The early empirical challenges to this view of individual deficiency found strong relations between social and cultural factors and psychological dysfunction (for example, Leighton 1959; Rennie et al. 1957). Other studies of that period as well as more recent ones have specifically identified an inverse relation between socioeconomic status and psychological dysfunction (Dohrenwend and Dohrenwend 1969, 1970; Hollingshead and Redlich 1958; Langner and Michael 1963; Myers, Lindenthal, and Pepper 1974; Roman and Trice 1967; Rushing 1969). A subsequent study by Dohrenwend (1973) moved this line of research from broad correlational data to measurement of the intervening variable of "more stressful life events." Dohrenwend postulated that (1) persons in low social status are disproportionately exposed to stressful life events and (2) this exposure provides an explanatory link between low social status and individual psychological stress. These hypotheses were tested in relation to lower versus higher socioeconomic status, women versus men, and disadvantaged ethnic groups versus advantaged ethnic groups. Support for the first hypothesis was obtained for socioeconomic status and sexual status, but not for ethnic status.

The second hypothesis was supported for sexual status and, with qualification, for socioeconomic status. The qualification refers to evidence that factors other than a high level of stressful life events would be required to account for the psychological stress of lower socioeconomic members. Dohrenwend's study makes an important contribution toward validating the relation between low social and economic status and individual stress. And the study suggests that this linkage is not identical for all types of reduced status, that is, status reduction based on socioeconomic status, sex, or ethnicity.

The results of the Dohrenwend (1973) study, as well as those of numerous other studies that have examined the relation between low social or economic status and psychological or physical dysfunction, are methodologically limited by the common use of the social readjustment rating scale (SRRS) (Holmes and Rahe 1967). The validity of the SRRS as a stress-measuring instrument has been questioned on a number of grounds, both methodological and theoretical. It has been charged that it is too vague in specifying the situation to be rated, that it is retrospective, and that it does not accurately account for the personal meaning of life events to different individuals (Brown 1974).

Typically, SSRS respondents report only stressful life events that have occurred in the past twelve months. This limit on the time span of reported events disallows measurement of the effect of chronic and cumulative psychological stress which accrues to minority-status individuals as a result of structural inequalities. In relation to the meaning of life events, the SRRS assigns a monolithic value to potentially stressful events; for example, it assigns a life-change score of 73 to divorce, 50 to marriage, and 40 to pregnancy, as compared to the highest value of 100 assigned to "death of spouse." These events may be desirable or undesirable and require much or little adaptation, according to the specific person-situation context. The same stressor, divorce, for instance, may have the effect of reducing psychological stress in one case and increasing it in another. The Holmes and Rahe (1967) method of attempting to rank various life events according to their stressor value can, at best, provide a crude index of an event's stressor value to diverse individuals in varying contexts.

A further defect in the SRRS, in my view, is that its items are largely slanted to life experiences of majority-group members, middle- to upper-class white males in particular, while essentially neglecting the types of stressful life events common to the daily experience of minority-group (lower-status) members. For example, nearly one-fourth of the items on the SRRS relate to work or school-associated changes, while there is no rating for stress associated with long-term or chronic unemployment or lack of resources for obtaining higher education. Three of four items concerning finances refer to mortgages, which are not obtainable for those without steady employment or sufficient financial resources. More than 30 percent of the items relate to changes contingent on being married or having a family, while there are no stress-rating items related to being single, or being a single parent, or holding some other nontraditonal relational status. It seems reasonable to assume that the type of stressful events which occur in the routine experience of either nontraditional or non-majority-group individuals would vary importantly from those which occur to traditional or majority-group individuals, differences which the SRRS does not measure. Nonetheless, the SRRS breaks empirical ground in validating the linkage between stressful life events and dysfunction. For social scientists who have advanced environmental theories of causation in relation to psychological and social dysfunction and therefore have moved toward the institutional-deficiency side of the theoretical continuum, the evidence resulting from this line of research should encourage improvement of measuring instruments and further research.

Why is one's theoretical orientation to the major causes of dysfunction important? What difference does it make? Response to a similar question regarding theories of racism provides a cogent answer to this question (Chesler 1976, p. 26):

> To the extent that sociological theory helps focus our treatment of change efforts on peripheral or malfunctioning persons or institutions, or on the basic character of our moral and social structure, it makes a great deal of difference. The difference theories make may not be with respect to truth and untruth, for truth about American racism may be multiple and undeterminate, resisting any single theory. But the differences in our theoretical preferences and priorities make a difference in our orientation to social policy or program—e.g., what we decide must be funded or what are social fringes. They make a difference in the way we interpret and support various change efforts. And they also make a difference in what social scientists see as important to study, in what we elect to report and not report, in how we relate to research content, in who we recruit and support into our ranks, and in what we implement as policies of our profession.

In the "helping" professions, then, the way in which a problem is defined determines the focus of intervention. As Rein (1970) suggested in regard to social work practice, the choice of an interventive approach is generally based on whether the social worker accepts social conditions as a constraint and concludes that change must start within the individual, or whether one views external conditions as the targets of change, rather than as constraints. Thus, even when helping efforts are directed at individuals rather than at policies and programs, the practitioner's perspective on the chief source of the problem to be solved (that is, either individual deficiency or social conditions) is translated into treatment goals, and effective treatment will rely on the practitioner's ability to accurately identify the major factors contributing to the individual's dysfunction.

Social psychological literature generally refers to negative outcomes of the minority condition as isolation, loss of identity or identity confusion, loss of self-esteem or loss of esteem by others, alienation, status inconsistency, social role conflict, and cognitive dissonance (Yinger 1965). Many of these descriptive terms represent internal states that do not lend themselves readily to objective measurement. Negative outcomes which are viewed as responses to social and cultural stress and which can be objectively measured are psychological dysfunction (Coates, Moyer, and Wellman 1969; Dohrenwend 1973; Dohrenwend and Dohrenwend 1969, 1970; Maslow and Mittelmann 1951; Myers, Lindenthal, and Pepper 1971, 1974; Myers et al. 1972; Noyes and Kolb 1963), drug addiction (Torrance 1965; Turner 1978), deviance (Teele 1970; Torrance 1965), and suicide (Durkheim 1951; Gibbs 1966; Gibbs and Martin 1964; Gove and Tudor 1973; Henry and Short 1954; Pierce 1967; Teele 1970; Torrance 1965).

In the absence of adequate instruments to directly measure the types of stressful life events that are recurrent for minority-group members and virtually nonexistent for majority-group members, a disproportionate occurrence of negative outcomes among minority-group members can be used as indicators of minority stress. However, comparable statistics are difficult to obtain, for separate studies provide different pieces of information using different measures and populations, and thus a comprehensive comparison of types of dysfunction among various groups still is lacking. Nonetheless, studies which have examined group differences in relation to stress and dysfunction provide some support for the phenomenon of minority stress.

For example, a recent summary ("Mental Illness: Escape Route from Poverty, Discrimination" 1979) of evidence indicating poor health and dysfunction among blacks attributed these outcomes to the stress of contending with institutional racism coupled with poverty. These outcomes include a lower life expectancy and a higher incidence of high blood pressure among black males than white males, higher infant mortality rates and higher frequency of paranoid symptoms among blacks than among whites, and an increasing suicide rate among blacks. However, since blacks constitute a disproportionate percentage of the poor, these data reflect the compounding of economic and social stress. Another recent report ("Stress Found Higher among Black Supergrades" 1979) discussed a survey that examined stress among black executives in the federal government and found that blacks exhibited significantly more stress than their white counterparts on 29 of 100 variables. Thus, even when the economic differential is not a factor, the reduced status of minority membership corresponds to higher stress. The investigator attributed this finding to the feeling of minority-group members that they must be twice as good as others in order to be treated equitably. Similarly, evidence from a number of other studies (Aiken and Ferman 1966; Bernard 1966; Pasamanick, Knobloch, and Lilienfeld 1956; Shanahan 1966; Udry 1966, 1967) that have compared rates of stressors between black and white groups has shown that black groups experience stressors more frequently than their white counterparts with socioeconomic status held constant for both groups. Thus it appears that an internalized sense of a stigmatized identity and its implicit status reduction are sufficient to create and perpetuate a state of stress.

The findings of another study (Kahn et al. 1964) further confirm the linkage of status, stress, and health, apart from the economic factor. Based on a national survey of male wage and salary earners, their data showed that those with less status report poorer health than those with higher status; for example, unskilled workers reported ten times more poor or fair health than the managerial force. The status differential corresponded to the health results even when the financial advantage was with the blue-collar worker rather than the white-collar worker. An important intervening variable between status reduction and poorer health appears to be its effect on self-esteem. Kasl and French (1962) found a positive relationship between status and self-esteem and a negative correlation between self-esteem and frequency of the use of medical services.

Thus, research from different disciplines conducted for dissimilar purposes points to the progression of phenomena that eventuate minority stress. The sequential systems events that ultimately register on the biophysical organism of the individual[1] as minority stress can be conceptualized as a communication process that begins with cultural antecedents which, in turn, are transmitted into social and psychological antecedents. Although these four dimensions—biophysical, psychological, social, and cultural—do not represent discrete territories in reality, they are conceptually useful in that they delineate bodies of knowledge which have different focal points in the analysis of human behavior. Representation of this systems sequence is shown in figure 5-3.

Minority stress, then, can be viewed as a state intervening between the sequential antecedent stressors of culturally sanctioned, categorically ascribed inferior status, resultant prejudice and discrimination, the impact of these forces on the cognitive structure of the individual, and consequent readjustment or adaptational failure. Obviously, individual members of minority groups are differentially affected by their categorical affiliation, so that certain members may represent a "population at risk" while others do not. *Populations at risk* may be defined as those who are in chronic jeopardy of reaching the upper limits of their adaptive range owing to excessive and persistent stress and to the absence of substantial mediating resources, which would sufficiently reduce the condition of chronic stress. Thus, although virtually all members of a minority are exposed to a disparaging sociocultural climate, the central factor in their varying responses is the availability of individual stress-mediating resources, which

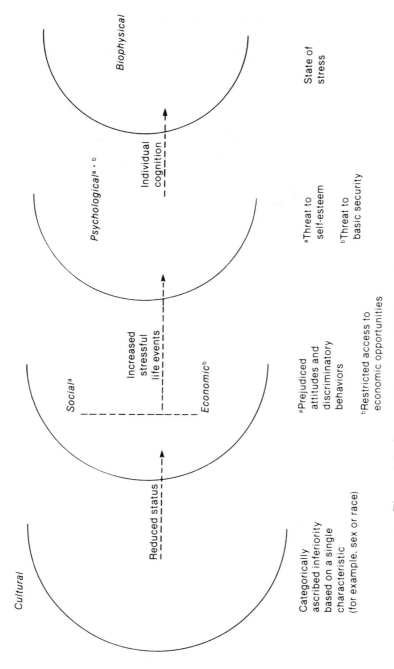

Figure 5-3. Systems Sequence of Minority-Stress Antecedents

are explored more fully in chapter 7. Evidence has been presented in this chapter indicating that minority stress can result from conditions other than insufficient economic resources; however, the probability of maladaptive outcomes would be expected to increase for individuals who occupy both low economic status and low social status, and such individuals would have a higher probability of constituting a population at risk.

Social and economic stratification in a society ensures that all strata will be identified by superordinate-subordinate statuses in relation to some type of hierarchy. In democratic Western societies, it is assumed that opportunities for upward mobility are available to everyone. Thus, although status differentials are inherent in our social and economic structures and could be viewed as structural sources of stress for all members of society, economic status per se is not necessarily a characteristic of life-long duration, and may or may not be at all times visible to others. Evaluation of the impact of different structural stressors would need to pay particular attention to the duration of the structural stressor and its degree of visibility, the latter being a significant factor in the frequency and intensity of associated stressful events.

Outcomes of minority stress also would be expected to vary according to whether membership in a minority group is based on a characteristic that is of lifelong duration. For example, sex and race are determined at birth and are always visible characteristics. Potential stress events related to inferior-status ascriptions based on sex or race, then, exist throughout the individual's lifetime and relate to a characteristic that is always visible. In contrast, minority-group status based on sociosexual preference is not of lifelong duration and may or may not be visible at all times. In evaluating the potential effect of a minority characteristic on behavioral outcomes, then, characteristics of lifelong duration would be expected to increase the probability of dysfunction more than those of lesser duration. However, qualifiers of this general assumption would include taking into account the compounded effect of occupying more than one minority status, as well as the availability of stress-mediating resources to the individual. Regarding the latter, an individual's stress-mediating resources *may* increase over time, thus decreasing the probability of dysfunction. This premise is explored further in chapter 7.

One further premise that relates to minority-stress theory concerns the linkage between minority stress and minority deviance. Although homosexuality and lesbianism are still viewed as "deviance" by current cultural norms, in this context deviance refers to law-breaking or nonconforming behaviors of minority individuals that may result, in part, from the inaccessibility of resources through legitimate means. This perspective, deriving originally from Merton's (1938) hypothesis regarding anomie, was later stated in the Cloward and Ohlin (1964, p. 152) paradigm that, "Given limited access to success-goals by legitimate means, the nature of the delinquent response that may result will vary according to the availability of various illegitimate means." Minority-group members who find the legitimate opportunity structure closed or restricted to them, then, may be more vulnerable to the illegitimate opportunity structure generally available to them. However, other factors would be expected to influence whether a minority person would actually engage in law-breaking or nonconforming behavior, such as socioeconomic status or level of self-esteem.

Minority deviance, then, may be viewed as a potential response to minority stress. That is, minority deviance is a potential means of readjustment or adaptation, although it may have negative secondary consequences. Minority deviance may be accompanied by the acceptance of a subcultural or countercultural value system which opposes that of the opportunity structures from which a person has been excluded. By opting out of the status struggle inherent in the legitimate opportunity structure, the minority individual ceases to contend with the ascription of inferiority and finds, instead, a less obstructed means to status in the illegitimate opportunity structure. In this sense, a response of minority deviance eliminates some aspects of identity confusion and role conflict, and a different set of norms supplants those of the original stress-producing culture.

The "correctness" of a theory regarding minority stress must be assessed by its applicability to various minority groups and must lend itself to testable hypotheses. The chief utility of a theory of minority stress is that it can provide a systematic method for identifying variables that make a difference between negative and positive outcomes for minority individuals, thereby contributing knowledge that may assist in resolving or reducing this stress. My research represents a beginning effort to employ this conceptualization of minority stress, and its hypotheses and findings are the subject of the next chapter.

Note

1. Selye's (1974) triphasic biological stress syndrome, which is discussed in *Stress without Distress*, consists of the alarm reaction, the stage of resistance, and the stage of exhaustion. This syndrome does not appear to allow for the intervention of environmental factors that would either irradicate the source of stress or allow the individual to reduce or eliminate the impact of a stressor; and this syndrome seems to suggest that the stage of exhaustion is inevitable. While this would appear to be valid in relation to the total life cycle culminating in death, it is unwarranted to assume that single stressors cannot be reduced or eliminated in the resistance stage. Nonetheless, Selye's model of the physiological consequents of prolonged

stress has been the pioneer work in this area from which subsequent research has proceeded, and it effectively illustrates the critical nature of persistent and unmediated stress on the human organism. In this context, the biophysical state of stress refers to the somatic effects of stressors characterized by the "fight or flight" reactions.

References

Aiken, M., and Ferman, L. "The social and political reactions of older Negroes to unemployment." *Phylon* 27 (1966):333-346.

Allport, G.W. *The Nature of Prejudice.* Reading, Mass.: Addison-Wesley, 1954.

Bernard, J. "Marital stability and patterns of status variables." *Journal of Marriage and the Family.* 28 (1966):421-439.

Brown, G.W. "Meaning, measurement and stress of life events." In *Stressful Life Events: Their Nature and Effects*, edited by B.P. Dohrenwend and B.S. Dohrenwend. New York: Wiley, 1974.

Chesler, M.A. "Contemporary sociological theories of racism." In *Towards the Elimination of Racism*, edited by P.A. Katz. New York: Pergamon Press, 1976.

Cloward, R., and Ohlin, L. "Illegitimate means and delinquent sub-cultures." In *Delinquency and Opportunity: A Theory of Delinquent Gangs*, edited by R. Cloward and L. Ohlin. New York: Free Press of Glencoe, 1964.

Coates, D.; Moyer, S.; and Wellman, B. "Yorklea Study: Symptoms, problems and life events." *Canadian Journal of Public Health* 69 (1969):471-481.

Coopersmith, S. *The Antecedents of Self-Esteem.* San Francisco: W.H. Freeman, 1967.

Davis, S.W. "Stress in combat." *Scientific American* 194 (1956):31-35.

Dohrenwend, B.P. "The social psychological nature of stress: A framework for causal inquiry." *Journal of Abnormal and Social Psychology* 62 (1961):294-302.

Dohrenwend, B.P., and Dohrenwend, B.S. *Social Status and Psychological Disorder: A Causal Inquiry.* New York: Wiley, 1969.

Dohrenwend, B.S. "Life events as stressors: A methodological inquiry." *Journal of Health and Social Behavior* 14 (1973):167-175.

Dohrenwend, B.S., and Dohrenwend, B.P. "Class and race as status-related sources of stress." In S. Levine and N. Scotch, *Social Stress.* Chicago: Aldine, 1970.

Durkheim, E. *Suicide, A Study in Sociology*, translated by J. Spaulding and G. Simpson. New York: Free Press, 1951.

Gibbs, J.P. "Suicide." In *Contemporary Social Problems*, 2d ed. edited by R. Merton and R. Nisbet. New York: Harcourt, Brace & World, 1966.

Gibbs, J.P., and Martin, W.T. *Status Integration and Suicide*. Eugene: University of Oregon Press, 1964.

Gove, W., and Tudor, J. "Adult sex roles and mental illness." *American Journal of Sociology* 78 (1973):812-835.

Henry, A., and Short, J. *Suicide and Homocide*. Glencoe, Ill.: Free Press, 1954.

Hinkle, L.E. "The effect of exposure to culture change, social change, and changes in interpersonal relationships on health." In *Stressful Life Events: Their Nature and Effects*, edited by B.S. Dohrenwend and B.P. Dohrenwend. New York: Wiley, 1974.

Hollingshead, A., and Redlich, F. *Social Class and Mental Illness*. New York: Wiley, 1958.

Holmes, T.H., and Rahe, R.H. "The Social Readjustment Rating Scale." *Journal of Psychosomatic Research* 11 (1967):213-218.

Janis, I.L. "Personality correlates of susceptibility to persuasion." *Journal of Personality* 22 (1954):504-518.

Kahn, R.L.; Wolfe, D.M.; Quinn, R.P.; Snoek, J.D.; and Rosenthal, R.A. *Organizational Stress: Studies in Role Conflict and Ambiguity*. New York: Wiley, 1964.

Kardiner, A., and Ovesey, L. *The Mark of Oppression*. New York: World Publishing, 1951.

Kasl, S., and French, J. "The effects of occupational status on physical and mental health." *Journal of Social Issues* 18 (1962):67-89.

Langner, T., and Michael, S. *Life Stress and Mental Health*. New York: Free Press, 1963.

Leighton, A.H. *My Name Is Legion*. New York: Basic Books, 1959.

Lieberman, M.A. "Adaptive processes in late life." In *Life-Span Developmental Psychology: Normative Life Crises*, edited by N. Datan and L.H. Ginsberg. New York: Academic Press, 1975.

Maslow, A.H., and Mittelmann, B. *Principles of Abnormal Psychology: The Dynamics of Psychic Illness*. New York: Harper, 1951.

"Mental Illness: Escape Route from Poverty, Discrimination." *National Committee on Minority Affairs Newsletter*, October 1979, p. 2.

Merton, R.K. "Social structure and anomie." *American Sociological Review* 3 (1938):672.

Myers, J.K.; Lindenthal, J.J.; and Pepper, M.P. "Life events and psychiatric impairment." *Journal of Nervous and Mental Disease* 152 (1971):149-157.

———— . "Social class, life events, and psychiatric symptoms: A Longitudinal study." In *Stressful Life Events: Their Nature and Effects*, edited by B.S. Dohrenwend and B.P. Dohrenwend. New York: Wiley, 1974.

Myers, J.K.; Lindenthal, J.J.; Pepper, M.P.; and Ostrander, D.R. "Life events and mental status." *Journal of Health and Social Behavior* 13 (1972):398-406.

Noyes, A.P., and Kolb, L.C. *Modern Clinical Psychiatry*, 6th ed. Philadelphia: Saunders, 1963.

Pasamanick, B.; Knobloch, H.; and Lilienfeld, A. "Socioeconomic status and some precursors of neuropsychiatric disorder." *American Journal of Orthopsychiatry* 26 (1956):594-601.

Pearlin, L. "Sex roles and depression." In *Life-Span Developmental Psychology: Normative Life Crises*, edited by N. Datan and L. Ginsberg. New York: Academic Press, 1975.

Pierce, A. "The economic cycle and the social suicide rate." *American Sociological Review* 32 (1967):457-462.

Rein, M. "Social work in search of a radical profession." *Social Work* 15 (1970):13-28.

Rennie, T.; Srole, L.; Opler, M.; and Langner, T. "Urban life and mental health." *American Journal of Psychiatry* 113 (1957):831-836.

Roman, P., and Trice, H. *Schizophrenia and the Poor*. Ithaca: New York State School of Industrial and Labor Relations, 1967.

Rushing, W. "Two patterns in the relationship between social class and mental hospitalization." *American Sociological Review* 34 (1969):533-541.

Selye, H. *Stress without Distress*. New York: J.B. Lippincott, 1974.

Shanahan, E. "Negro joblessness up—why?" *The New York Times*, September 11, 1966, 6E.

"Stress Found Higher among Black Supergrades." *ADAMHA News* (U.S. Dept. of Health, Education, and Welfare, Alcohol, Drug Abuse, and Mental Health Administration) 5 (November 2, 1979):4.

Teele, J. "Social pathology and stress." In S. Levine and N. Scotch, *Social Stress*. Chicago: Aldine, 1970.

Torrance, E.P. *Constructive Behavior: Stress, Personality, and Mental Health*. Belmont, Calif.: Wadsworth, 1965.

Turner, R.J. "International vs. external control as predictor of abstinence rate among opiate addicts." Doctoral dissertation, University of Michigan, 1978.

Udry, J.R. "Marital instability by race, sex, eduction, and occupation using 1960 census data." *American Journal of Sociology* 72 (1966):203-209.

———. "Marital instability by race and income." *American Journal of Sociology* 72 (1967):673-674.

Vinokur, A., and Selzer, M.L. "Desirable versus undesirable life events: Their relationship to stress and mental distress." *Journal of Personality and Social Psychology* 32 (1975):329-337.

Yinger, J.M. *A Minority Group in American Society*. New York: McGraw-Hill, 1965.

6 Stress-Response Variables among Lesbian Women

Lesbian women are a double minority, for categorical status reduction results from two characteristics, sex and sociosexual orientation. The double-minority status of lesbian women in relation to the dominant society presents two major structural stressors for all members of this double minority, although, as previously stated, the impact of these structural stressors will vary widely according to specific characteristics of the antecedent event (duration, frequency, intensity) and specific characteristics of the individual (meaning of event).

Some studies (Harris, Mackie, and Wilson 1956; Miller 1953; Torrance 1959) have shown that mild stress tends to result in improved performance, increased activity, and more learning, but that extremely intense stress results in deterioration of performance and breakdown. Also, as previously noted, prolonged stress has been found to be more damaging than brief stress (Davis 1956). Similarly, the frequency of events that require adaptation will influence outcomes as each change draws on available resources. Other than stressor characteristics, diverse outcomes of minority stress may be accounted for by examining the varying adaptational resources of individual minority members.

Outcomes among lesbian women reported in the literature do vary widely. My research and other studies (Kenyon 1968; Wilson and Greene 1971) found that lesbian women comprise a disproportionate number of high-achieving women; yet other studies (Saghir et al. 1970; Swanson et al. 1972) report that lesbian women, as compared to nonlesbian women, have higher rates of alcoholism, drug addiction, and suicide attempts.

The Saghir et al. (1970) study reported that alcohol dependence occurred in 10 percent of the lesbian sample, but in none of the controls, and that over one-half (51 percent) had used nonprescription drugs, primarily marijuana and amphetamines, as compared with 9 percent of the controls. The Swanson et al. (1972) study reported that more than four times as many lesbian women as controls (thirteen to three) were habituated to alcohol, amphetamines, or barbiturates. Concerning suicidal behaviors, the Saghir et al. (1970) study reported that 23 percent of the lesbian sample had made attempts, compared to 5 percent of the controls. The Swanson et al. (1972) study indicated that suicidal behavior (thoughts, threats, attempts) was common to both groups (lesbian, 58 percent; control, 40 percent) with twice as many suicidal attempts (fourteen to seven) by lesbian women.

The issue of psychological adjustment has been addressed extensively in preceding chapters, and a preponderance of evidence supports the view that lesbian women are extraordinarily well adjusted. On the surface, these two themes—that lesbian women evidence high rates of dysfunction and that lesbian women are psychologically well adjusted—appear to be in contradiction. To resolve the contradiction, it should be noted that on the basis of available evidence, it cannot be stated with any certitude that lesbian women do or do not exceed other population groups in relation to various types of dysfunction. The methodological issues discussed in chapter 2 apply to these studies just cited which report higher rates of dysfunction among lesbian women. Also, another plausible explanation, irrespective of lower or higher rates of dysfunction, is that adaptation to a stigmatized identity entails cognitive processes and behavioral adjustments over time, as opposed to an all-or-nothing capacity inherent in some but not in others. Part of this explanation is clarified in chapter 7, which addresses minority responses as they occur in phases or stages. The point addressed here is that at any time rates of dysfunction or levels of psychological adjustment are measured, it is probable that participating lesbian women would reflect these different stages or phases or adjustment in the areas being measured.

Another fundamental issue here is the comparative approach to data collection and its utility. Studies reporting high rates of dysfunction among lesbian women generally have implied that these indexes of dysfunction confirm psychiatric aberration. This bias invites the counterargument that there are no differences in these rates between lesbian and nonlesbian women (for example, Oberstone 1974). On the basis of currently available evidence, the question of greater or lesser incidence of dysfunction among lesbian women cannot be answered conclusively. Further, until the causative implication of "individual deficiency" is removed from the interpretation of such data, the extent of these stress responses among lesbian women as compared to other groups is not likely to be obtainable.

From the perspective of the helping professions, little is gained from comparative rates between lesbian and nonlesbian women, but much could be gained from studies that lead to a better understanding of factors which contribute to dysfunction among minority members and which identify variables that contribute to resistance to these factors. My study presents more comprehensive data on the incidence of dysfunction among lesbian women would reflect these different stages or phases of adjust- gathering data on these behaviors was to ascertain if selected variables were associated with functional and dysfunctional outcomes. The remainder of this chapter reports these findings.

Stress Indexes

Dysfunctional outcomes of stress were measured by three indexes. Respondents indicated whether they had ever been hospitalized for "mental illness," amount (if any) of drug use, both past and present, and whether they had ever felt suicidal or attempted suicide. Responses to these three indexes were combined to form a composite measure of stress, here referred to as the *stress index* (for additional information see Appendix A), the range of which included low, moderate, and high stress levels. Values were assigned to responses, and the range was determined, as shown in table 6-1.

Results on the three components of the stress index indicate that about one in eleven respondents had been hospitalized for psychiatric reasons, more than one in six had attempted suicide, over half had felt suicidal, and more than one in six had been drug-dependent. Both past and present levels of drug use were obtained to provide a measure of change in drug use, and this indicator is discussed later in this chapter. The composite of these three indexes—the stress index—shows that about one in nine respondents were in the high-stress category. These results are shown in table 6-2.

Other possible consequences of minority stress that were measured relate to behaviors designated as "deviant" by prevailing cultural norms, specifically, whether a respondent had an illegal source of income and/or had ever engaged in prostitution, defined here as providing sexual services for monetary gain. Of the total sample, 4.4 percent reported having an

Table 6-1
Stress Index: Assigned Values and Range

Assigned Values	Index			
	Drug Use	Suicidal Behavior	Psychiatric Hospitalization	Range
Never or occasionally	0			
Frequently	2			
Dependent	3			
Never		0		
Felt suicidal; no attempt		2		
Attempted		3		
No			0	
Yes			3	
Low stress				0-2
Moderate stress				3-5
High stress				6-9

Table 6-2
Stress Indexes: Results

Index	Percentage
Psychiatric Hospitalization	
Yes	9.4
No	90.6
Past Drug Use	
Dependent	17.4
Moderate	47.1
None	35.5
Suicidal Behavior	
Attempted	18.6
Felt, no attempt	51.2
Never	30.2
Stress Index	
High	11.6
Moderate	43.8
Low	44.6

illegal source of income, and 13.2 percent reported engaging in prostitution one or more times. Of those who reported having provided sexual services for monetary gain, only 1.2 percent reported doing so regularly; 1.7 percent, occasionally; 5.4 percent, a few times; and 4.8 percent, once only. The overlap between the two indexes of deviance—that is, those who reported both having an illegal source of income and engaging in prostitution—was 1.9 percent.

In order to examine factors which might be associated with changed levels of stress, a drug-change score was obtained which provided a measure of increased or decreased drug use. It was assumed that a decrease in drug use represented a decrease in an individual's stress level. The score was derived by subtracting present drug-use scores from past drug-use scores. Inclusion in the decreased drug-use group was restricted to only those respondents who had no increased use on any drug. That is, a single respondent may have decreased in the use of one or more drugs but increased in the use of another drug. With increased use of *any* drug, that case was excluded from decreased drug use statistics.

Hypotheses

Evidence has been reviewed supporting the view that the net effect of categorically reduced status, or the minority condition, increases the probability of stressful life events. I examined behavioral outcomes in a population which is, by definition, a double minority and thus is subjected to increased stress on the basis of both statuses.

The hypotheses addressed the relation of selected independent variables to the dependent variables of stress and "deviance" among lesbian women. Stated otherwise, factors which may contribute to maladaptive behaviors among members of a minority group, as well as factors which appear to mediate the impact of minority status, were explored. By studying within-group differences, the effects of occupying two minority statuses were held constant for each respondent. The hypotheses, then, focus on other variables which might account for adaptational differences.

The first hypothesis anticipated a relationship between low socioeconomic status (SES) and high life-stress scores. The assumption was that, for the low-SES lesbian woman, stress-reducing or mediating factors without a negative secondary consequence would be less available, and the probabilities of altering her reduced status (for instance, through education and career achievement) would be notably decreased. A second and related hypothesis predicted a relationship between low SES and deviance, based on the above assumption and on the premise that deviant behavior (as defined in this research) is associated with stress which arises from lack of access to legitimate opportunity structures.

A third hypothesis expected a relationship between public visibility as a lesbian woman and increased life stress. This expectation was predicated on the concept of visibility as developed in Goffman's (1963) work on stigma. According to Goffman, *stigma* indicates the situation of the individual who is disqualified from full social acceptance and refers to an attribute that is deeply discrediting. The concept of *visibility* and its relation to stress requires a brief discussion of Goffman's assumptions. In order for a characteristic to be effective as a basis for exclusion or discrimination, it must be, in general, socially discernible. Sex, color, and behavior are visible characteristics; language, names, and other distinguishing characteristics may communicate "difference" in social situations. Whether or not the distinguishing characteristic is apparent, the same outcome would result with knowledge of its possession.

Goffman refers to this distinction in terms of being "discredited" or "discreditable." The person whose stigmatizing characteristic is visible must cope with the tension of social situations "at all times during his daily round and by all persons he encounters therein" (Goffman 1963, p. 48). The person whose stigmatizing characteristic is not visible and who is "passing" must cope with the psychological price of "living a life that can be collapsed at any moment" (Goffman 1963, p. 87). He differentiates the two positions by stating that one position requires tension management (the discredited), while the other position (the discreditable) requires information management.

Lesbian women, by the Goffman criteria, are "discredited" persons as women and, if disclosed, as lesbian women. If not disclosed, lesbian women are "discreditable" persons, and it was postulated that the extent to which they fear that others may discern their gay identity would affect their level of stress. To assess self-perceived level of visibility, respondents checked one of the following choices: "I feel like anyone who looks at me could guess I'm gay," "I feel like only other gay people might think I'm gay," or "I don't think it would occur to anyone that I'm gay." *Disclosure,* on the other hand, represents a self-determined option and is defined in this context as affirming one's lesbian identity to others. *Visibility,* then, denotes an assessment of one's belief that others can or cannot discern one's sociosexual orientation, whereas disclosure is not mandated by socially observable characteristics. That these two variables represent distinct psychological phenomena was supported by the finding that high visibility and high disclosure were inversely related ($p = < .00001$).[1] Distributions on the variables of visibility and disclosure are shown in table 6-3.

A fourth hypothesis anticipated that one's degree of disclosure would affect one's employment options and thus that high disclosure would increase the probability of participation in illegal activities (deviance). The undisclosed lesbian woman, as Abbott and Love (1972, p. 45) noted, "can pass for straight and is accorded the privileges attendant upon . . .'the heterosexual assumption.' " These authors describe the double-bind, no-win situation as one in which the lesbian woman "can either have external approval and no internal integrity by keeping silent, or can achieve integrity and lose approval by coming out publicly" (Abbott and Love 1972, p. 14). The disclosed lesbian woman can lose or be denied employment, and admission to or continuation in many professions can be prohibited. As legitimate opportunities for economic self-sufficiency diminish, the probability of pursuing this objective through illegitimate means was hypothesized to increase.

A fifth hypothesis predicted that, of the two minority statuses, female and lesbian, being female would produce the greater stress to the individual. As previously indicated, the majority of lesbian women are not "visible" as such, but all are visibly female. Discrimination on the basis of lesbian status, then, would be expected to be intermittent, in contrast to discrimin-

Table 6-3
Visibility and Disclosure Distributions

Variable	Response	Percentage
Self-perceived level of visibility	In-group only	48.8
	Not visible	37.0
	Highly visible	14.2
Disclosure	Low	37.5
	Moderate	20.6
	High	41.9

ation on the basis of female status, which would be potentially present throughout one's life.

A sixth hypothesis anticipated that increased age may be associated with increased stress. This hypothesis was based on the assumption that the older lesbian woman is likely to have experienced a more hostile environment for a longer time than her younger counterpart (Martin and Lyon 1972). That is, both the greater stigma attached to lesbianism prior to the resurgence of the feminist movement and the beginning of the gay movement and the extended duration of the attendant stress were expected to relate to an increased probability of dysfunction.

In the stress paradigm, an important variable in the net effect of a stressor is the stress-reducing resources available to the individual. In my research two variables, "feminist exposure" and "minority reference group," were postulated to act as stress-reducing agents. Both variables were intended to measure an aspect of the same assumption. This assumption is that lesbian women who view other women, and in particular other lesbian women, as a reference group will evidence less dysfunction than those with a negative view of women or of lesbian women.

The concepts of the in-group and reference group help to distinguish two levels of belongingness. Allport (1954) stated that the former relates to the sheer fact of membership, the latter to whether the individual values that membership or seeks to relate to another group. Thus, a reference group may be an in-group that is valued or an out-group in which inclusion is desired. Rinder (1954) described the process of identification as signifying involvement in some way with a reference group. In his view, identification with a reference group implies an involvement by the individual with the group, so that the group is seen as important and its social patterns and norms are seen as meaningful. An individual incorporates these norms which help to fashion his or her attitudes, interests, values, and behavior.

Lewin (1948) hypothesized that positive in-group identification for minorities was necessary to overcome feelings of group self-hatred which could stem from the internalizaton of negative stereotypes from the out-group culture. Positive minority-group identification is viewed as a function of self-acceptance and thus acceptance of others like oneself. When the self-referential aspects of group membership no longer feed back a negative self-image, it is reasonable to assume that stress is decreased. This may occur as a by-product of recognizing that discrimination is a consequence of societal attitudes and forces rather than a matter of personal defect. Positive minority-group identification, then, may strengthen in-group bonds and improve social interaction. That is, just as a minority-group member who has incorporated the negative stereotypes of the out-group would tend to reject others of that minority, a positive attitude toward one's minority would enhance social relatedness to the in-group.

Thus, exposure to feminist ideology, either through participation in consciousness-raising groups or by reading feminist literature, was expected to result in a greater awareness of social forces that have historically defined and constrained women.[2] This awareness was expected to be a stepping-stone to a more positive identification with other women in general and to a more positive attitude toward lesbian women. If a negative group identification is assumed to increase dysfunction, then change to a positive group identification should be related to a reduction of dysfunction. Thus, both feminist exposure and positive minority-group identification were expected to be associated with decreased stress.

Of the total sample, only 9 percent (61) were found to not have had any exposure to feminist groups or books, 31.1 percent (210) had had exposure to one or the other, and 57.6 percent (389) were exposed to both books and groups. Regarding positive attitudes toward "others like oneself," 34.8 percent (235) indicated their most prevalent affiliations were with other lesbian women, and 61.5 percent (415) extended this affiliation to women in general.

Summary of Hypotheses

1. Lesbian women of lower socioeconomic status will evidence higher life-stress scores than lesbian women of higher socioeconomic status.
2. Lesbian women of lower socioeconomic status will utilize illegitimate opportunity structures more frequently than lesbian women of higher socioeconomic status.
3. Public visibility as a lesbian woman will be associated with higher life-stress scores.
4. Lesbian women with high disclosure scores will utilize illegitimate opportunity structures more frequently than lesbian women with low disclosure scores.
5. Lesbian women will associate greater life stress with their status as female than with their status as lesbian.
6. Increased age among lesbian women will be associated with higher life-stress scores.
7. Lesbian women with exposure to feminism will evidence lower life-stress scores.
8. Lesbian women who view other lesbian women as a reference group will evidence lower life-stress scores.

Factors Associated with Negative and Positive Outcomes

Higher stress scores were found to correlate with lower socioeconomic status ($p < .0001$). The overall relation between the stress index and socioeconomic status is shown in table 6-4.

Table 6-4
Stress Index, by Socioeconomic Status

Stress Level	Socioeconomic Status, [a] Percentage				
	I	II	III	IV	V
High	6.3	8.0	10.1	15.9	26.0
Moderate	31.3	44.0	43.3	45.5	54.0
Low	62.5	48.0	46.6	38.6	20.0

[a]Determined by the two-factor index of social position (Hollingshead 1957).

Lower socioeconomic status was found to correlate also with higher deviance scores ($p < .0001$). Although 84.4 percent of the sample reported no deviance as defined in this context (illegal source of income and/or prostitution), those who did report deviant activity included a disproportionate number of respondents of low socioeconomic status, as may be seen in table 6-5.

The relation of low socioeconomic status to the incidence of both high stress and greater deviance strongly emphasizes the critical role of socioeconomic resources in adaptation to minority stress. However, simply occupying a low socioeconomic status, one determined by educational level and occupation, does not necessarily identify the components of occupying that status which produce the most stress. Both limited economic resources and psychosocial factors associated with occupying low socioeconomic status may contribute to higher stress and greater deviance, and these aspects are considered in chapter 9. However, one psychosocial factor emerged in the results of the next hypothesis.

The hypothesized relation between self-perceived high public visibility as a lesbian woman and increased life stress was supported ($p = < .002$). However, further data analysis modified this relation, for self-perceived high visibility was found to be associated with low socioeconomic status ($p = < .005$), indicating that the variables of socioeconomic status and visibility are not independent. The association between visibility and high stress was no longer significant with socioeconomic status controlled.

Table 6-5
Deviance, by Socioeconomic Status

Deviance	Socioeconomic Status, [a] Percentage				
	I	II	III	IV	V
Both indexes	0	0.8	0.6	2.2	7.3
One or the other	2.8	8.4	12.5	18.7	25.5
Neither index	97.2	90.8	86.9	79.1	67.3

[a]Determined by the two-factor index of social position (Hollingshead 1957).

(The relation between socioeconomic status and stress was unchanged with visibility controlled.) It appears, then, that self-assessed higher public visibility is a stress-producing component of lower-class status, although it is not exclusively a characteristic of lower-class respondents, as can be seen in table 6-6.

It can be seen that more than two and one-half times as many lower-class respondents were in the high-visibility category as compared to upper-class and upper-middle-class respondents (classes I and II, 19.3 percent; classes IV and V, 49.0 percent).

These results contradict Goffman's (1963) dichotomization of tension management as related to being discredited and information management as related to being discreditable. In fact, stress increased for respondents as their self-perception of being discreditable (visible) increased: stress was lowest for those who believed only other gay people would think they were gay, higher for those who believed no one would think they were gay, and highest for those who believed everyone would know they were gay. Stress increases, then, with increased fear and anxiety regarding one's undisclosed sociosexual identity. The relation between stress and self-perceived level of visibility is shown in table 6-7.

Self-perceived visibility was not related to deviance, and the relation between socioeconomic status and deviance was not affected when controlled for visibility. These results suggest that whatever characteristics lead one to feel that one's lesbian identity is always socially discernible are in contrast to characteristics associated with prostitution, since the latter contributed disproportionately to the deviance index.

However, high disclosure scores *were* found to be associated with high deviance scores ($p < .0001$). A caution is in order here, however, since 42 percent of the sample had high disclosure ratings while only 15.6 percent engaged in any deviance as defined here. The relation between disclosure and deviance is shown in table 6-8.

These findings lend support to the theory that, given limited access to success goals by legitimate means, the nature of the deviant response will

Table 6-6
High Visibility, by Socioeconomic Status

Socioeconomic Status[a]	High Visibility, Percentage
I	8.8
II	10.5
III	12.5
IV	18.8
V	30.2

[a]Determined by the two-factor index of social position (Hollingshead 1957).

Table 6-7
Stress Index, by Visibility

Stress Level	Self-Perceived Visibility, Percentage		
	In-group	Not Visible	Highly Visible
High	8.6	12.5	17.3
Moderate	41.6	43.4	51.0
Low	49.6	43.8	31.5

vary according to the availability of various illegitimate means (Cloward and Ohlin 1964; Merton 1938). Prostitution may be one of the most easily available illegitimate avenues for women, and accessibility to legitimate means in many cases would be affected by disclosure (see, for example, the findings related to job jeopardy in table 4-3).

As previously noted, twice as many respondents attributed greater stress to being female than to being lesbian (58.3 versus 28.6 percent). This finding suggests that the negative impact of economic discrimination against women in general is of considerably greater magnitude than social discrimination from the heterosexual majority. In the latter instance, alternative social resources are generally available to lesbian women, whereas in the first instance restriction of economic opportunities is culturally endemic.

The expectation that stress scores would increase with increased age was based on the assumption that older lesbian women have encountered a more hostile social environment than younger lesbian women. While this assumption was not necessarily negated, the hypothesis was not supported. The possibility of stress-reducing factors accruing with age was not anticipated; but, in fact, increased age was found to correlate both with higher socioeconomic status ($p < .0001$) and with higher income level ($p < .0001$). The sample, of course, included only lesbian women who were to some extent a part of the lesbian communities tapped for this research, and of the total sample, only 9 percent were over 40 years of age.

Both feminist exposure and positive minority-group identification were expected to be associated with decreased stress, as measured by reduced

Table 6-8
Deviance, by Disclosure

Deviance	Disclosure, Percentage		
	Low	Moderate	High
Both indexes	1.2	0.7	3.2
One or the other	9.5	10.8	18.7
Neither index	89.3	88.5	78.1

drug use. In relation to feminist exposure, the results were not at an acceptable level of statistical significance ($p < .07$). The absence of a stronger relation between decreased stress and exposure to feminism may relate to differences among respondents which were not controlled. Developing a feminist consciousness, which, simply stated, means recognizing that many "personal" problems experienced as a woman in our society are rooted in sociocultural phenomena rather than in individual deficiency (Kirsch 1974), occurs in phases. These phases, which may be seen as phases of resocialization toward a feminist identity, may initially increase frustration, anger, or depression and thus result in increased dysfunctional behaviors (Brodsky 1976; Lerman 1976). If these stress-producing phases are successfully resolved, the outcome of developing a feminist identity has been shown to be an enhanced sense of self-acceptance and self-worth, an improved self-image as reflected in higher ambitions, more independence and more confidence, decreased prejudice toward other women, and seeing other feminist women as a positive reference group (Newton and Walton 1971; White 1971; Whiteley 1973). The positive but insufficient correlation obtained between decreased stress and feminist exposure, then, could reflect the fact that the measure represents the effects of feminist exposure on women in various phases of resocialization into a feminist identity.

Viewing other lesbian women as a reference group *was* found to correlate significantly with decreased stress scores ($p < .001$). The stronger correlation between these two variables may more accurately reflect the effects of possessing a feminist identity. Since this sample consisted of women who view themselves primarily as lesbian women, two separate criteria were utilized for reference-group indexes, one reflecting a positive identity with lesbian women and the other reflecting a positive identity with women in general. Decreased stress also related to viewing women in general as a reference group ($p < .009$).

The results of other studies which reported positive outcomes for women who developed a feminist identity (Newton and Walton 1971; White 1971; Whiteley 1973) were supported by my findings. A more positive self-image as a lesbian woman and as a woman and a more positive attitude toward other lesbian women and other women in general appear to be favorably related to stress reduction.

Another factor found to relate to decreased stress was high disclosure ($p < .0001$). Thus, in contrast to self-assessed high visibility, which as a component of lower socioeconomic status was associated with increased stress, high disclosure was found to be related to decreased stress. Stress relating to the self-perception that one has a stigmatizing identity which is socially discernible suggests a psychological state of anxiety or fear. Decreased stress associated with disclosure suggests that choosing to disclose one's lesbian identity is interrelated with the attainment of a more positive self-image.

This view is consistent with Jourard's (1971) hypothesis that self-acceptance is a factor in self-disclosing behavior in general, as well as with the psychological premise that stress is reduced through self-acceptance.

Figure 6-1 places the variables found to be related to decreased stress in the context of the basic stress paradigm. The interaction of the three variables—minority-group identification, socioeconomic status, and disclosure—with levels of stress is explored more fully in chapters 8, 9, and 10, respectively.

To summarize my findings, low socioeconomic status and self-perceived public visibility as a lesbian woman were found to be associated with higher stress levels, and respondents assessed the minority characteristic of being female as being more stress-producing than the minority characteristic of being lesbian. Low socioeconomic status and high disclosure were found to be related to deviance. Although not at an acceptable statistical level, a trend was indicated showing exposure to feminist ideology to be associated with less stress, and viewing women in general and particularly lesbian women as a reference group was found to be positively related to less stress. The expectation that older lesbian women would evidence higher rates of stress was not substantiated, a finding which may be partly attributable to the fact that, as a group, older respondents were of higher socioeconomic status and enjoyed higher income levels.

Need for Further Research

Correlational analysis can point to relations between dependent and independent variables and provide some measure of the level of interaction between or among variables. The relevance of relations found between or among variables is largely contingent on the soundness of the theoretical

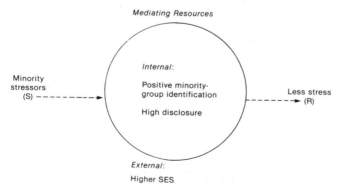

Figure 6-1. Variables Associated with Less Stress in Lesbian Women

and empirical underpinnings which have guided the investigation. Both the complexity of the subject matter of my research and the massive ignorance about it required a broad and exploratory approach to data gathering. Accordingly, while the findings provide new and relevant information pertaining to differential outcomes of categorical status reduction and consequent stress, they also raise many further questions which require additional, indepth research.

It is unlikely that any single research effort can provide a definitive explanation of why some individuals appear to master the art of coping with stress while others appear to succumb to stress and become dysfunctional, given apparently similar situational or structural factors. The complexity of individual differences precludes that any single cause-effect relation will provide an explanation. Nonetheless, cumulative results of investigations of stress phenomena are leading to a more precise identification of contributing factors to functional and dysfunctional outcomes.

The next chapter discusses various definitions of "coping" and examines types of stress-mediating resources. These observations form the basis of the other half of the framework, which identifies variables in the effect of a stressor on an individual.

Notes

1. Significance levels reported in this and remaining chapters are based on Pearson product-moment correlation coefficients.

2. No singular definition of "feminist ideology" has been accepted by the different components of the women's movement. *Webster* (1971, p. 360) defines feminism as "the doctrine advocating that social and political rights of women be equal to those possessed by men; a movement to acquire such rights." Another, more elaborate conceptualization of feminism has been presented by Mander and Rush (1974) which relates to the themes of integration, trust, politics, sex, and play/work. In my view, a feminist may be defined as one who resists barriers to the personal growth and development of women that impair their self-concepts and perceptions of other women, and who seeks to eliminate social, cultural, and institutional stratification on the basis of sex which perpetuates sex-role stereotypes and obstructs women's achievement of autonomy and equality.

References

Abbott, S., and Love, B. *Sappho Was a Right-on Woman: A Liberated View of Lesbianism.* New York: Stein and Day, 1972.

Allport, G.W. *The Nature of Prejudice.* Reading, Mass.: Addison-Wesley, 1954.

Brodsky, A.M. "The consciousness-raising group as a model for therapy with women." In *Female Psychology: The Emerging Self,* edited by S. Cox. Palo Alto, Calif. :Science Research Associates, 1976.

Cloward, R., and Ohlin, L. "Illegitimate means and delinquent subcultures." In *Delinquency and Opportunity: A Theory of Delinquent Gangs,* edited by R. Cloward and L. Ohlin. New York: Free Press of Glencoe, 1964.

Davis, S.W. "Stress in combat." *Scientific American* 194 (1956):31-35.

Goffman, E. *Stigma: Notes on the Management of Spoiled Identity.* Englewood Cliffs, N.J.: Prentice-Hall, 1963.

Harris, W.; Mackie, R.; and Wilson, C. *Performance under Stress: A Review and Critique of Recent Studies.* Los Angeles: Human Factors Research, 1956.

Hollingshead, A. *Two-Factor Index of Social Position.* New Haven, Conn.: privately printed, 1957.

Jourard, S.M. *Self-Disclosure: An Experimental Analysis of the Transparent Self.* New York: Wiley-Interscience, 1971.

Kenyon, F.E. "Studies in female homosexuality, 4 and 5." *British Journal of Psychiatry* 114 (1968):1337-1350.

Kirsch, B. "Consciousness, raising groups as therapy for women." In *Women in Therapy,* edited by V. Franks and V. Burtle. New York: Brunner/Mazel, 1974.

Lerman, H. "What happens in feminist therapy." In *Female Psychology: The Emerging Self,* edited by S. Cox. Palto Alto, Calif.: Science Research Associates, 1976.

Lewin, K. *Resolving Social Conflicts.* New York: Harper, 1948.

Mander, A., and Rush, A. *Feminism as Therapy.* New York: Random House, 1974.

Martin, D., and Lyon, P. *Lesbian/Woman.* New York: Bantam Books, 1972.

Merton, R.K. "Social structure and anomie." *American Sociological Review* 3 (1938):672.

Miller, J.G. *The Development of Experimental Stress-Sensitive Tests for Predicting Performance in Military Tasks.* Washington: Adjutant General's Office, 1953.

Newton, E., and Walton S. "The personal is political: consciousness-raising and personal change in the women's liberation movement." In B.G. Schoepf (Chw.), *Anthropologists Look at the Study of Women* (American Anthropological Association). Symposium presented at the American Anthropological Association, 1971.

Oberstone, A.K. "Dimensions of psychological adjustment and style of

life in single lesbians and single heterosexual women." (Doctoral dissertation, California School of Professional Psychology, 1974. *Dissertation Abstracts* 35/10-B (1974):5088 (University Microfilms No.
75-8510).

Rinder, I.D. "Identification reaction and intergroup conflict." *Phylon*
15 (1954):365-370.

Saghir, M.; Robins, E.; Walbran, B.; and Gentry, K. "Homosexuality, IV.
Psychiatric disorders and disability in the female homosexual."
American Journal of Psychiatry 127 (1970):147-154.

Swanson, D.; Loomis, S.; Lukesh, R.; Cronin, R.; and Smith, J. "Clinical
features of the female homosexual patient: A comparison with the
heterosexual patient." *Journal of Nervous and Mental Disease* 155
(1972):119-124.

Torrance, E.P. "An experimental evaluation of 'no pressure' influence."
Journal of Applied Psychology 43 (1959):109-113.

Webster International Dictionary of the English Language, vol. 1. New
York: Grolier, 1971.

White, H.R. "Becoming a feminist." Unpublished honors paper,
Douglass College, 1971.

Whiteley, R.M. "Women in groups." *The Counseling Psychologist* 4
(1973):27-43.

Wilson, M.L., and Greene, R.L. "Personality characteristics of female
homosexuals." *Psychological Reports* 28 (1971):407-412.

7

Coping Resources

Minority stress has been defined as a state intervening between the sequential antecedent stressors of culturally sanctioned, categorically ascribed inferior status, social prejudice and discrimination, the impact of these environmental forces on psychological well-being, and consequent readjustment or adaptation. Also, it has been stated that although virtually all members of a minority are exposed to a disparaging cultural and social climate, the central factor in their varying responses is the availability of mediating resources, both external and internal. My research identifies variables that are related to decreased levels of stress among lesbian women, and thus these variables may be viewed as stress-mediating resources. To the extent that these and other stress-mediating resources can be more clearly specified, more effective coping responses to minority stress can be developed or enhanced.

Whether the process of improving an individual's ability to cope more effectively with minority stress is pursued through self-help, group or organizational efforts, or in the context of traditional or nontraditional psychotherapy, a cognitive map of the minority-stress terrain may assist in clarifying some ingredients of the process. The helping process in any form is essentially an effort to minimize obstructions to self-actualization and to maximize the accessibility of stress-mediating resources. Analysis of the components of this terrain began in chapter 5 with a framework for conceptualizing the antecedents of minority stress. Further analysis begins with an overview of what is meant by "coping."

Defining Coping

In its general use, the term *coping* refers to a psychological process that allows one to manage current stressors. Coping has been defined as the heightened ability to operate in a new set of circumstances and the ability to perform roles under crisis (Lieberman 1975). This definition suggests that the breadth and flexibility of an individual's role repertoire may contribute to effective coping abilities. Miller (1957) has stated that effective coping involves the economical utilization of available resources. In relation to behavior, this definition suggests that coping is the ability to select from one's repertoire of behaviors the least costly response—that is, one which utilizes the least amount of resources. This adaptive principle of using the least costly response can be seen as employing a "psychic economy" in relation to the social milieu to which the individual must respond (Myers, Lindenthal, and Pepper 1974).

Both Lieberman's (1975) and Miller's (1957) contributions to a definition of coping refer to psychological resources, behavioral and cognitive respectively, and psychological correlates of effective coping have been the prevalent interest in stress research. However, a broader view of variables that assist in effective coping also must include biophysical, affiliative, and economic resources, and these will be discussed in this chapter.

Most attempts to define coping aptly describe abilities which contribute to adaptation, but the more difficult task of explicating how these abilities are developed and maintained has not been undertaken in a comprehensive manner. However, the findings of several authors are helpful in providing an overview of developmental processes that lead to effective coping abilities.

Beginning in early childhood, evidence suggests that development of effective coping abilities comes through encountering frustration and learning mastery skills (Murphy 1962; Torrance 1965). Obviously, the type and level of frustration that a child encounters or is allowed to encounter and the cumulative ratio of "successes" versus "failures" in resolving frustration are a part of the child's developing self-concept. Initially, the child's efforts are designated as "successful" or "unsuccessful" by adults in the environment, but later the child's own criteria may become increasingly important to this evaluation. For example, if by the age of around 4 a child succeeds in tying her own shoes, but her mother insists on retying them, their criteria of "successful" shoe tying may conflict. The mother may be assessing what others will think of her if they see her daughter's uneven tie; the child may be quite satisfied that her shoes did not fall off when she walked. The child may continue attempts to tie her shoes in a more precise manner until her mother stops redoing her work, for the sake of her own independence, but the achievement may be less important to the child than the initial one.

The relevance of a child's sense of competence to her adult self-evaluation is a part of the theoretical controversy discussed previously; that is, behavioral theorists differ in relation to the relative weight that should be attributed to childhood socialization in the formation of adult characteristics. Common sense dictates that a child who is brutally beaten for a performance failure will be affected differently than a child whose attempt at a task is favorably acknowledged, followed by encouragement to improve. Either experience may influence the child's developing self-image, but adult self-image is subject to alteration by ongoing life experiences, as well as by the adult's ascription of meaning to these experiences, both past and present. In general, it is agreed that there is a generalized "net result" of childhood experience which mitigates for or against a positive self-evaluation as an adult, and the continuity between childhood and adult experience may be better understood through the learning concept of "response sets." In his classic work on self-esteem, Coopersmith (1967) defined *response sets* as attitudes that engender a readiness to respond to particular stimuli along predetermined lines which may reflect an individual's expectancies as to what will occur in a new situation. It seems reasonable to assume, then, that a child whose early life experience with frustration results in an attitude of self-competency will be more open to successive trials of ability and will seek new challenges to reinforce this self-concept. As Allport (1955) indicated, psychological resources are developed through risk taking and testing one's limits, and early life experience may predispose a child to seek or avoid new risks.

The concept of self-esteem is addressed more fully in the next section of this chapter, but for purposes of this discussion, it is important to note Coopersmith's (1967) finding that the self-appraisals of children aged 10 to 12 were largely global rather than area-specific; that is, children who tended to rate themselves positively in any performance area tended to rate themselves positively in all areas. This evidence supports the view that self-appraisals of competency in early life stages are based on a somewhat generalized response set, that is, "I can do everything well," or "I can't do anything well." This predisposition appears to be the essence of the life-position theory of transactional analysis; similarly, it is alterable through ongoing life experiences which allow the adult to differentiate levels of competence in specific areas and under certain conditions.[1] To the extent that the more rational and less affective processing of information is developed in adulthood, self-evaluations are likely to become less uniform and subject to elaborate compartmentalization.

Stress-research findings tend to elucidate under what conditions the more affective life position may temporarily prevail over more rational, later-learned coping responses. Evidence indicates that in sudden emergencies a person relies largely on early-learned and overlearned behaviors; in adaptation to stress over time, later-learned behaviors play a more important role in constructive adaptation (Funkenstein, King, and Drolette 1957; Wolf 1943). These findings suggest that early-learned problem-solving behaviors which tend to be more affectively determined are more likely to be elicited in severe crisis situations, but more rational stress-management skills acquired in later years are more critical in adaptation to stress over time (for example, structural stressors). This does not imply that only one or the other set of responses is elicited by a particular type of situation, only that one or the other may dominate according to situational contingencies.

This discussion of some various facets of coping suggests that the development of affective coping abilities is a life-long learning process and that different sets of responses from the same individual may prevail according to the nature of the situation. Variables in the impact of a stressor on an individual, discussed in chapter 5 and outlined in figure 5-2, included characteristics of the stressor and individual characteristics. Regarding the latter, the meaning of the stressor to the individual is critical to the individual's response to the stressor. In turn, the meaning is derived on the basis of the stressor's degree of threat to need fulfillment and the amount of change required. In systems terms, coping infers a continual psychological processing of information (input), whose aim is adaptation to intrinsic and extrinsic demands on the system. The result of this processing is behavior (output). Thus, coping entails the continual psychological processing of stimuli through which meaning is attributed to events, and the meaning of an event is contingent on the availability of various types of internal and external resources. The efficacy of this process is evidenced in consequent behavior.

Stress-Mediating Resources

Stress-mediating resources have been referred to previously as "internal" or "external." Any attempt to classify types of stress-mediating resources as internal or external is encumbered with an array of philosophical and semantical difficulties; therefore, the choice and meaning of these terms in this context require some elaboration.

In Western thought and language, we are confronted philosophically with centuries of debates about the separation of mind, body, and spirit; semantically, we encounter various dichotomies of human experience and behavior, such as objective or subjective, rational or affective, and instrumental or expressive. As Singer (1976) observes in her work on androgyny, mechanistic theories began to break down in the early twentieth century, succeeded by a heightened interest in sets of interacting relationships. Eventually, this shift in approach led to the employment of systems theory in many disciplines to organize increasingly complex phenomena and their interrelationships.

A central tenet of systems theory is that the whole is greater than the sum of its parts. Thus, a social scientist with a systems perspective acknowledges the necessity of studying various components of human behavior as separate entities, but recognizes that each component is simultaneously a part of larger and smaller systems. Living systems are open systems that allow for inputs and outputs across their boundaries.

The classification of stress-mediating resources as internal or external, then, does not refer to a fixed boundary, but instead refers to the person (internal) at the interface with the environment (external), the common boundary at which energy and information exchange occur. For conceptual purposes, resources may be viewed as properties of the person or the environment, prefaced on the awareness that individual systems and environmental systems are in dynamic interaction. Internal stress-mediating resources may be viewed as capacities and abilities that an individual could access in any environment or situation, whereas external stress-mediating resources are in various degrees environment- or situation-dependent. For example, achieved socioeconomic status may result from an individual's capacities and abilities, but the idea of "status" is dependent on a comparative hierarchy in a given society. The concept of "self-esteem" provides another example. From birth, environmental forces contribute importantly to an individual's self-concept. As the individual incorporates definitions of self reflected from her or his environment, they add to or take away from the individual's self-esteem. Over time, a person's level of self-esteem may become more autonomous and less dependent on environmental inputs, and to the degree that it is autonomous, it becomes an internal resource.

In general, internal stress-mediating resources may be further categorized as biophysical and psychological; and external stress-mediating resources, as social (affiliative) and cultural (economic). These dimensions correspond to those presented in figure 5-3 (the schema for minority-stress antecedents) and similarly provide a means for conceptualizing the dimensions from which resources may be drawn. Figure 7-1 illustrates the location of these dimensions in the systems paradigm, indicating their concurrency with the systems processing stage.

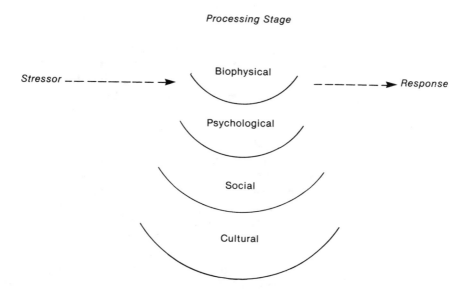

Figure 7-1. Resource Dimensions in the Systems Paradigm

Internal Resources

One's genetic inheritance appears to be the only type of resource that is irrevocably determined at birth, and the extent to which genetic factors set limits on other types of resources is still a matter of considerable debate. Cognitive and intellectual capacities evidence consistency throughout the life span, in contrast to social behavior which evidences little consistency (Mischel 1969). For purposes of this discussion, then, it is assumed that cognitive and intellectual capacities, to the extent that they have genetic perimeters, would proscribe the limits of psychological processes and resources available for making adaptive responses. However, inherent capacities are not necessarily developed and utilized, and coping abilities are ultimately a product of life-long socialization.

The ability to utilize psychological, social, and cultural resources obviously is based on the available biophysical resources. Beyond genetic perimeters, such factors as general level of health, stamina, and level of attractiveness are important biophysical resources that interact with other stress-mediating resources.

Psychological resources may be subcategorized as cognitive (although cognitive capacities apparently have a biophysical perimeter) and behavioral. The previously mentioned definitions of coping underscore these two categories of psychological resources: a broad and flexible response repertoire and the ability to economically utilize this repertoire. The first refers to available behaviors, and the second refers to cognitive skills which allow an individual to select specific behaviors for specific situations that minimize stress.

This distinction may clarify the continuity between early-learned and later-learned coping skills. It would seem that early-learned coping skills would contribute more importantly to the breadth and flexibility of behavioral repertoires, and that later-learned coping skills would contribute more importantly to the economical utilization of this repertoire.

The positive relation between androgyny and self-esteem (Orlofsky 1977; Spence, Helmreich, and Stapp 1975; Wetter 1975) is illuminated through this perspective on role breadth and flexibility as a major psychological resource in stress mediation. A role repertoire which includes both instrumental and expressive behaviors and skills optimizes coping resources, and the employment of this repertoire provides opportunities for increasing self-esteem. These resources, in turn, would be expected to be diminished among sex-typed individuals, and as Orlofsky (1977, p. 574) noted in regard to her related findings, such evidence calls into question "the socialization process which requires that girls suppress or fail to properly learn the very behaviors (assertive, instrumental) that lead to high self-esteem in males (and in masculine and androgynous females)."

Differences in socialization that lead to more sex-typed or more androgynous behavioral repertoires among females appear to correspond to developmental differences in sources of self-esteem. Self-esteem of sex-typed females has been found to depend more on external rewards, such as acceptance by others, than the self-esteem of more androgynous females which is based more on internal rewards, such as having a wide range of competencies, even if sometimes at the cost of social disapproval (O'Connell 1976).

The source of a person's self-esteem appears to be as critical as its level in relation to effective coping with severe crisis. As postulated in the example of the Hungarian refugees who coped most effectively, self-esteem based largely on an internal reward system seemed to provide a buffer to outer changes. It can be speculated that the more adaptive refugees had previously formed response sets which enabled them to cognitively restructure the crisis as less threatening. Similarly, in the example of the Korean prisoners of war who later were found to have had the most resistance, the accessibility of prelearned behavioral responses apparently enabled them to cope more competently with the threat in their environment.

These examples elucidate the meaning of "internal" resources. The availability of a broad and flexible response repertoire and cognitive skills that allow for the most economical utilization of this repertoire represent behavioral and cognitive psychological resources, and thus are internal resources. Ultimately, internal resources are the biophysical and psychological equipment that an individual can access in any environment. Self-esteem as a central psychological resource for coping with severe stress, then, could be more specifically described as self-esteem based largely on one's internal resources. Obviously, self-esteem also is derived from external sources, such as social status and wealth; however, these sources are environment-dependent, whereas internal sources are not.

As previously noted, measures of self-esteem among preadolescents were found to reflect somewhat global self-appraisals. However, with maturation, self-appraisals would be expected to become more discriminant (that is, more "area-dependent") as a result of the multiplication of feedback systems which act as corrective linkages. Coopersmith (1967) suggests that self-esteem may vary across different areas of experience and according to variables such as sex, age, and other role-defining conditions.

With an interest in improving the measurement of self-esteem, French (1968) proposed that self-identity has three major dimensions: abilities, physical characteristics, and behavioral characteristics. A fourth major dimension, reflecting Coopersmith's thinking, may be called demographic or status-defining roles and characteristics, such as being Irish or occupying the position of senator. Each of these four major dimensions contains subidentities, or sets of attributes. Since it is unlikely that all attributes under one dimension contribute equally to that dimension's esteem level, each attribute would be weighted according to its centrality in that dimension. Similarly, each dimension's contribution to total self-esteem would be weighted according to its centrality.

Ideally, then, measures of self-esteem would differentiate among the four dimensions that contribute to total self-esteem, and by designating these dimensions as internal or external it could be ascertained whether total self-esteem is more internally based or externally based. According to the framework presented in this chapter, abilities, physical characteristics, and behavioral characteristics are internal sources of self-esteem, and demographic characteristics or status-defining roles are external sources of self-esteem.

The component approach to self-esteem, in contrast to the more global approach, allows for specification of subidentities which detract from total self-esteem and are amenable to change, as well as those which contribute most importantly to high self-esteem and constructive problem solving. Coopersmith (1967, p. 248) has addressed the relation between levels of self-esteem and overall coping abilities:

> Inasmuch as the definition, interpretation, and response to a stimulus play an essential role in determining what is deemed to be a threat, the prevailing level of self-esteem would appear to be an important determinant of whether, how, and how well an individual will defend himself. Meaning is, after all, imposed upon a situation and persons who feel powerful and adequate to deal with threat are less likely to have their confidence shaken than are persons who are fearful and unsure of their abilities.

Thus, persons with low self-esteem would be expected to experience anxiety or a sense of helplessness when confronted with devaluating stimuli or adverse events; persons with high self-esteem would be expected to have the ability to resist or reject devaluating stimuli and to deal with adversity.

Self-esteem, then, is essentially a cognitive appraisal of one's assets and liabilities along the dimensions of abilities, physical and behavioral characteristics, demographic characteristics, and status-defining roles; and self-esteem represents a balance sheet reflecting net worth. Entries on the ledger may refer to both internal and external resources. However, the most enduring and advantageous entries in relation to increasing individual adaptivity to stress are those which describe biopsychological (internal) characteristics.

Psychological resources that have been discussed thus far include prior learning of broad and flexible behavioral repertoires and the ability to economically utilize the available repertoire. This latter ability and its relation to stress mediation warrant further explication. Miller (1957) reported a number of propositions regarding systems and stress which were developed in an interdisciplinary effort of the Mental Health Institute at the University of Michigan. One of these propositions states (Miller 1957, p. 779): "Systems which survive employ the least expensive defense against stress first and increasingly more expensive ones later." By example, Miller notes that a person unable to achieve a goal may follow a pattern such as this: First, lower his or her level of aspiration (least expensive); second, rationalize that the goal could have been reached with more time (more expensive if given more time and the goal is still not reached); third, repression, perhaps resulting in psychosomatic symptoms; and finally, catatonia, which Miller believes results from a total denial of reality (extremely expensive). Responses which would constitute the least to most expensive options for a specific individual in a specific situation would be highly variable, of course, although general consensus could be found on what would constitute extreme options such as alcoholism and suicide.

The ability to select the least costly response to a stressor as a psychological coping resource suggests the function of some types of patterned behavior. Habits may serve to routinize regularly occurring events with a minimal expenditure of time and energy. For instance, behaviors that begin upon waking and that precede going to sleep are often ritualized to economize both time and energy. In some measure, order and stability are prerequisites for either positive or negative habit formation. Thus, one way that the amount of change required by a stressor is a critical factor in its impact is in its relation to the disruption of habits. Events which alter one's ability to economize on behavioral expenditures through routinization or habit temporarily increase the cost to resources. In this regard, any change temporarily increases stress until new patterns are stabilized that can lead to an overall decrease in stress.

As previously indicated in figure 5-2, both the amount of change required and the degree of threat to need fulfillment comprise the meaning of a stressor. This formulation highlights both the strength and weakness of the social readjustment rating scale (SRRS) (Homes and Rahe 1967). Its use in stress research has provided some measure of the relative weight of some events in people's lives in terms of the amount of change it requires. The SRRS lists forty-three events, most of which could be viewed as disruptive of habit patterns. "Change in residence," for example, is assigned a mean value of 20 on a 100-point scale. Obviously, the meaning of a change in residence in relation to its degree of threat to need fulfillment, if any, would vary widely from person to person; but in all cases it would disrupt some habit patterns. However, another type of psychological resource that may be more determinant of coping strategies than having available adaptive behavioral repertoires or having the ability to selectively employ the least costly response is one's belief or value system. Even with these assets, an individual's belief system, depending on its strength, would more or less govern their expression. Belief systems may derive from religious institutions, political convictions, professional commitments, the *I Ching,* witch doctors, or any source that provides a philosophy of life to which one ascribes and which influences one's behavior.

These acquired values shape or accommodate human motivation. For example, if a part of one's belief system is the Protestant (or "work") ethic, the individual is motivated to work diligently for the reward of feeling "worthy," whether that feeling is based on self-evaluation or social and economic reward. An individual's values generally can be prioritized, but often one or more values are in conflict with each other and compete in influencing behavior. Values, then, may be a source of stress as well as a part of one's coping armamentarium.

The example of geographic mobility as a stressor illustrates that belief systems may be both sources of stress and determinants of stress resolution. Also, it can illustrate the interrelatedness of types of psychological resources. The amount of change required in a move would vary, in part, according to whether a person has a prior history of relocating. Prior learning of "moving" behaviors would allow for a more economical utilization of available resources. Depending on the degree of similarity between the present and future locations, the breadth and flexibility of one's behavioral repertoire also may be a critical variable in stress mediation. In his studies of the elderly before and after they underwent radical shifts in living arrangements, Lieberman (1975) found that there was a positive relation between frequency of breakdown and amount of environmental discontinuity and concluded that people whose adaptive pattern fits or matches the new environment are less likely to be stressed. Thus, the level of environmental discontinuity would be affected by the congruence of the individual's available adaptive patterns with the prevalent regional patterns of the new environment. Regions in the United States reflect diverse belief systems along some dimensions, and the level of environmental discontinuity for mobile individuals may frequently hinge on the compatibility of belief systems. For example, a person's sex-role ideology may be more congruent with some regions than with others and thus be a determinant of a "best fit" environment. In the interest of a "best fit" environment, the least costly option in relation to sex-role stress would be to avoid the regions that posed the most environmental discontinuity. However, if other aspects of one's belief system or goal orientation prevailed over interpersonal "best fit," such as professional or family commitments, the less desirable region may be selected even though it presents a more stressful environment along the interpersonal dimension. In this instance, evaluation of greater versus lesser stress would require contextual analysis of the individual in a specific situation at a given time, but the example raises the relevance of long-versus short-term goals and their relation to one's hierarchy of values.

Achievement of long-term goals often necessitates short-term increases in stress. Thus, based on the order of the value hierarchy, the individual may have to select the most costly response regarding interpersonal "best fit" to achieve career aims in relation to which the selection is the least costly response.

What can be assumed about the role of belief systems or value hierarchies in mediating stress is that beliefs or values can importantly alter the meaning of an event. It is unlikely that a value per se can directly alter the duration, frequency, or intensity of a stressor. And so in the example of environmental discontinuity, characteristics of the stressor may increase the cost to psychological resources. However, an individual's superordinate values may provide a cognitive appraisal of a situation that serves as a buffer and reduces the overall impact of a stressor.

An example of the influence of a belief system on coping processes that arises often in reports of stress adaptability can be seen in the concept of "hope." Lieberman (1975) refers to hope as a process of time binding. It is assumed that hope—as a psychological state—must be attached to both a belief system that legitimizes it and a vision of a desired goal or reward which one believes is attainable in the future.

Apart from the philosophical aspects of beliefs and values, another aspect that represents a potential psychological resource for coping with stress can be described as "cognizance of external resources." Since the actual availability of various external resources may or may not concur with an individual's beliefs about their availability, belief in this context remains a potential internal resource, although in general it would have some external basis.

External Resources

Resources which are in various degrees environment- or situation-dependent (that is, outside the boundary of the individual system) are considered external resources. In the conceptual model shown in figure 7-1, their locus is largely in the social and cultural dimensions, although other outer dimensions (larger systems) also may provide resources. More specifically, external resources may be categorized as affiliative and economic. As stress mediators, economic resources refer to goods and services available to the individual system. *Affiliative* resources may be any external system to which the individual has emotional or affective ties.

Primary ties are typically to one's mate, family, and friends, but they also can be to groups, communities, nations, or larger aggregates. Allport (1954) formulated a schema to illustrate that the potency of affiliative ties is commonly believed to lessen as the distance from personal contact grows larger (figure 7-2). Allport (1954) added some qualifications to the

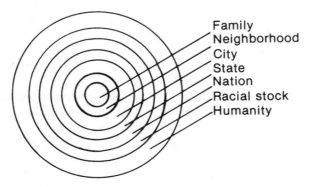

Family
Neighborhood
City
State
Nation
Racial stock
Humanity

Source: G.W. Allport, *The Nature of Prejudice* © 1954, Addison-Wesley Publishing Company, Inc., Chapter 3, page 43, figure 2., "Hypothetical Lessening of In-Group Potency As Membership Becomes More Inclusive." Reprinted with permission.

Figure 7-2. Hypothetical Lessening of In-Group Potency as Membership becomes More Inclusive

interpretation of his schema in an important footnote, pointing out that the innermost circle of loyalty is not necessarily the family, but could be any entity to which one's foremost loyalty is given, such as self or love of God. Allport (1954, p. 47) states that the schema is "an approximate representation of the fact that for many people the larger the social system the less easily do they encompass it in their span of understanding and affection." Allport advanced two corollary assumptions about loyalties. First, concentric loyalties need not clash; that is, attachment to a larger circle (for example, a nation) does not negate attachment to a smaller circle (for example, a state). Second, loyalties that clash are almost invariably those of identical scope (for example, two states). Despite these observations which were used to analyze in-group-out-group phenomena, Allport believed that there is no intrinsic reason why the outermost circle of membership (humanity) needs to be the weakest. Although his vision of a "human in-group" seems as remote a reality today as it was in 1954, the technology is now in place with satellite communications available, and perhaps people in general have greater awareness of our global interdependence.

This expanded perspective is useful in conceptualizing affiliative resources in increasingly larger social systems. It allows for the formulation of a further hypothesis in relation to stress and coping resources: the effectiveness of affiliative resources in stress mediation will vary in relation to their potency in an individual's set of concentric loyalties. Another hypothetical map of concentric loyalties can be used to examine the implications of this hypothesis (figure 7-3).

The potency of various loyalties at any given time relates both to one's

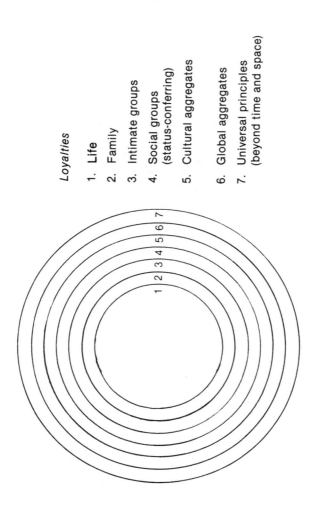

Loyalties

1. Life
2. Family
3. Intimate groups
4. Social groups (status-conferring)
5. Cultural aggregates
6. Global aggregates
7. Universal principles (beyond time and space)

Example

1. Self
2. Biological family
3. Social families
4. Majority/Minority groups
5. Gynocentric/Androcentric cultures
6. Humanity
7. Evolutionary requirements

Figure 7-3. Map of Concentric Loyalties: Example

"survival" needs and to one's life-goal priorities, which in turn reflect one's belief or value system. By definition, loyalty infers an affiliation of duration, in contrast to more transient attachments. For many people today, transient attachments may include geographical locations, work organizations, or social groups, and loyalties may be formed more often in relation to a larger sense of "common destiny." Communities may be geographical or functional, and Lewin (1948, p. 184) stated that "A community is best defined as a dynamic whole, based on an interdependence of fate rather than on similarity." Thus, in addition to representing affiliative resources, an individual's set of concentric loyalties may represent a scale of perceived interdependencies in decreasing order from inner to outer circles. In contemplating various types of crises, however, it seems clear that the order of these circles' potency may be dramatically altered according to the nature of the crisis.

Consider, for example, differences in the reactions of gay citizens and nongay citizens when San Francisco's mayor, George Moscone, and gay supervisor, Harvey Milk, were murdered on November 28, 1978. Undoubtedly, for many gay people throughout the country, the response of grief, anger, or fear relates to their perception of an interdependence of fate. Among those who grieved, Harvey Milk symbolized a rapprochement between the gay minority and society, and his elected role as a supervisor reinforced the hope that by working with and within the political institutions of the country, greater equality for gay people could be attained. Thus, among gay people who shared a sense of interdependency of fate with Harvey Milk, the most potent affiliative resources for coping with stress at that time more than likely would have been other gay people.

Concentric loyalties, then, may be relatively stable over time, but their positions may alter according to situational variables. This qualification can be stated in the form of a hypothesis: The potency of aggregate loyalties, and thus their effectiveness as affiliative resources, will vary according to characteristics of the stressor and its meaning to the individual.

As previously stated, the second category of external resources, economic resources, refers to goods and services available to the individual system. The evidence cited in chapter 5 showing a relation between low socioeconomic status and greater maladaptation to stress, a finding supported by my research, emphasizes the centrality of economic resources to effective coping. Just as one's genetic inheritance establishes the perimeters of biophysical resources, economic resources establish the perimeters of one's ability to mobilize other adaptive processes.

The crisis-potential of many events is either buffered or intensified according to the economic resources available to a person. As an example, for middle-income people with a good credit rating, the option is generally available to move to a more desirable residence if their current one is in a deteriorating neighborhood or to get their car repaired if it has a mechanical failure. For low-income people, these inconveniences can escalate into crises. The inability to move from a dwelling with faulty plumbing, inadequate heat or ventilation, pealing lead paint, or rat infestation ultimately will take its toll on the health of the inhabitants. The lack of resources to repair a car may result in the loss of employment in cities without adequate public transportation.

The ability to isolate and resolve one stressor before it escalates into numerous other stressors, then, is often a function of economic resources. Having sufficient economic resources, however, does not ensure adaptive success, and not having them does not preclude adaptive success, as hundreds of biographies attest. Effective coping as an ongoing achievement, then, must depend on a combination of internal and external resources.

Variables in the effect of a stressor on an individual have been examined, beginning with characteristics of the stressor and the individual presented in chapter 5 (summarized in figure 5-2) and including through this discussion types of stress-mediating resources. Figure 7-4 summarizes this framework, indicating that the response to a stressor would vary according to the balance of these variables.

The next section focuses on the response side of the stress paradigm, specifically in relation to identification and goal patterns of minority groups, as well as stages of adaptation of individual minority members. As outcomes of the minority condition, these patterns and stages provide a broad overview of responses which have been observed to be characteristic among minorities, and they do not represent specific patterns or stages that individual minority members may find to cope with minority stress.

Individual Responses and Minority-Group Patterns

Minority-group patterns are essentially a composite of individual responses to the minority condition, and to speak of a pattern, there must be a notable proportion of a given minority group that exhibits a relatively common response. If individual responses to minority stress were determined in an environmental vacuum, they could be said to precede and therefore shape minority-group patterns. Obviously individual responses are formed in a particular sociocultural climate, so that individual and group responses are reciprocally influential. Options available to minority groups along the dimensions to be discussed are reactions to a sociocultural climate that has assigned to them a categorically reduced status; thus, the range of options to a common stressor would be expected to narrow into a few identifiable patterns.

Wirth (1945) characterized minority patterns according to different goals in relation to majority groups. These goals were described as

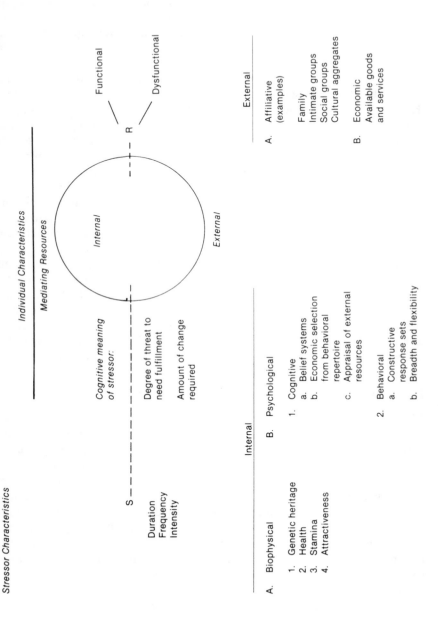

Figure 7-4. Variables in Effect of Stressor on Individual

assimilation (to disappear as a group and to be judged only as individuals), *pluralism* (to maintain group identity while still acknowledging loyalty to the larger society), *separation*[2] (to establish group's own society), and *domination* (to reverse present status arrangement).

Historically, goals of most minority groups in the United States have been considerably more complex than these four distinctions would indicate. Nonetheless, the common denominator of these four positions is a reaction to differential and unequal treatment by majority groups, and each one reflects a belief system about how inequality can best be eliminated.

Wirth's classification of minority-group goals corresponds to Allport's (1954) description of individual response patterns of minority-group members. These responses were viewed as identification patterns and were distinguished as follows: the *out-group reaction*: the minority-group member identifies with a dominant majority and rejects the minority (goal: assimilation); the *mediating reaction*: the minority-group member identifies with both the in-group and the out-group, exhibits an attitude of rapprochement, and functions as an interpreter, a conciliator, and a teacher (goal: pluralism); and the *ingroup reaction*: the minority-group member strongly identifies with her or his minority and tends to reject the out-group (goal: separatism or domination).

Again, while these broad descriptions are recognizable as varying tendencies among minority-group members, they do not offer postulates regarding the antecedents or correlates of these response patterns. Also, they suggest that a minority-group person has one or the other type of response, as opposed to conceptualizing potential responses as sequential, that is, as occurring in logical stages.

Symor (1977) proposes a framework that corrects for both these errors. Its theoretical basis is transactional analysis, and its central premise is that "Redecision of life positions may . . . result from effective personal therapy" (Symor 1977, p. 37). Symor's (1977) framework, the dependency cycle, "postulates that individuals or groups in a dependent relationship $(-/+)$ must move through clear phases of counter-dependence $(-/-)$ and independence $(+/-)$ in order to attain interdependence $(+/+)$."

Applying the cycle to women as a minority group, Symor states that in the dependence phase, the "I'm not OK/you're OK" position, a woman responds with compliance, accepts the limitation of her options, and manipulates her social system to get positive strokes. In the counter-dependence phase, the "I'm not OK/ you're not OK" position, with the emphasis on the other party being not OK, a woman is angry, hostile, and blaming; chooses negative strokes from those in her previous environment; and seeks a new support system for herself. This phase is one in which a woman seeks freedom "from" dependence on men to be OK. In the independence phase, the "I'm OK/you're not OK" position, a woman withdraws, stops expressing resentments, and explores the question of what she wants instead. She is defining her own state of being OK, gives herself positive strokes, and both gives and accepts strokes from other women. In the interdependence phase, the "I'm OK/you're OK" position, a woman has a strong sense of options, behaves autonomously, and enjoys both freedom "from" and freedom "to." Symor's dependency cycle is viewed as cyclical and as moving in a spiral; that is, as each new issue is worked through, the client's freedom of choice increases, and progress through the cycle on further issues is made more quickly.

Symor's phases appear to have some correspondence to Wirth's (1945) goal patterns and to Allport's (1954) identification patterns, although the counterdependence phase in this schema is seen as something of a half-way house between the dependence and the independence phase and has no direct correlate in the other two frameworks. These correspondences are shown in figure 7-5.

More tentatively, these phases could be used to describe the prevalent pattern of any one minority group at a given time. Differences in phase progression within groups would reflect a number of important variables such as region, socioeconomic status, age, and other factors, and members

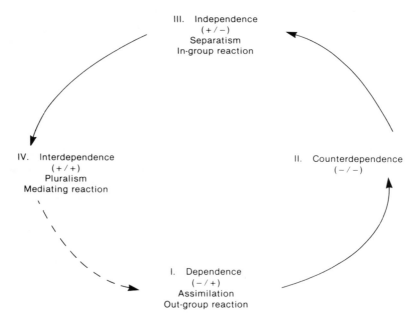

Figure 7-5. Correspondence of Minority Phases and Patterns

of any one minority group probably would be expressing attitudes typical of more than one phase in any specific period. Nonetheless, a modal description may have some utility. These phases represent the spectrum of reactions to sociocultural negation, but one phase of reaction may dominate within a particular group during a particular period. A modal description of a minority group may describe the sociocultural climate perpetuated by majority groups as well as the prevalent pattern of minority responses.

Drawing from the similarities of the minority phases and patterns just discussed, another framework is proposed here that lends itself to the systems model employed in this book's analysis of minority stress. This framework addresses both identity and goal patterns and contains elements of Symor's phases as well. The progression of minority response patterns in this framework includes (1) redefinition of self, (2) establishment and maintenance of positive minority-group identification, (3) the ability to join in collective efforts with others of one's minority group, and (4) a desire to achieve cultural pluralism that is reflected in support of equal rights for other minorities as well as one's own.

The cornerstone of this progression is obviously self-acceptance, and the primary obstacle in relation to minority identity is separating negative cultural stereotypes from one's personal belief system about oneself. As these false assumptions are eliminated from self-concept, wider acceptance of others of one's minority generally follows. The phenomenon often referred to as "horizontal hostility" or group self-hatred disappears at this stage, and empathy with other members of one's minority group increases. An attitude of devaluation becomes one of valuation, and through any of a number of channels the minority individual enters into an active pursuit of equal treatment for one's minority.

Movement beyond this stage to a broader empathy with other minorities may be the slowest in development because of a number of factors. At the macro level, majority members benefit from divisiveness both within and among minority groups, for the orchestration of their common efforts would present a formidable political coalition. To the extent that separate groups must overcome their mutual stereotypes toward one another before effective coalitions can be formed, the perpetuation of group stereotypes serves to diminish the effectiveness of any single group's social-change efforts. Further, even when stereotypical perceptions are altered, intergroup hostility based on competition for social and economic rewards affords the continuation of majority self-interests.

At the micro level, impediments to movement from the third to the fourth stage can be analyzed by application of the model presented in figure 7-4, which represents variables in the effect of a stressor on an individual. If the stressor is identified as "altering stereotypic beliefs," stress is increased in relation to its degree of threat to need fulfillment and the amount of change required. Regarding intergroup relations, the degree of threat may be influenced by one's belief that if another minority group's grievances gain public attention, one's own will receive less. The amount of change required may be influenced by the extent of one's false assumptions and their relevance to one's self-esteem. For example, if being white or heterosexual is an important component of one's self-esteem, allowing someone who is black or homosexual to be OK may make demands on self-concept that increase the amount of change required.

It has become an axiom in stress research to recognize that change invariably requires a temporary increase in stress in order to attain an overall reduction of stress. The systems model again can be employed to illustrate the relation of the progression of minority response patterns to stress levels. Self-redefinition and self-acceptance imply a mastery of stress at the psychological level, positive minority-group identification indicates effective coping at the social level, joining collective efforts toward equality merges the social and cultural, and seeking equality for all minorities (that is, having pluralistic goals) demonstrates stress-management ability at the cultural level.

Three important premises accompany this theoretical framework. First, integration at one level allows for movement to the next. Second, movement from one level to the next signifies a reduction in stress associated with the previous level and an increase in stress associated with the present level. Third, movement through the progression provides a net increase of stress-mediating resources. In regard to the latter, the assumption is that movement through each stage of the progression requires cognitive restructuring and the development of new skills and behaviors, therefore increasing one's internal resources. Regarding external resources, one would expect some losses but also some gains as one's sphere of activities broadened, therefore, over time, resulting in a net gain in external resources.

In sum, both individual and collective minority responses to minority stress act back on dimensions that correspond to those from which the stress conditions originate. To complete the systems analysis, these actions continue on through feedback loops to impact the antecedents; thus, responses become additional stimuli. This reaction-action cycle is illustrated in figure 7-6.

This discussion of minority responses has focused on those which appear to follow general patterns across and within minority groups and refer to a minority person's position in relation to his or her own minority group, other minorities, and the larger society. Perhaps the most important utility of the phase or sequence conception of individual responses to minority stress is that it diminishes the notion that functional or dysfunctional outcomes reflect essential differences in types of people who exhibit one or the other response patterns. As previously stated, adaptation to a stigmatized

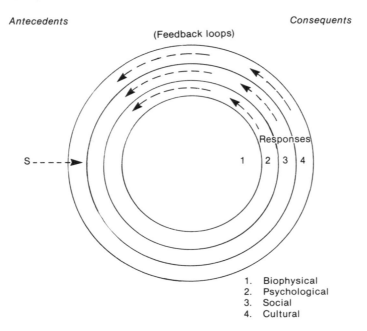

Figure 7-6. Minority Responses in Systems Cycle

identity entails cognitive processes and behavioral adjustments over time, as opposed to an all-or-nothing capacity inherent in some but not in others. Thus, as an individual achieves integration at one stage, for example, the stage of redefining self, a negative habit such as excessive alcohol intake may decrease or be eliminated. As the individual progresses toward a positive minority-group identity, a depressive pattern, often associated with anger turned in rather than out, may disappear and be replaced by a channelization of energy toward group goals.

Components of the model for analysis of minority-stress variables have been presented in chapter 5 and in this chapter, and these components now can be integrated as an overall systems model.

Model for Analysis of Minority-Stress Variables

The separate representations of antecedents, mediating resources, and consequents can be viewed holistically in figure 7-7. The antecedents of minority stress, as summarized in figure 5-3, begin with the cultural ascription of inferiority based on a single characteristic. This cultural communication of

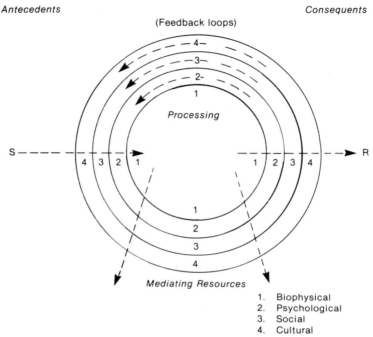

Figure 7-7. Model for Analysis of Minority-Stress Variables

reduced status gives license to majority social groups to exhibit prejudice and to practice discrimination against minority groups and, overtly or covertly, grants permission to majority-controlled institutions to restrict minority access to socioeconomic opportunities. In turn, these forces precipitate an increase in stressful life events for minority individuals, the impact of which, in part, varies in relation to the meaning of these events to the individual's self-esteem and basic security. The impact of minority-related stressors is more definitively affected by the variables summarized in figure 7-4 which include characteristics of the stressor (duration, frequency, and intensity) and characteristics of the individual. The latter include the meaning assigned to the event, based on its degree of threat to need fulfillment and the amount of change required, and the availability of internal and external resources that can modify the stressor's impact. Finally, the results of the processing stage impact back on the environment as aspects of minority behavior, which then feeds back to alter subsequent inputs.

Issues which relate to some of the sequential stages of minorities and their associated stresses are the focus of Part III. Although some of the issues are relevant to minorities in general, the remaining chapters specifically address these issues as they affect lesbian women.

Notes

1. The four possible life positions (for example, "I'm OK/you're OK") represent central emotional (affective) attitudes established early in life. The extent to which an early-formed "life position" is alterable in later life also is debated among transactional analysts; for example, see Harris (1967, chap. 3).

2. Wirth's (1945) actual term for the minority-group goal of wanting to establish a separate, homogeneous society was *secession*. The same idea is more commonly expressed today as separatism, as in lesbian separatism.

References

Allport, G.W. *The Nature of Prejudice.* Reading, Mass.: Addison-Wesley, 1954.

———— . *Becoming.* New Haven, Conn.: Yale University Press, 1955.

Coopersmith, S. *The Antecedents of Self-Esteem.* San Francisco: W.H. Freeman, 1967.

French, J., Jr. "The conceptualization and measurement of mental health in terms of self-identity theory." In *The Definition and Measurement of Mental Health.* Washington: U.S. Department of Health, Education, and Welfare, Public Health Service, Health Services and Mental Health Administration, National Center for Health Statistics, 1968.

Funkenstein, D.; King, S.; and Drolette, M. *Mastery of Stress.* Cambridge, Mass.: Harvard University Press, 1957.

Harris, T.A. *I'm OK—You're OK.* New York: Avon, 1967.

Holmes, T.H., and Rahe, R.H. "The Social Readjustment Rating Scale." *Journal of Psychosomatic Research* 11 (1967):213-218.

Lewin, K. *Resolving Social Conflicts.* New York: Harper, 1948.

Lieberman, M.A. "Adaptive processes in late life." In *Life-Span Developmental Psychology: Normative Life Crises*, edited by N. Datan and L.H. Ginsberg. New York: Academic Press, 1975.

Miller, J.G. "Mental health implications of a general behavior theory." *American Journal of Psychiatry* 113 (1957):776-782.

Mischel, W. "Continuity and change in personality." *American Psychologist* 24 (1969):1012-1018.

Murphy, L.B. *The Widening World of Childhood.* New York: Basic Books, 1962.

Myers, J.K.; Lindenthal, J.J.; and Pepper, M.P. "Social class, life events, and psychiatric symptoms: A longitudinal study." In *Stressful Life Events: Their Nature and Effects*, edited by B.S. Dohrenwend and B.P. Dohrenwend. New York: Wiley, 1974.

O'Connell, A.N. "The relationship between life style and identity synthesis and resynthesis in traditional, neotraditional, and nontraditional women." *Journal of Personality* 44 (1976):675.

Orlofsky, J.L. "Sex-role orientation, identity formation, and self-esteem in college men and women." *Sex Roles* 3 (1977):561-575.

Singer, J. *Androgyny: Toward a New Theory of Sexuality.* Garden City, N.Y.: Anchor, 1976.

Spence, J.T.; Helmreich, R.; and Stapp, J. "Ratings of self-peers on sex role attributes and their relation to self-esteem and conceptions of masculinity and femininity." *Journal of Personality and Social Psychology* 32 (1975):29-39.

Symor, N.K. "The dependency cycle: Implications for theory, therapy, and social action." *Transactional Analysis Journal* 7 (1977):37-43.

Torrance, E.P. *Constructive Behavior: Stress, Personality, and Mental Health.* Belmont, Calif.:Wadsworth, 1965.

Wetter, R. "Levels of self-esteem associated with four sex role categories." Paper presented at the 83d Annual Convention of the American Psychological Association, Chicago, 1975.

Wirth, L. "The problem of minority groups." In *The Science of Man in the World Crisis,* edited by R. Linton. New York: Columbia University Press, 1945.

Wolf, A. "The dynamics of the selective inhibition of specific functions in neurosis: A preliminary report." *Psychosomatic Medicine* 5 (1943): 27-38.

Part III
Redefining
Self, Group,
and Social Context

8 Identity Conflicts, Cognitive Dissonance, and Resolution

The preceding chapters have identified some faulty premises regarding lesbianism which are embedded in the belief systems of the larger society and create personal conflict for lesbian women who have internalized them. Internalization of these premises undermines the achievement of positive self-identity and consequently negatively impacts a lesbian woman's level of self-esteem in relation to its sociosexual component. This chapter reviews these false assumptions and addresses historical and current rationales for their perpetuation vis-à-vis patriarchal necessity.

Even for those lesbian women who have effectively rejected these premises as invalid, conflicts may arise between the sociosexual component of self-identity and one's larger individual or personal identity. Recognizing that the aversive stimuli which encourage maintenance of a dichotomized identity are largely products of cultural and social misinformation serves to identify means by which this dichotomy can be reduced and self-concept can be more fully integrated.

Faulty Premises and Self-Concept

The most pervasive and deeply embedded assumption, which serves as the cornerstone for other assumptions, is that *lesbianism has to be explained.* This pervasive cultural mandate derives its credibility from the individual-deficiency model, which requires that any "difference" (in this case, from patriarchal norms) be explained by normative concepts of "deviance" and "psychopathology." Thus, any woman who at any stage of life acknowledges feelings of sexual attraction to another woman is confronted with the "why" question, either in relation to accepting her own experience as valid and not indicative of "psychopathology" or in relation to justifying her experience to others, or both. The onus of explanation, either to oneself or to others, which accompanies same-sex attraction often impels women to seek psychotherapy.

Psychotherapists who cooperate in the search for causes generally utilize one or more of the etiological assumptions reviewed in chapter 2, which, with the exception of the biological explanation, have as their common denominator a second major distortion: *adult sexual orientation is determined by early-childhood experience.* Cultural indoctrination, which has largely derived from the psychoanalytic assumptions prevalent in Western societies, most frequently directs the client-therapist's search for an explanation to a thorough review of the client's childhood, and any imperfection in parenting abilities may serve as an accounting system for the client's "defect." For example, any degree of deviation from traditional sex-role norms on the part of either parent, such as an "expressive" father or an "instrumental" mother, may render them culpable.

Viewing one's parents as culpable for one's outcome affects adversely offspring and parent alike. If it is believed that lesbianism is a negative outcome which requires a psychological explanation, and if the prevailing explanation is defective parenting, the consequence may be parental guilt, expressed as anger toward or rejection of the daughter, or a lesbian adult who views herself as a victim of defective parents and thus experiences ongoing stress in familial relationships.

As detailed in chapter 2, there is no empirical evidence to support the notion of childhood causality of adult sexual orientation. While parental modeling and reinforcement are clearly important factors in character and personality development of children, these influences, relative to the ongoing and continual process of adult socialization, have not been demonstrated to be sufficient to either impel a child toward or repel a child away from any specific adult sociosexual orientation. Conversely, there is no evidence to support the belief that children reared by homosexual or lesbian parents are any more likely to become homosexual or lesbian adults than are children reared by heterosexual parents.

Therapeutic focus on early childhood serves to reinforce in the lesbian client the belief that her sociosexual receptivity to another woman requires an explanation and that this explanation may be supplied by a dissection of parental imperfections. The associated premise is the third major cultural fallacy: *lesbianism is a negative outcome of childhood socialization.*

As discussed in chapter 3, outcomes associated with lesbianism are in accord with culturally sanctioned values and goals, including positive mental health and high educational and occupational achievement. Evidence has been presented, however, that there is a double standard of mental health for men and women and that although the personality profiles of lesbian women closely parallel those of mentally healthy adults, they do not conform to the culturally prescribed expectations for women. To the extent that any woman who deviates from the single-model role system (marriage and children) is still considered an anomaly in our society, opportunities for positive evaluations from others also may be restricted as a result of nonconformity to the conventional female sex role. For the role-breaking heterosexual woman, social approval may be diminished by her career pursuits, but she will still be accorded the benefits of being a "normal" woman, at least as long as there is some visible indication of her heterosexuality (that is, husband, boyfriend, child). Without such visible badges of conformity, as is the case for most lesbian women, their essential gender identity as "feminine" is challenged, for feminine in our society largely equates with male dependency (Keller 1974). Again, since cultural indoctrination induces guilt for other than "feminine" behavior in women, the internalization of these cultural prescriptions frequently results in self-negation for women who have not conformed. Thus, the lesbian client who has internalized the view that being lesbian is a negative outcome may experience guilt and a proportionate decrease in self-esteem.

Another potential consequence of internalizing a negative societal view of being lesbian is that it can provide a ready rationale for all one's failures. By building on the cornerstone of "I am a victim," it is an easy step to abdicate self-responsibility for one's lack of achievement or for one's dysfunctional behavior, such as substance abuse. The error lies not in the perception that there are added and frequently overwhelming constraints imposed by society for a lesbian woman, but in the perception of self as "defective" and thus powerless to affect one's own outcome. An individual holding this belief may evidence a very low level of aspiration and a high level of dependency on others. Generally, the crux of this negative self-assessment constitutes the fourth faulty premise: *lesbian women are "masculine"; "masculine" women are pathological.*

Chapter 3 has provided evidence that lesbian women are, in fact, highly androgynous and not singularly "masculine." However, sociocultural negation of sex-role nonconformity may prevent a lesbian woman from accepting or expressing various facets of her personality, either those considered "masculine" or "feminine," depending in part on what characteristics have been most rewarded or punished in her interpersonal relations.

Lowered self-esteem may be the frequent result for the lesbian woman who has incorporated these false assumptions into her belief system. First, she has been taught that her sexual feelings for a member of her own sex must be either denied or explained. The explanation process typically requires ascribing negative characteristics to one's family of origin or assigning some developmental defect to oneself. Further, self-deprecating behavior is expected of lesbian women who have not met the culturally prescribed mandates of the conventional female sex role. Since lesbian self-deprecation satisfies the cognitive expectancies of the larger society, this behavior is often rewarded or reinforced while the rewards of independent or achievement-oriented behavior are often withheld to the extent that they are perceived as inappropriate for a woman.

Prior to examining some means of altering this cycle of rewarded self-negation, a second identity conflict that appears to confront most lesbian women is identified and discussed. This conflict—one's personal versus one's lesbian identity—emerges irrespective or whether a lesbian woman has internalized faulty assumptions about her sociosexual identity, although it may be heightened as a result of acceptance of a same-sex sociosexual orientation. With self-acceptance, the cultural and social constraints that impinge on one's behavior as a consequence of this self-definition often become less tolerable.

"Personal" Identity versus "Lesbian" Identity

A person's struggle for an individual identity is part of an ongoing developmental process ultimately aimed at, in Maslow's (1954) terms, self-actualization. For one whose "master status"[1] is categorically ascribed on the basis of one characteristic, and particularly when this categorical ascription is culturally associated with reduced status, the struggle for an individual identity may be intensified. In this context, the dilemma may be expressed as, "Can I be lesbian and still be myself?" The problem is common to minority-group members, whether ethnic or cognitive, who require political organization and unity of purpose in the struggle for social justice and legal rights, and yet whose quest for individual identity is made more difficult by an all-encompassing master status. Just as a black person may seem to communicate simultaneously "I'm proud to be black" and "Can you stop describing me as black?" so lesbian women today may be caught between expressing positive self-identity as lesbian and the desire to be considered uncategorically, that is, as an individual.

On an interpersonal basis, it is important to remember that the minority individual has not asked to be group-labeled on the basis of a "different" characteristic and discriminated against legally, economically, and socially on this basis. That the minority person is viewed primarily as a part of this group, that is, that this categorical description has become the master status of the individual in the eyes of majority-group members usually results in stereotypical attributions and assumptions being made about the individual. Thus, to convey that one relates positively to that characteristic which is typically stigmatized is a healthy assertion against the implied status reduction which accompanies a negative stereotype. The second assertion is simply the other side of the same coin, enjoining the perceiver to see beyond their stereotypes and to see the individual as an individual rather than as a representative of a category.

However, interpersonal labeling responses would produce only intermittent stress events for most lesbian women; in contrast, fixed social and cultural constraints pose continual limits on her options, thus continually reducing her opportunities to evolve a self-identity independent of the culturally imposed master status. Many of these constraints have been previously identified, such as those which deny her access to legitimate family formation and present her with a "Catch 22" situation in relation to the effect of disclosure on job security and achievement orientation. Some of the effects of these constraints become more apparent by examining their impact on the social options available to lesbian women. The limitations can be illustrated by considering the shift in behavioral settings that would be experienced by a woman making a transition from a heterosexual to a lesbian sociosexual orientation.

As a heterosexual woman, almost any setting or interpersonal transaction has the potential of providing an opportunity for meeting a member of the other sex to or from whom interest or attraction could be communicated. By contrast, similar behavior between two women is tabooed in almost all settings and interpersonal transactions. Thus it becomes clear that "courting" behavior for lesbian women is largely confined to a few, if any, environs such as lesbian bars or clubs. This restriction requires a careful monitoring of one's behavior, reduces spontaneity, and may increase self-consciousness in relating to other women.

According to the model of minority-stress antecedents (figure 5-3), the sequence begins with cultural stigmatization of same-sex relationships (to support patriarchy), this culturally ascribed stigma dictates limiting the social opportunities of lesbian women, and these social restrictions in turn diminish the individual's self-esteem. Thus, in an effort to restore self-esteem, a lesbian woman may spend much of her social time in a lesbian club talking about how she hates the place and denying the frequency of her visits. Closer examination may find that it is not the club or its inhabitants that cause this resentment as much as it is the simple fact that there are often few, if any, alternative settings in which she could spontaneously communicate attraction to other women without fear or anxiety. This unparalleled constraint on relational processes is a constant reminder to single lesbian women of their reduced status and denies them the prerogatives accorded to heterosexual relational processes.

Although it can be argued that lesbian women may avail themselves of most of the same social opportunities as anyone else, the subjective reality for lesbian women is that doing so is often at the psychic cost of social fabrications which veil their sociosexual orientation. Many lesbian women are not willing to sacrifice their psychic well-being by routinely performing according to majority expectations and prefer to socialize predominantly with other gay people. The salience of sociosexual roles in structuring social exchange could be expected to be less observable to heterosexual individuals since their roles and identities are consistent with cultural expectations. However, for lesbian women, both the traditional subordinate behavior expected of women and the disassociation from her sociosexual identity make most heterosexual milieus uninviting. On the other hand, if one's social milieu is determined solely on the basis of sociosexual orientation, a lesbian woman may feel that other significant parts of her identity are submerged. This occurs since characteristically in our society social gathering places are somewhat self-stratified according to level of income or education, focus of interest, marital status, or other differentiating variables. In contrast, the only common denominator which can be assumed to be present in lesbian gathering places is sociosexual identity. The cost in this instance may be that all other sources of self-identity or status enhancement are subordinated to one's lesbian identity. Thus, the dilemma may be posed as, "Which part of myself do I abdicate for the benefit of social relations?" An all too common solution to this social dilemma is withdrawal, or at least a markedly circumscribed social existence.

Awareness of these conditions may illuminate certain feeling states expressed by lesbian women during various stages of coming to terms with a minority identity. For example, statements such as "I don't have any real friends" or "I never meet anyone I really like" may indicate the frustration of compartmentalized associations from the perspective of the perceived and the perceiver—that is, "only one part of me is seen by others, and I see only one part of others."

Statements that express social isolation may be the tip of the iceberg sitting atop the rage that emerges when a lesbian woman confronts the social limitations imposed on her on the basis of her sociosexual orientation. Social acceptance often seems to be contingent on her hiding her sexual identity or, conversely, based entirely on her orientation. Either condition presents enormous obstacles to establishing and maintaining an integrated sense of self, as well as to the formation of meaningful and fulfilling social relationships since significant relationships are not formed or nourished among fragmented "selves."

The self-referential effects of "lesbian" identity, then, may be negative if they are derived from having internalized cultural stereotypes or if they result from the external social constraints imposed by the larger society based on those stereotypes. Negative effects are subject to modification because they depend in some degree on maintaining the belief systems that reinforce them. The cultural stigmatization of lesbianism must rely on a belief system (and for some, on evidence) that supports the superior status of heterosexuality. The next section examines some of the majority-controlled institutions that perpetuate the stigmatization of lesbian women and offers some arguments for challenging their allegedly normative prescriptions for sociosexual behavior. Suggestions are then proposed for modifying the negative self-referential aspects of lesbian identity.

Reassessing Social Reality

"Functionalism in sociology posits that established social institutions or patterns of behavior would cease to exist if they did not serve some function for the society'' (Traub and Little 1975, p. 1). A minority group's reassessment of social reality, then, must examine the purpose and function of established social institutions and related patterns of behavior in order to identify and distinguish issues that present the greatest resistance to social change and those that are more amenable to change.

As stated previously, categorical ascription of inferior status on the basis of sex, sociosexual orientation, race, ethnicity, or any other group characteristic reduces social, sexual, and economic competition and thus protects the vested interests of those who control resources. What, then, are the vested interests of those who control resources that are threatened by the changing status of women or by lesbianism?

Historically, the social control of sexuality has been linked to male supremacy (patriarchy). The property status of women supported through monogamous marriage has ensured paternity and other patriarchal rights. Other modes of sexual expession such as homosexuality and premarital or extramarital sexual activity were tabooed because they threatened to disassociate sexual experience from reproductive experience and to violate the property and paternity rights ensured by monogamous marriage. In regard to the latter, the legal notion of an ''illegitimate'' child, for example, one that has been abolished in Sweden and Russia, has no meaning except in terms of patriarchal property rights. In regard to the former, easily available contraception and abortion further undermine the linkage of sexual and reproductive experience, and it is not coincidental that the most emotional controversies in the current sociopolitical arena of the United States are abortion and homosexuality—both perceived as threatening the vested interests of heterosexual males and their wives who depend on the institution of marriage for their social and economic survival (during and after). By assigning to women the singular function of reproduction and the rearing of children, controlling their access to economic resources, and prohibiting other modes of sexual expression except that which occurs within legally sanctioned monogamous marriage, social, economic, and sexual competition are effectively reduced, thus protecting the vested interests of patriarchy.

The status-quo support of male supremacy, in spite of much rhetoric to the contrary, bears no relation to supporting the function of families. The purpose of the family is to benefit the young (May 1930), that is, to provide for the nurturance and socialization of children. Just as there are many avenues to meaningful and enduring relationships besides marriage, there are many alternative social arrangements for rearing and caring for children. Mitchell (1972, p. 337) argues for a plural range of institutions where the traditional family is one, but that also includes legitimation and social recognition of ''couples living together or not living together, long-term unions with children, single parents bringing up children, children socialized by conventional rather than biological parents, extended kin groups, and so on—all these could be encompassed in a range of institutions which matched the free invention and variety of men and women." Obviously these relational structures now exist and rival the nuclear model that is heralded as the form which now must be protected.

Given the observation that established social institutions or patterns of behavior would cease to exist if they did not serve some function for the society, an objective appraisal of the institutions of marriage and the nuclear family might lead to the conclusion that they are diminishing as institutions because they no longer serve the needs of society. In regard to marriage, the Census Bureau reports that between 1970 and 1977 the number of women aged 25 to 34 who had never been married increased by 111 percent, and the number divorced and not remarried was up 170 percent. According to the National Center for Health Statistics, the annual divorce rate rivals the marriage rate, and the current annual divorce rate is 1.6 million. These statistics further support the trends noted in chapter 4 indicating that women are increasingly choosing economic independence over marriage.

The assumption that conventional family structures provide an optimum environment for rearing children must be questioned in view of statistics indicating that more than half (28 million) of the nation's married women are physically abused by their husbands (Levy and Langley 1978). Whether or not the children in these homes also are physically abused, and evidence suggests that 65 percent of them are, the "modeling" of wife battery raises critical questions about the benefit of a man in the home versus the potential costs. Child abuse itself is estimated to include 1 million cases per year, and of these about 2,000 children die (U.S. Department of Health, Education, and Welfare 1978). These statistics appear to support the Adlerian theory that the most basic psychological drive is the need for superiority or domination. If this is so, and given the fact that male physical aggression is encouraged and rewarded by male society, the insecure male whose power strivings are frustrated in other arenas may be more likely to use physical aggression to satisfy his need for dominance in the family arena.

To draw these facts together, the institution which seems to no longer serve a useful function for society is patriarchy and its doctrine of male supremacy. A plurality of forms of "marriage" and "family" are apparently rising to serve the needs of a society that can no longer tolerate the results of male dominance. The insecurity of men who have depended on institutionally supported supremacy and asymmetrical relations with women to shore up their self-esteem is apparently reverberating through all our social institutions, and their protest is often echoed by their wives whose economic dependence and borrowed sense of power are similarly threatened.

One of the most critical examinations of "the nature of man" to appear recently comes from male ranks. Drawing from the work of Sutherland

and Cressy (1966), Gilder (1973, p. 5) reports that "The chief perpetrators of . . . problems are men. Men commit over 90 percent of major crimes of violence, 100 percent of the rapes, 95 percent of the burglaries. They comprise 94 percent of our drunken drivers, 70 percent of suicides, 91 percent of offenders against family and children." Gilder states clearly that "It is male behavior that must be changed to create a civilized order" (p. 24), but strongly advocates that this be accomplished by greater suppression of women, that is, by all women accepting that their place is in the home ["every cent of our employment money should be spent on males" (p. 136)]. Gilder's analysis *could* lead to the conclusion that the best way to serve the family function of protecting and nurturing the young would be to limit this privilege to women exclusively, and one could assume that two or more women would be better than one. However, Gilder seems to be less concerned with the child-rearing function of the family than with the opportunity it provides for male dominance. For example, he decries the existence of other child-support mechanisms, such as the Aid to Families with Dependent Children program, and notes that such an alternative "qualms and frightens every lower-class male" (Gilder 1973, p. 147).

That the greatest threat to patriarchy is female reproductive freedom seems nowhere more clearly stated than in Gilder's (1973, p. 142) description of male potency: "Throughout the centuries, men could imagine their sexual organs as profoundly powerful instruments. If they performed a normal amount of sexual activity—'spread their wild oats'—they could assume that they would cause a number of women to bear their children. Male potency was not simply a matter of erectile reliability; it was a fell weapon of procreation." If, in general, the male sense of sexual potency relies on female pregnancy (the having-my-baby syndrome), and considerable evidence supports this premise (Lewis 1956; McGinn 1966; Patch 1970; Williamson 1970), what other affirmation of sexual power could support male self-esteem since prolific paternity has ceased to benefit society?

However heretical the cumulative evidence appears to be, other outcomes of male sexuality are apparently of dubious value to women as well. According to Cox (1976, p. 262), the equal right to fulfilling sexual expression has been denied to women under patriarchy:

> Unequal sexual expression is one more way in which men are ensured dominance and mastery over women. . . . For men, sexuality and power are interwoven. . . . Underlying the patriarchal creations of the Whore and the Madonna, then, may be both men's desire and their fear that women be fully sexual. . . . Women's sexual lives at present may be indicative of the toll that patriarchy has taken on the lives of women.

Hite's (1976) survey concerning female sexuality indicates that increasing numbers of women are less willing to pay this toll. About 30 percent of the women in her sample of 3,019 could attain orgasm regularly from intercourse, and Hite notes that many women are interested in trying a sexual relationship with another woman, believing it would be a more symmetrical relationship. Although I doubt that many lesbian women are interested in being "tried," the patriarchal suppression of women's sexuality is nonetheless capsulized in the Hite finding that more women regularly attain orgasm by what have previously been considered "lesbian practices" than by coition.

As pointed out in chapter 2, there is a physiological component which contributes to this difference in outcome relating to the decrease in female orgasmic intensity caused by the penis holding the vaginal walls apart (Kline-Graber and Graber 1975). Masters and Johnson (1979) elaborate in great detail other differences between intrasexual and intersexual eroticism, as well as between lesbian and heterosexual male approaches to sexual expression. Based on their extensive research on human sexuality, Masters and Johnson (1979, p. 208) state:

> The safe conclusion can be drawn that, from a purely functional point of view, woman has the physiologic potential to be a more responsive sexual entity than man. These laboratory returns also lead to the speculation that, in this country at least, man's culturally established role as the sex expert, as the more facile sexual responder, or as the more effective sexual performer will not be supported much longer.

Other dysfunctional outcomes for women associated with heterosexuality, as noted in chapter 2, include the fact that experiments have confirmed the possibility that sperm can trigger cervical cancer by invading the nonsexual cells of the cervix (Nelson 1975) and the finding (Kenyon 1968) that lesbian women had fewer gynecological operations and significantly less premenstrual tension than nonlesbian women. Further, in Bell and Weinberg's (1978) study of 686 homosexual men and 293 lesbian women, they found that while about two-thirds of the men had contracted a venereal disease, virtually none of the women had. One must conclude that the doubling of the syphilis rate for women in the past twenty years (U.S. Department of Health, Education, and Welfare 1976) is also an outcome of heterosexuality. Finally the effects of many birth-control drugs and repetitive abortions on women's health, although still debated, do not add confidence in the efficacy of heterosexuality.

As noted in chapter 3, according to the Keller (1974) criteria of the conventional female sex role, the two major departures from this role are economic and sexual independence from men. Lesbian women symbolize both areas of independence; thus, what better assurance against the erosion of patriarchy than to negate this alternative and to maintain its cultural invisibility? Except through authoritarian totalitarianism, the only means for suppressing sociosexual minorities is through cultural indoctrination that they threaten the "rightness and goodness" of majority patterns of behavior, and this is a fait accompli if the minority acquiesces to this cultural indoctrination by remaining virtually invisible. More importantly, the perpetuation of this cultural indoctrination impairs the life opportunities and satisfactions of millions of gay men and women and unnecessarily creates divisiveness in a society that can ill afford the global publicity of still another Achilles heel that weakens its posture as the champion of human rights and social justice (the first being its inability to effectively deter the social reality of racism). From this perspective, both the short- and long-range goals of a democracy are well-served by the efforts of social scientists to unravel the psychological principles at work that mitigate against the achievement of cultural pluralism. In my view, no such effort can surpass that of Gordon W. Allport's (1954) *The Nature of Prejudice,* but new knowledge can elaborate and expand his ideas as they apply to majority-minority relations today.

A more recently added psychological concept—cognitive dissonance—explains some aspects of the heterosexual-homosexual tug-of-war. Cognitive dissonance can be viewed as the stressor in the struggle for lifestyle equality, and one of the more effective resources for reducing states of stress induced by cognitive dissonance is called, not surprisingly, cognitive restructuring. Festinger's (1962) theory of cognitive dissonance centers on the idea that if a person "knows" various things that are not psychologically consistent with one another in his or her frame of reference, the person will try to make them more consistent. *Cognitive* emphasizes the theoretical focus on items of information, and *dissonance* refers to a breach in a person's expectations about what things go together and what things do not (that is, a state of incongruence is produced in one's assumptive world). Resolving dissonance generally leads to an increase in the desirability of the chosen alternative and a decrease in the desirability of the rejected alternative. Thus, for the heterosexual person with vested interests in traditional social institutions, a reduction in dissonance can be achieved by negation of alternative lifestyles such as single parenthood and homosexuality. This resolution is made even simpler by the fact that it is reinforced by cultural prohibitions against or sterotypes attached to alternative lifestyles, as well as by the fact that a negative description of one's chosen alternative (heterosexuality, monogamous marriage, and so on) is rarely (if ever) presented. Conversely, a gay person may reduce dissonance by negating heterosexual patterns of behavior, although this is a less easily defended position in a culture that supports the heterosexual majority.

In either case, another option is available through cognitive restructuring, that is, the systematic modification of faulty patterns of thinking (Shaw 1977), or a reappraisal of the situation based on new information.

This reappraisal can result from new evidence indicating that the dissonance-producing stimuli are nonthreatening and benign. Regarding alternative lifestyles, it may entail new information that enables a person to accept a plurality of lifestyles as opposed to a rigid defense of only one.

Cognitive restructuring as a therapy approach with lesbian women seems particularly appropriate for those who have internalized cultural stereotypes and whose behavior appears to be self-destructive (for example, chronic depression, substance abuse, and suicidal ideation). The objective is not the total negation of heterosexual social institutions, but self-affirmation that lesbian lifestyles merit cultural parity. An approach such as Beck's (1967, 1974), designed for intervention with depressed individuals, seems highly applicable to the dysfunctions associated with lesbian self-negation. As summarized by Shaw (1977, p. 544), the cognitive framework of depressed individuals, according to Beck, is described as follows:

> A primary position [is assigned] to a cognitive triad, which consists of a negative conception of the self, the external world, and the future . . . the depressed client sees himself as deficient and inadequate, he consistently construes his experience in a negative way, and he believes his current difficulties will continue indefinitely.

A therapeutic approach to altering these cognitions could include identifying the client's depressant automatic thoughts about self, the external world, and the future; training the client to challenge their validity; and modifying the client's assumptions that underlie the faulty cognitions. Thus, a reappraisal of social reality that examines the deficits of "normative" patterns of behavior can assist in challenging the validity of a lesbian woman's depressant automatic thoughts about self.

The faulty assumptions presented at the beginning of this chapter that may contribute to lesbian self-negation can be deconditioned and replaced with positive self-affirmations on the basis of this new information. The replacement automatic thoughts would depend on the specified person-situation configuration, but they need to be sufficiently assertive to dissipate the I'm-not-OK life position. Some suggestions are:

Faulty assumption: Lesbianism has to be explained.
New message: "Be serious."
                     or
                     "It's heterosexuality that needs explaining."

Faulty assumption: Adult sexual orientation is determined by early-childhood experience.
New message: "If it were true, why did I waste all that time experimenting with heterosexuality?"
                     or

"If it were so, I'd feel very grateful to my parents."

Faulty assumption: Lesbianism is a negative outcome of childhood socialization.

New message: "Negative for patriarchy, but not for me."

or

"Then why am I at the top of the heap?"

Faulty assumption: Lesbian women are "masculine"; "masculine" women are pathological.

New message: "Lesbian women are androgynous, and androgyny is good for your health."

or

"If 'masculine' means power and privilege, maybe I should 'butch-up' my act."

The different perspectives discussed in this chapter can be placed in the larger context of the effects of sex-role transitions since in many respects the hetrosexual-homosexual xenophobia represents a microcosm of competing belief systems. The psychological responses are similar for both those with vested interests in maintaining conventional sex roles (majority-identified) and those with vested interests in modifying conventional sex roles (minority-identified). The two groups differ in their designation of the stressor, and this identification is posited as majority-minority related as opposed to heterosexual-homosexual related, in recognition of the fact that many heterosexual people support changing sex-role prescriptions and that not all gay people do. The conflict is shown in figure 8-1, using the systems-sequence paradigm of stress antecedents.

While these maps emphasize the common outcome of cognitive dissonance, they do not underscore the differential effect of the stressors on majority- and minority-identified individuals. Currently, the external resources available to minority-identified groups are minimal, whereas for receives continuous sociocultural reinforcement. Thus, in considering the variables in the effect of a stressor on an individual, important differences are found in stressor characteristics (duration, frequency, and intensity), in the cognitive meaning of the stressor as it impacts need fulfillment and amount of change required, and in the external resources available with which to reduce the impact of the stressor. (Since internal resources are person-specific, general comparisons would not apply.)

The different effect in relation to stressor characteristics is summarized by Allport's (1954, p. 145) statement quoted previously, which bears repeating: "A minority group member has to make many times as many adjustments to his status as does the majority group member . . .the awareness, the strain, the accommodation all fall more heavily and more

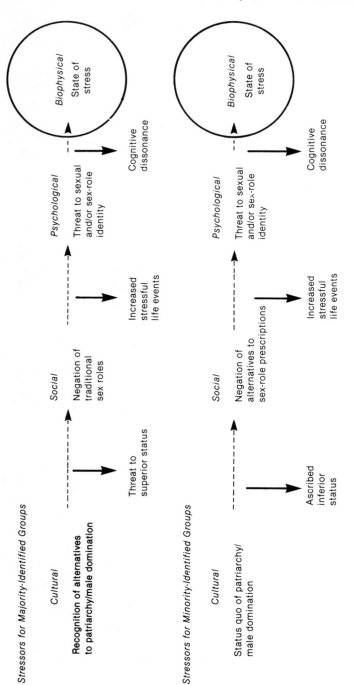

Figure 8-1. Stressors for Majority- and Minority-Identified Groups in Relation to Changing Sex Roles

frequently on the minority group members." This perspective leads to the conclusion that interactions with dominant-group members often require minority-group members to maintain a degree of vigilance in regard to the minority component of their identity, and that these interactions increase the frequency of events which require adaptation.

To apply the cognitive-reappraisal approach to the personal versus "lesbian" identity conflict assumes that the redefinition-of-self stage has increased self-acceptance and, concurrently, has increased esteem for other lesbian women. However, even if one's self-esteem is not threatened by "lesbian" identity, the tendency to maintain a dichotomized identity is reinforced by the external world's use of the categorical label as a master status indicating a host of cultural stereotypes. The label as stressor could be expected to vary according to numerous variables, including region, occupation, and level of social disclosure, since these and other factors would influence the duration, frequency, and intensity of the stressor. The effect of the label also will vary in relation to characteristics of the individual and the availability of internal and external resources. The foundation of internal resources—level of self-esteem—is the pivotal factor in coping with devaluation, but external resources such as socioeconomic status and positive minority-group identification also are significant factors in stress reduction, as indicated by the findings of my research.

For minority-identified individuals, one outcome of a cost/benefit cognitive reappraisal of patriarchally prescribed sex roles can be an unwillingness to passively acquiesce to this demand for adaptation to the cognitive expectations of majority-identified groups. Effective cognitive restructuring is generally accompanied by behavioral change and in the context of therapeutic approaches, assertive training techniques can be utilized to identify specific interpersonal transactions that are stress-producing and to provide "rehearsal" opportunities for establishing stress-reducing responses. Fensterheim and Baer (1975, p. 26) state as a criterion of assertive behavior: "If you have doubts whether a specific act was assertive, ask yourself whether it increased your self-respect even slightly. If it did, it was assertive. If not, it was unassertive." The cognitive expectations of majority-identified individuals, as encountered in interpersonal transactions, may include the entire gamut of cultural stereotypes, but their common denominator is the assumption of majority-superior and minority-inferior statuses in relation to sex, sex roles, and sociosexual orientation. Expected minority behaviors might include an apologetic, self-disparaging demeanor; and overreaction to social overtures such as displayed by an overeagerness to please and placate; and a total denial or suppression of one's sexual self.

For example, heterosexual patronage of homosexual and lesbian associates, a corollary to white liberal patronage of black associates in the 1960s, often takes expession in such remarks as, "What difference does it make what you do in bed?'' While the overt intent is to demonstrate a charitable tolerance for sexual nonconformity, in effect it reduces the choice of an alternative lifestyle and its full meaning to one simple characteristic of that choice—a sexual act. The tolerant heterosexual person thus reduces his or her cognitive dissonance by minimizing the "difference," that is, by inferring that acceptance is contingent on the confinement of gay lifestyle to the bedroom and by continuing the higher-status prerogative of bestowing "acceptance" on the lower-status individual. Gay people who have internalized faulty assumptions about themselves may not recognize the inherent devaluation of such a remark and, in fact, may use it themselves as a rationale for their acceptance. For those who regard their sociosexual orientation positively and have chosen to be disclosed, however, a response would be selected that may shift the cognitive dissonance back to the devaluing remarker in order to break up the game of superior/inferior status and to make clear that the remark is not considered to be benign.

Paradoxical techniques (for example, Fay 1978) are well suited to the game of "bedroom-only lifestyle" as they are intended to disrupt fixed habit patterns and games by nonreinforcement of the existing pattern. Of particular value in this situation may be the "anti shame" exercise originated by Ellis (Fay 1978) which recommends that easily embarrassed or inhibited individuals do outrageous things in public in order to overcome their inhibitions. Also, a similar technique, Hoffman's (1971) "deviation amplification" method, which recommends exaggeration of the "different" behavior, may effectively alter the game, based on the principle that introducing distortion into a system tends to change the individuals in it and their habitual communication patterns. Thus, to respond to "What difference does it make what you do in bed," a gay person might respond, "Not much. It's when I do it in the middle of a busy intersection that people get mad," or, "None, so long as I don't try to marry her/him," or, "My once-heterosexual partner says it makes a big difference."

An individual's manner of responding to devaluation was identified by Coopersmith (1967) to be a major factor in the development of self-esteem. With the input of new information, a gay person can reevaluate both the benefits of gay lifestyles and the deficits of heterosexual patterns and thus be better equipped to respond assertively to devaluations of gay cultural alternatives. Logically, it also would diminish the heterosexual inclination to continue the devaluation.

The provision of new information about lesbianism should enable lesbian women to eliminate the faulty assumptions that undermine the lesbian component of their self-esteem, and, in turn, the consequent redefinition of self provides a basis for coping more effectively with devaluation. With each successful counter to devaluation, in relation either to one's internal thoughts or to external sources, self-esteem is further developed. In the stress framework, cognitive restructuring provides an internal resource—knowledge—that reduces stress by changing the meaning of the stressor. The meaning of devaluative stimuli is changed as a result of the lessened impact on self-esteem; that is, it no longer threatens need fulfillment to the same degree because the "reasons" or motivations for the devaluation are known to be ill founded. In a very real sense, then, drawing on one's internal resources initiates a cycle of self-reinforcement and nets an increase in these resources for coping with future stress.

This psychological phenomenon may partly explain why many successful people credit their enemies for helping them to achieve success and may be part of the reason that advice such as "When you get a lemon, make lemonade" is psychologically valid. By putting obstacles in a person's course, the person has the option to retreat from the obstacle or to confront it; and if it is confronted effectively, the person increases her self-esteem, leaving her better prepared to cope with subsequent obstacles. In essence, redefinition of self by cognitive reappraisal minimizes environmental constraints by maximizing individual strengths.

Further, as internal resources increase (for example, knowledge, self-esteem), the laws of attraction (Murstein 1971) suggest that external resources will be enhanced as well. Among the most important external resources for lesbian women are other lesbian women, as shown by my finding that positive minority-group identification correlated with reduced stress. This sense of reference group is not ensured by virtue of self-acceptance, however. The dichotomized identity conflict also may result from intragroup dissonance. Aspects of lesbian milieus that may inhibit reference-group identity are the topic of the next chapter.

Note

1. The concept of "master status" was first developed by E.C. Hughes ["Dilemmas and contradictions of status," *American Journal of Sociology* 50 (1945):353-359]. It is intended to emphasize that membership in a stigmatized minority group confers a "master status" that tends to overpower any other characteristics which might run counter to it, for example, professional standing. A master status is accompanied by a complex of auxiliary characteristics expected of its incumbents.

References

Allport, G.W. *The Nature of Prejudice*. Reading, Mass.: Addison-Wesley, 1954.

Beck, A. *Depression: Clinical, Experimental and Therapeutic Aspects.* New York: Harper & Row, 1967.

———— . "The development of depression: A cognitive model." In *The Psychology of Depression: Contemporary Theory and Research,* edited by R.J. Friedman and M.M. Katz. New York: Wiley, 1974.

Bell, A., and Weinberg, M. *Homosexualities: A Study of Diversity among Men and Women.* New York: Simon and Schuster, 1978.

Coopersmith, S. *The Antecedents of Self-Esteem.* San Francisco: W.H. Freeman, 1967.

Cox, S. *Female Psychology: The Emerging Self.* Palo Alto, Calif.: Science Research Associates, 1976.

Fay, A. *Making Things Better by Making Them Worse.* New York: Hawthorne Books, 1978.

Fensterheim, H., and Baer, J. *Don't Say Yes When You Want to Say No.* New York.: Dell, 1975.

Festinger, L. "Cognitive dissonance." *Scientific American* 107 (1962): (Scientific American Offprint 472).

Gilder, G. *Sexual Suicide.* New York: Bantam Books, 1973.

Hite, S. *The Hite Report: A Nationwide Study of Female Sexuality.* New York: Dell, 1976.

Hoffman, L. "Deviation amplifying processes in natural groups." In *Changing Families,* edited by Jay Haley. New York: Grune & Stratton, 1971.

Keller, S. "The female role: Constants and change." in *Women in Therapy* edited by V. Franks and V. Burtle. New York: Brunner/Mazel, 1974.

Kenyon, F.E. "Physique and physical health of female homosexuals." *Journal of Neurology, Neurosurgery and Psychiatry* (London) 31 (1968):487-489.

Kline-Graber, G., and Graber, B. *Woman's Orgasm: A Guide to Sexual Satisfaction.* New York: Bobbs-Merrill, 1975.

Levy, R.C., and Langley, R. *Wife Beating—The Silent Crisis.* New York: Pocketbooks, 1978.

Lewis, O. *Five Families.* New York: Basic Books, 1956.

McGinn, N. "Marriage and family in middle-class Mexico." *Journal of Marriage and the Family* 28 (1966): 305-313.

Maslow, A.H. *Motivation and Personality.* New York: Harper & Row, 1954.

Masters, W.H., and Johnson, V.E. *Homosexuality in Perspective.* Boston: Little, Brown, 1979.

May, G. *Social Control of Sex Expression.* New York: William Morrow, 1930.

Mitchell, J. "The situation of women." In *The Capitalist System: A*

Radical Analysis of American Society, edited by R.C. Edwards, M. Reich, and T.E. Weisskopf. Englewood Cliffs, N.J.: Prentice-Hall, 1972.

Murstein, B.I., *Theories of Attraction and Love.* New York: Springer, 1971.

Nelson, H. "Experiments indicate sperm may trigger cancer." *Los Angeles Times,* March 23, 1975, I, p. 23.

Nicassio, P.M. "Social class and family size as determinants of attributed machismo, femininity, and female planning." *Sex Roles* 3 (1977):577-598.

Patch, R. "Attitudes toward sex, reproduction, and contraception in Bolivia and Peru." *West Coast South American Series* no. 2 (1970).

Shaw, B.F. "Comparison of cognitive therapy and behavior therapy in the treatment of depression." *Journal of Consulting and Clinical Psychology* 45 (1977):543-551.

Sutherland, E.H., and Cressy, D.R. *Principles of Criminology.* Philadelphia: Lippincott, 1966.

Traub, S., and Little, C. *Theories of Deviance.* Itasca, Ill.: F.E. Peacock, 1975.

U.S. Department of Health, Education, and Welfare, Public Health Service, Center for Disease Control. V.D. Statistical Letter, May 1976, p. 124.

U.S. Department of Health, Education, and Welfare, Office of Human Development Services. "New light on an old problem: Nine questions and answers about child abuse and neglect" [DHEW Publication No. (OHDS) 78-31108]. Washington: Government Printing Office, 1978.

Williamson, R. "Role themes in Latin America." *Sex Roles in Changing Society,* edited by G. Seward and R. Williamson. New York: Random House, 1970.

9 Intragroup Differences

Conflict in relation to one's lesbian identity may be less frequently and indirectly related to the larger social stigma attached to it and more frequently and directly related to the incongruities of self-identity posed within lesbian social milieus. Coopersmith (1967) concluded that a person's affective interpersonal environment seemed more salient to self-esteem than broader or more distant social variables, which suggests that identity conflicts based on intragroup dissonance would be more stress-producing than those based on intergroup dissonance. My finding that reduced stress is significantly related to positive lesbian group identity underscores the importance of intragroup relations to minority individuals who must continuously confront majority stereotypes. Threats to self-esteem from more affectively distant social groups are, in effect, minimized or eliminated by the major affiliative resource of positive minority-group identification.

The benefits for lesbian women of affiliation with some part of the lesbian community have been addressed by several authors (Chafetz et al. 1974; Hedblom 1972; Simon and Gagnon 1967). Simon and Gagnon (1967) suggest that within the lesbian community lesbian women can find suitable partners, feel less socially isolated, receive social and emotional support, and, through the exchange of experiences, learn a variety of practical survival tactics. In an empirical study (Chafetz et al. 1974), using a sample of fifty-one lesbian women, the most frequent response to the question "What do you like about gay bars?" was that the women could "be themselves," that is, act without the behavioral constraints imposed by the presence of "straights" or males. In a sense, then, lesbian milieus provide a refuge from the assumptive world of the majority and may permit a lesbian woman to express her sociosexual identity more freely and spontaneously.

These findings are consistent with some psychological principles regarding group affiliations. Skinner (1953) noted that by joining a group, the individual increases her power to achieve reinforcement. Allport (1954), referring to the principle of "least effort," observed that it requires less effort to deal with people who have similar presuppositions; that is, people can "let down" with those who share their beliefs and assumptions. This observation concurs with Miller's (1957) adaptive principle of employing a "psychic economy" in relation to the selection of responses from one's behavioral repertoire that utilize the least amount of resources.

The psychological significance of positive intragroup affiliation for lesbian women seems evident; thus, potential sources of intragroup stress which also may create cognitive dissonance in relation to self-identity require analysis. Although the notion that gay subcultures have a monolithic character has been largely disspelled in recent works (for example, Abbott and Love 1972; Bell and Weinberg 1978; Martin and Lyon 1972), class differences as a major variable in intragroup diversity have not been fully explored. In fact, among some sectors of the gay-rights movement, to acknowledge that class differences may significantly impair a lesbian woman's ability to relate positively to lesbian women as a group may be considered anathema. The focus of this chapter, however, is to examine intragroup differences that may obstruct positive minority identification and therefore detract from the psychological well-being of the lesbian community as a whole.

Differences among lesbian women that derive from class background may be transcended as a result of psychological growth and maturity, and it is my view that this process is expedited by becoming more aware of the behavioral areas in which class differences are most prominent. By examining some of these differences that may create conflict in both the self-identity and group identity of lesbian women, a more durable universalistic attitude may be achieved.

Group Identity and Class Differences

Learned behavioral norms have been found to differ in many respects according to class background. Miller (1958) has described six focal concerns of lower-class culture which differentiate lower-class behavioral patterns from those of middle- and upper-class cultures. He identifies the avoidance of "trouble" as a dominant feature of lower-class culture, with *trouble* meaning behavior which results in unwelcome or complicating involvement with official authorities or agencies of middle-class society. The avoidance of law-violating behavior "is often based less on an explicit commitment to . . . legal standards than on a desire to avoid . . . the complicating consequences of the action" (Miller 1958, p. 8). A second focal concern is *toughness,* which may include demonstrating physical prowess, an absence of sentimentality, bravery in the face of physical threat, and the conceptualization of woman as conquest object. *Smartness,* according to Miller, is conceptualized in lower-class culture as the ability to outwit, dupe, or "con" others, perhaps gaining money as a result, and requires adroitness in aggressive repartee. At the same time, intellectualism is overtly disvalued and associated with effeminacy. A fourth characteristic of lower-class life is the search for *excitement.* This may involve the use of alcohol, gambling of all kinds, and the highly patterned practice of the recurrent "night on the town," including alcohol, music, and sexual adventuring. The sought situations of stimulation are counterbalanced by periods of passivity, or just "hanging out." Regarding the fifth characteristic, fatalism, Miller (1958, p. 11) states: "Related to the quest for excitement is the concern with fate, fortune, or luck. . . . Many lower class individuals feel that their lives are subject to a set of forces over which they have relatively little control." Thus, one is either "unlucky" or "in luck," implying the ultimate futility of directed effort toward a goal. The sixth focal concern, *autonomy versus dependency,* is seen as related to both "trouble" and "fate." Miller describes a cycle of involvement in trouble-producing behavior (assault, sexual adventure, a "drunk"), followed by active seeking of a locus of imposed control (a spouse, jail, a restrictive job) and, after a period of subjection to this control, resentment toward it and a breaking away to search for involvement in further trouble. Thus, Miller concluded, the pose of tough, rebellious independence often assumed by the lower-class person frequently conceals powerful dependency needs. The need for belonging may also provide the incentive to conform to the norms of this reference group (that is, toughness, smartness, excitement, and so on), even though by doing so, one may violate norms of other reference groups.

To the extent that this description of lower-class focal concerns may apply to some portion of lesbian culture, perhaps particularly in parts of the "bar" culture, conflicts incurred in the process of trying to acculturate to an environment dominated by these characteristics would be predictably difficult for non-lower-class members seeking social and emotional relationships in such environments. The Chafetz group's (1974) study reported that what their lesbian sample disliked most about gay bars was the behavior of some of the patrons—the role playing, fighting, or drug use. These "dislikes" suggest at least two broad criteria by which lesbian intragroup social assessments are made: class-related behaviors and sex-role behaviors. As noted previously, middle-class females have been found to define their sex roles much more broadly and inclusively than working-class females (Hartley 1964; Rabban 1950), which suggests that socioeconomic status and sex-role orientation are interdependent.

Evidence from my research as well as from others (see chapter 3) indicates that lesbian women are highly androgynous in both psychological characteristics and desired behavioral options. Yet, cultural stereotypes stigmatize lesbian women as "masculine." As I found, higher "public visiblity" as lesbian was significantly related to lower socioeconomic status (table 6-6). Additionally, a significant correlation ($p < .0001$) was found between self-ascription as "more masculine" and self-rated higher visibility. These findings suggest that lesbian women who were socialized in lower-class backgrounds may carry the lower-class norm of more rigid adherence to traditional sex roles into lesbian milieus and particularly into lesbian "bar" culture. Given the evidence that middle- and upper-class women are generally less "visible" and that a lesbian woman's impressions of other lesbian women are often formed in bar cultures, differences in sex-role behavior may be a chief source of intragroup stress. From a middle-class perspective, other behavioral norms prevalent among lower-class members—the emphasis on toughness, smartness, excitement, and so on—also would be sources of intragroup stress.

Additionally, intragroup social assessments generally reflect the status-conscious judgments and pecking-order hierarchies operative in the larger social context. When the group is, in fact, a minority group and is also labeled a "deviant" group, the internal and external pressures to conform to "acceptable" behaviors may be greatly intensified. Thus any behavior which tends to confirm the majority group's stereotype of the minority group will be denigrated by those within the minority group who still seek approval or acceptance from the majority group. The key psychological factor may be the norm and value disparities between the group to which the person aspires to belong (for example, a high-status occupational group) and those of the stigmatized group with which the individual is categorically identified (lesbian). Behaviors rewarded in one group may be devalued or disparaged by the other group, thereby creating social role conflict for the individual wanting acceptance by both groups.

Class as a variable in behavioral norms may serve to distinguish which members of a stigmatized group most adamantly pursue acceptance by the group of aspiration. In a summary of class cultures, Collins (1975) identifies the lower middle class as the most distinctive type, characterized by a rigid, religious morality and a belief that hard work and self-discipline will make success possible. "Least sure of his own authority and most pressed to stay on the top side of the sharpest division among power classes, he identifies with the values of the organization and of respectability and authority in the most rigid way" (Collins 1975, p. 70). Collins suggests that the nearby "bad" example of lower-class hedonism has something to do with the vehemence with which lower-middle-class persons drive themselves to keep up their respectability. That there is an inherent futility in their power strivings is also suggested: "In compensation for the deference he must give to his superiors . . . he can exact deference from a class of subordinates who have no power at all. But the last are outside the realm of power and hence have no reason to identify with it" (Collins 1975, p. 70).

To better understand the impact that lower-middle-class socialization may have on lesbian women, other characteristics of this group need to be identified. Lower-middle-class groups in the larger social context could be expected to be the most vehement opponents of gay rights, in that the movement represents to them defiance of conventional morality, strict adherence to which provides them with their major, and perhaps sole, source of respectability. Studies of the homophobic personality support this thesis. Negative views toward homosexuality have been found to correlate with authoritarianism, components of which are intolerance of ambiguity and cognitive rigidity, and with support of the double standard between the sexes (MacDonald 1974; MacDonald et al. 1973; MacDonald and Games 1974; Smith 1971). These characteristics of the authoritarian personality parallel those of the lower-middle-class. A socializing background that is characterized by a driving need for respectability—coupled with extreme homophobia—may result in a lesbian personality that tries to reduce her value dilemma by living as "respectably" as possible in the narrowest sense of the word.

The original conceptualization of the authoritarian personality (Adorno et al. 1950), although criticized for various methodological flaws, nonetheless stimulated a vast quantity of research which has assisted in clarifying the psychology of prejudice (Ashmore and Del Boca 1976). Kirscht and Dillehay (1967) reviewed a number of studies which found that social class and education are inversely correlated with prejudice. Ehrlich (1973) reviewed a large number of studies that demonstrated a strong relationship between low self-esteem and rejection of others. Conceptually linking these characteristics, Porter (1971) found that the higher the social class, the higher was self-esteem and the lower was antiblack prejudice. By extrapolation, it could be postulated that both lower-class and lower-middle-class lesbian women would experience lower levels of self-esteem and thus a greater need to exhibit prejudice toward and rejection of others. The targets of their rejection within lesbian milieus, however, could be expected to be primarily one another; that is, intragroup stress may often pivot around the value tug-of-war between rigid adherence to "respectable behavior" and antirespectable behavior.

It follows that lower-middle-class lesbian women may be those who would internalize negative stereotypes of themselves and other lesbian women more than lesbian women from other social strata, given their values of rigid religious morality and strict adherence to "authority." Thus, they may be the most circumspect in monitoring their own behavior as well as that of other lesbian women for the purpose of maintaining respectability and propriety in the eyes of the majority. Behavioral norms that could emerge from lower-middle-class values among lesbian women might be characterized by an emphasis on "should-nots"—for example, should not use illegal drugs (alcohol is permissible), should not engage in sex for pleasure (one must be "in love"), should not be "visibly" lesbian in public ("passing" seen as contingent on conventional "femininity"), and should not fail to embrace the work ethic (that is, work equals worthiness). These norms (antideviance, denial of sexual pleasure for its own sake, maintaining appropriate "feminine" behavior in public, and political conservatism) obviously are in conflict with behavioral norms which may emerge from lower-class values among lesbian women—for example, wide use of illegal drugs, measuring sexual prowess by number of conquests, displaying dichotomized and accentuated sex-role behaviors, and outwitting the system either by managing to live on government aid programs or through illegal activities. Here the emphasis is more aptly understood as antirespectability. Believing their social and economic conditions to be unalterable, they abandon efforts to satisfy majority demands, and "having a good time" becomes the alpha and omega of existence.

This profile may serve to depict some of the divergent norms which coexist in lesbian milieus. It does not yet include, however, reference to upper-middle- or upper-class values. The "bar" culture in general appears to serve the social needs of predominantly lower- or lower-middle-class groups, and the norms of these groups seem to prevail in this culture. As in the larger society, lesbian women who are members of upper-middle- and upper-class groups (most frequently professional women) are more likely to have other and more varied resources for social enjoyment which allow for greater exclusiveness and privacy and which provide a higher level of material comfort. With the availability of more economic resources, the primary locus of social activity is the home. Parties in private homes, though, cannot sufficiently meet the social needs of many lesbian women, irrespective of class position. The reasons are varied. First, the private circuit is composed largely of stable couples; singles are generally excluded, and, if included, their options for initiating an intimate relationship are minimal. Second, a potential outcome of narrowly circumscribing one's social group is eventual boredom with one another and an over-intrusiveness into one another's lives. Third, given the high mobility that characterizes the United States, those who move from place to place do not have the opportunity to develop ready access to these private networks. Most important, by withdrawing to elitist conclaves, one sacrifices the benefits of a sense of belonging to a larger lesbian community, and the community loses the special contributions which professional women may have to offer.

It is reasonable to assume that the majority of lesbian women at one time or another will look to some part of lesbian culture as an avenue for social relationships and partners, whether or not they seek total submersion in lesbian communities. In lesbian communities just as in the larger society, belief systems and behavioral norms vary considerably from region to region and from place to place within the same urban area. Most often, the only common denominator among the clientele of lesbian establishments is their sociosexual orientation. Beyond that, the full range of human diversity may be present. The purpose of describing the differing value systems and consequent behavioral norms which derive from the socioeconomic status of family of origin is to delineate and underscore the fact that characteristics often labeled "lesbian" (by both those who are and those who are not members of this group) are unrelated to sociosexual orientation per se, but are the same products of social stratification which are apparent in the larger society. This delineation may be particularly important in relation to both the self-referential impact of a "lesbian" identity and one's ability to positively identify with other lesbian women.

My finding that stress levels decreased as positive regard for other lesbian women increased supports the psychological axiom that a positive group identity provides an important psychological buffer for a minority person against prejudice in the larger social realm. The affiliative resource of a lesbian group may be the most critical component of psychological well-being for lesbian women; thus, any efforts aimed at reducing intragroup stress attributable to class differences can benefit both individuals and the lesbian community as a whole.

Upward and Downward Mobility

In the analysis of class differences and consequent variations in behavioral norms, I was seeking to identify variables that could account for greater dysfunction among some lesbian women than others. In my own observations and to the extent that class origins were apparent in individual behavior, there seemed to be no correlation between effective coping with minority stress and class of origin. If anything, lesbian women evidencing middle-class backgrounds behaviorally seemed to display greater dysfunction than those from the lower socioeconomic strata. I then realized that in my finding that higher socioeconomic status was positively correlated with reduced stress, respondents' achieved status had been used as the independent variable. Hollingshead's (1957) two-factor index of social position yields a class level based on factor weighting of occupation (7) and education (4) and thus reflects an individual's achieved status. A separate item in my research obtained a rating of the economic status of respondents' families of origin. It was possible, then, to ascertain whether respondents had achieved higher socioeconomic status than their families of origin, maintained the same status level, or had fallen below their family of origin's status level. The results provided a *mobility* index, the distribution of which can be seen in table 9-1.

It can be seen that 54.2 percent evidenced some degree of downward mobility, 34.6 percent showed some degree of upward mobility, and 11.2 percent remained at the same level. Further data analysis revealed that both high stress and high deviance were related to downward mobility ($p < .01$ and $p < .004$, respectively). Of those in the high-stress category, 62.8 per-

Table 9-1
Socioeconomic Mobility of Respondents

Category	Percentage
High downward (two levels down)	21.5
Downward (one level down)	32.7
Same	11.2
Upward (one level up)	33.3
High upward (two levels up)	1.3

cent were downwardly mobile, 10.3 percent had no mobility, and 26.9 percent were upwardly mobile. Similarly, of those in the high-deviance category, 75 percent were downwardly mobile, 12.5 percent had no mobility, and 12.5 percent were upwardly mobile. These findings add another dimension to the relationship between levels of socioeconomic status and stress, and they support the view that degree and direction of socioeconomic mobility are more salient factors in stress levels than is the static determination of socioeconomic status based on family of origin.

The question remained, however: Why did more than half (54 percent) evidence downward mobility? Given that the sample was entirely female, the difference in economic status of families of origin and achieved status of the "downwardly mobile" respondents may well reflect inequalities of opportunity for women. Remarkably, in spite of unequal socioeconomic opportunities, over one-third of respondents were upwardly mobile, a few moving as much as two class levels forward. Since all respondents would be subjected to the sex barrier to upward mobility, other variables had to be operative that would explain the variation in achievement levels. However, two cautions are necessary in interpreting the findings before we consider additional explanatory variables. First, the median age of the sample was about 28 years of age, with over two-thirds of respondents being 30 years of age or under. Since socioeconomic status (achieved) rose with increased age ($p < .0001$), it can be assumed that many respondents would continue to increase their status over time. Second, 19 percent, almost one out of five, were college students (by coding convention entered in class III) and also would be expected to increase their status over time. These two factors suggest that the high percentage who appeared to be downwardly mobile may be, in part, in a transition stage toward upward mobility. Even with these modifications regarding the downwardly mobile group, one hypothesis is suggested that would account for the variation in upward and downward mobility, based on a theory advanced by other researchers.

Allport (1954, p. 223), reporting on the results of an empirical study by Bettelheim and Janowitz (1950), stated that people who were falling on the status ladder were more prejudiced than those who were rising and concluded that "the dynamic concept of social mobility turns out to be more important than any static demographic variable." In a complex and comprehensive approach to the measurement of stress and coping resources, Antonovsky (1974) indicated that the gap between aspirations and perceived reality would provide the best measure of stress. Antonovsky (1974, p. 250) states: "We would expect the individual who perceives upward movement from the past to feel less tension than one who feels he has remained at the same level or moved down." Together these perspectives suggest that a lesbian woman who perceives her status to be falling would be experiencing greater stress than one who perceives her status to be rising, and that the experience of downward mobility would result in greater prejudice toward others. The stressor of categorically reduced status based on one's lesbian identity would be expected to differentially impact various individuals according to the meaning of the stressor to their self-concept and the availability of internal and external resources. If the meaning of lesbian identity to an individual were negative and resources were lacking to cope effectively with stigma, conceivably the stress could result in a pattern of downward mobility. On the other hand, if the individual had previously developed problem-solving skills, particularly those related to reduced status, the stress could conceivably lead to increased effort resulting in a pattern of upward mobility.

As the evidence relating to stress and coping suggests, early-learned cognitive patterns and behavioral repertoires figure prominently in crisis management, and early-learned problem-solving skills are developed through encountering frustrations and mastering them. Successful experiences, in turn, increase self-esteem, and self-esteem provides the foundation for coping more effectively with devaluation. If it is assumed that early experiences of respondents whose families were in the lower socioeconomic strata involved more stressful life events (in terms of duration, frequency, and intensity) than those whose families were in the middle to upper categories, and that these events necessitated more early learning and practice of adaptive abilities, then the consequent gains in self-esteem would provide a buffer to a later reduction of status, a buffer which may be less available to those from more affluent backgrounds who, although they enjoyed acquired status, may not have developed as many internal sources of self-esteem. There are, of course, other factors in one's family of origin that would equip one with effective coping mechanisms for dealing with stigma or categorically reduced status, such as ethnicity and religion. Any condition in early life that encourages the development of adaptive behaviors and problem-solving skills would contribute to the internal resources of the adult and may serve as an internal "bank account" that can be drawn on during later life crises.

The finding that downward mobility related significantly to high stress supports the view that internal resources are more critical than external resources in coping with a stigmatized identity and that the development of dysfunctional behaviors may be directly related to the inability to integrate one's sociosexual identity as a positive part of one's self-concept. In some instances, this lack of self-integration may be due in part to an individual's negative perception of other lesbian women who differ from her in values and behavior. Although there are no simple solutions to group identity conflicts, it may be beneficial to clarify the issues and to discuss some of their psychological implications.

Collective Diversity

Irrespective of whether a lesbian woman chooses to submerge herself in lesbian groups or chooses from a range of other options, it is clear that the question of group affiliation can add still another stressor to her life. Being designated as a member of a particular group by the majority appears to necessitate that the individual so designated confine most of her social activities to that particular group. Many may do so because these social milieus provide an optimal level of satisfaction. Yet for others, perceiving that lesbian milieus have been designated as their only legitimate social option, both by the majority and by lesbian groups, may be considered a major form of oppression.

From the perspective of psychological well-being, one of the aims of any social reform movement should be to increase the social and economic options available to members of a minority; yet the effect often seems to be the opposite. The early stages of such movements frequently produce a set of minority-defined mandates that occasionally seem more restrictive than the majority-defined mandates they attempt to replace. The crux of the matter is that a minority group which hopes to achieve civil rights and social justice must develop a political base and achieve a degree of political unity to work effectively on its own behalf. This task is made all the more difficult by the fact that members of the gay minority can remain "invisible" if they so choose. Thus, political realities call for self-disclosure and the presentation of a united front to majority groups. Unfortunately, the politicalization of the gay minority during the 1970s which requires an acknowledgment of one's interdependence of fate with other gay people has had a secondary consequence that negatively impacts the possibilities for achieving the needed political unity.

This secondary consequence may be described as the factionalization of the interpersonal environment of lesbian women. In some instances, this factionalization has greatly altered the psychological distance a lesbian woman may have to travel in order to find an interpersonal milieu that "fits," that is, one in which she feels that similarities outweigh dissimilarities and in which she can feel socially at ease. Biographical factors that influence one's belief systems and behavioral patterns can impede change in lesbian women just as they do in other people. Yet the rapid change that has been expected of lesbian women in recent times has disregarded this psychological precept, has merely added to her identity struggles, and at times has further obstructed her opportunities to fulfill her social needs.

It may be recalled that a major variable in the impact of a stressor on an individual is the meaning of the event, and the meaning is determined by the event's degree of threat to need fulfillment and the amount of change required. Thus, how much change a group's norms and sanctions require and to what degree these changes would interfere with the fulfillment of other needs would be major variables in the level of stress produced in developing a positive group identity. If, for example, a group norm of antimonogamy is encountered by a lesbian couple in a long-term relationship, group affiliation is weighed against the amount of change required to conform to this norm and the degree of threat the change poses to need fulfillment. This conflict can be described as a choice between affiliative need fulfillment and making an overwhelming amount of change in one's beliefs or behavior.

For lesbian women, the sole common denominator around which group affiliation is based is their sociosexual identity. If in seeking group affiliation she is confronted with group membership contingencies of subscribing to unfamiliar ideologies and/or dogmatic behavioral norms, rather than finding a nonconflicted interpersonal environment that should serve as a refuge from majority judgments, the lesbian woman is faced with still further conflicts. In the long run, minority members who begin to define new mandates for one another are ensuring that large portions of that minority group will feel even more alienated from them than they did from the majority.

The cognitive restructuring that can reduce this stress entails the recognition that there are many options for affiliation other than ideologically laden groups. While no attempt is made here to minimize the importance of all groups who seek institutional remedies for injustice and inequality, the psychological perspective must examine potential affiliative resources in lesbian communities in relation to their contribution to the overall mental and emotional well-being of lesbian women. Groups based on ideological positions may meet the affiliative needs of some members of the lesbian minority, but assuredly not all. The potential benefits of any group must be weighed against the costs, and these equations can be expected to vary according to the individual and her situation.

In sum, a by-product of the politicalization of gay issues in the 1970s has been increased factionalization in lesbian communities, at a time in which greater unity is critically needed in order to deal more effectively with majority oppression. Thus, I advocate a policy of collective diversity which respects individual differences yet enables the lesbian minority to coalesce around common concerns. With the enormous range of diversity that exists among lesbian women in relation to beliefs and value systems, socio-economic status, age, race, and other variables, it would appear that the psychological well-being of this minority would be best served by a focus on the common need for civil rights in the political arena and on the common need for group affiliation in the social arena, and by encouraging the growth and greater accessibility of settings in which these interests can be pursued separately. These settings do not necessarily have to be limited to gay establishments; yet the availability of other options may vary according to a number of variables, including one's level of social disclosure. Some of the potential stresses associated with disclosure and nondisclosure are the subject of the next chapter.

References

Abbott, S., and Love, B. *Sappho Was a Right-on-Woman: A Liberated View of Lesbianism.* New York: Stein and Day, 1972.
Adorno, T.W.; Frenkel-Brunswik, E.; Levinson, D.J.; and Sanford, R.N. *The Authoritarian Personality.* New York: Harper, 1950.
Allport, G.W. *The Nature of Prejudice.* Reading, Mass.: Addison-Wesley, 1954.
Antonovsky, A. "Conceptual and methodological problems in the study of resistance resources and stressful life events." In *Stressful Life Events: Their Nature and Effects,* edited by B.S. Dohrenwend and B.P. Dohrenwend. New York: Wiley, 1974.
Ashmore, R.D., and Del Boca, F.K. "Psychological approaches to understanding intergroup conflicts." In *Towards the Elimination of Racism,* edited by P.A. Katz. New York: Pergamon Press, 1976.
Bell, A.P., and Weinberg, M.S. *Homosexualities: A Study of Diversity among Men and Women.* New York: Simon & Schuster, 1978.
Bettelheim, B., and Janowitz, M. *Dynamics of Prejudice: A Psychological and Sociological Study of Veterans.* New York: Harper, 1950, chap. 4.
Chafetz, J.; Sampson, P.; Beck, P.; and West, J. "A study of homosexual women." *Social Work* 19 (1974):714-723.
Collins, R. *Conflict Sociology.* New York: Academic Press, 1975.
Coopersmith, S. *The Antecedents of Self-Esteem.* San Francisco: W.H. Freeman, 1967.
Ehrlich, H.J. *The Social Psychology of Prejudice.* New York: Wiley, 1973.

Hartley, R.E. "A developmental view of female sex-role definition and identification." *Merrill-Palmer Quarterly* 10 (1964):3-16.

Hedblom, J.H. "Social, sexual, and occupational lives of homosexual women." *Sexual Behavior* 2 (1972):33-37.

Hollingshead, A. *Two-Factor Index of Social Position*. New Haven Conn.: privately printed, 1957.

Kirscht, J.P., and Dillehay, R.C. *Dimensions of Authoritarianism: A Review of Research and Theory*. Lexington: University of Kentucky Press, 1967.

MacDonald, A.P., Jr., and Games, R.G. "Some characteristics of those who hold positive and negative attitudes toward homosexuals." *Journal of Homosexuality* 1 (1974):9-27.

MacDonald, A.P., Jr., and Games, R.G. "Some characteristics of those who hold positive and negative attitudes toward homosexuals." *Journal of Homosexuality* 1 (1974):9-27.

MacDonald, A.P., Jr.; Huggins, J.; Young, S.; and Swanson, R. "Attitudes toward homosexuality: Preservation of sex morality or the double standard?" *Journal of Consulting and Clinical Psychology* 40 (1973):161.

Martin, D., and Lyon, P. *Lesbian/Woman*. New York: Bantam Books, 1972.

Miller, J.G. "Mental health implications of a general behavior theory." *American Journal of Psychiatry* 113 (1957):776-782.

Miller, W.B. "Lower class culture as a generating milieu of gang delinquency." *Journal of Social Issues* 14 (1958):5-19.

Porter, J.D.R. *Black Child, White Child: The Development of Racial Attitudes*. Cambridge, Mass.: Harvard University Press, 1971.

Rabban, M. "Sex-role identification in young children in two diverse social groups." *Genetic Psychological Monograph* 42 (1950):81-158.

Simon, W., and Gagnon, J. "Femininity in the lesbian community." *Social Problems* 15 (1967):212-221.

Skinner, B.F. *Science and Human Behavior*. New York: MacMillan, 1953.

Smith, K.T. "Homophobia: A tentative personality profile." *Psychological Reports* 29 (1971):1091-1094.

10 Social Disclosure

Stratification by sociosexual orientation serves as an effective means for reducing competition for social and economic rewards. The overarching "heterosexual assumption" that pervades patriarchal cultures places the burden of correcting this assumption or conforming to this assumption on the victims of sociocultural negation and discrimination. The "forced choice" social situation for gay people, then, brought about by the structural expectation that all adults are heterosexual—in spite of the fact that an estimated 20 percent of adults are gay—is either one of communicating that one is not heterosexual or one of maintaining behaviors that allow others to continue their heterosexual assumption.

As "gay consciousness" has grown in the 1970s, more and more gay people are choosing disclosure in both their interpersonal and occupational environments. Although prodisclosure political efforts have resulted in a greater willingness to disclose among some gay people, these efforts also may result in greater stress for gay individuals as they confront disclosure decisions. This chapter discusses the disclosure question as a stressful life event which requires thoughtful consideration of possible outcomes and identifies factors that may influence individual decisions. Changes that may result from full disclosure are addressed, and finally stress in general and life goals are considered.

Stress of Disclosure versus Nondisclosure

Self-disclosure has been described as the process by which one person allows him- or herself to be known by another person, and *reciprocal disclosure* has been viewed as an essential component in the development of deep interpersonal relationships (Derlega and Chaikin 1975). Jourard (1971, p. 17) stated: "Self-disclosure produces consequences, influencing the behavior of others toward oneself for better or for worse. Possibly, then, persons disclose or fail to disclose themselves in accordance with the consequences that they expect to follow." Thus, while self-disclosure is, in general, considered necessary to the formation of authentic interpersonal relationships, the potential consequences of disclosure of a stigmatized sociosexual identity frequently act as an effective deterrent to self-disclosure. One stress-producing aspect of disclosure decisions, then, may be viewed as an approach-avoidance dilemma; that is, in seeking authentic relationships (prosocial), a gay person often must risk social rejection and being defined as deviant (antisocial).

Disclosure of one's sociosexual identity to others would occur infrequently as an all-or-nothing phenomenon, but instead it appears to be more often a specific person-situation phenomenon. Nontheless, in most instances, disclosure represents a stressful life event for a gay person, and as such, the model representing variables in the impact of a stressor (table 5-2) can be applied. Both the decision-making process that is utilized and the resources available for coping with the life situations that are affected by those decisions also will impact the outcome of disclosure/nondisclosure events (variables represented in table 7-4).

By using the stress paradigm, the question can be stated: How stress-producing is nondisclosure, and how stress-producing is disclosure? Responses to this question, of course, will vary from individual to individual and from situation to situation. Evaluation of stressor characteristics (that is, the duration, frequency, and intensity of potential disclosure situations) clearly requires person-situation specificity in relation to potential outcomes, both short-range and long-range. Consideration of stressor characteristics would include the following questions: How long will contact with this person/group/community last? If responses to disclosure are positive/negative in this situation, how will this affect subsequent encounters with this person/group/community? In sum, how long will disclosing/nondisclosing responses affect the individual, how often, and to what degree?

The meaning of the event to the gay individual is interrelated with characteristics of the stressor: Does disclosure/nondisclosure threaten the individual's need fulfillment (for example, self-esteem, affiliative or economic needs)? How much change does disclosure/nondisclosure require (for example, in self-presentation, relational requirements, employment circumstances)? The potential impact of disclosure on one's ability to meet one's affiliative and economic needs, and thus to maintain or to gain external resources, is generally the primary concern in difficult disclosure decisions.

First, the meaning of disclosure in interpersonal relations would vary in direct proportion to the degree of need fulfillment provided by the other person or persons. A series of concentric circles can be utilized to chart the significance of various interpersonal contacts for a specific person, with self represented in the center circle. The most significant other or others would be in the second circle, and the following circles can represent progressively more distant associations. The degree of risk in disclosure, then, can be assessed in relation to the potential threat to need fulfillment that the associations represent, with the assumption being that those who occupy the innermost circles are more important to need fulfillment than those in the outermost circles. This process can help to evaluate which relationships entail greater potential stress by disclosure or greater potential stress by nondisclosure. Figure 10-1 provides an example.

It can be seen in this example that although disclosure or nondisclosure with work associates might be of primary economic importance, the socioemotional risk in that setting is considerably less than that in relation to family and close friends. On the other hand, economic need fulfillment,

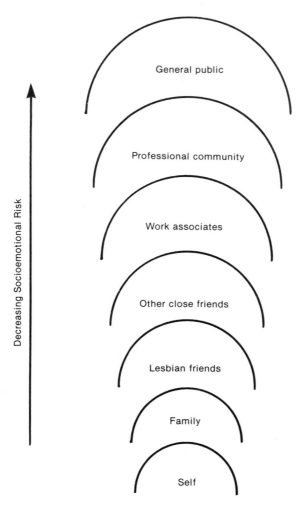

Figure 10-1. Interpersonal Distance and the Meaning of Disclosure: An Example

if threatened by disclosure, could result in long-term stress that supersedes interpersonal stress in its cumulative impact on economic well-being. Obviously, the effect of disclosure is person-situation-specific and will vary according to its potential impact on interpersonal and economic need fulfillment, both representing major external resources.

The second component shaping the meaning of the event (disclosure/nondisclosure) is the amount of change required, and it should be recalled that both positive and negative events require change. Stress relating to disclosure decisions, however, often may be more related to anticipated consequences than to actual consequences. I found that nearly two out of three respondents felt that their jobs might be jeopardized if their sociosexual orientation were known. Clearly disclosure in one's work environment is perceived by lesbian women as a high-risk event, and the perceived risk very likely is based on the amount of change that loss of one's job would require (for example, looking for another job, moving to another location, trying to maintain one's standard of living, and so forth).

The amount of change that may be required in the interpersonal dimension as a result of disclosure to one's family and social groups would depend, in part, on the response of these significant others to the disclosure and, in part, on the amount of change required in the discloser's behavior. If there has been a high degree of inauthenticity in the discloser's behavior before disclosure, self-presentation after disclosure may require considerable change in the discloser's behavior and may create considerable cognitive dissonance for those relating to the discloser. In anticipating potential disclosure consequences, then, the amount of change required by shifting to authentic self-presentation may be an important component of disclosure stress.

Essentially, then, lesbian women must evaluate whether the level of fear or anxiety that may be perpetuated by nondisclosure is more or less costly than the potential negative consequences which may or may not result from disclosure. In any specific situation, a gay person must evaluate which response—a disclosing or nondisclosing one—will best reduce his or her state of stress. Further, she or he must evaluate potential responses from others and assess how these may impact further interactions. By using the stress paradigm, variables in disclosure decisions are presented in figure 10-2.

The optimal decision-making process would include (1) sufficient time to rationally assess the degree of risk in disclosure or nondisclosure and (2) an appraisal of one's internal and external resources that would mediate stress irrespective of the outcome of disclosure or nondisclosure. In the behavioral paradigm, decisions would be based on answers to questions such as "Which response will be the most rewarding for me?" or "Will

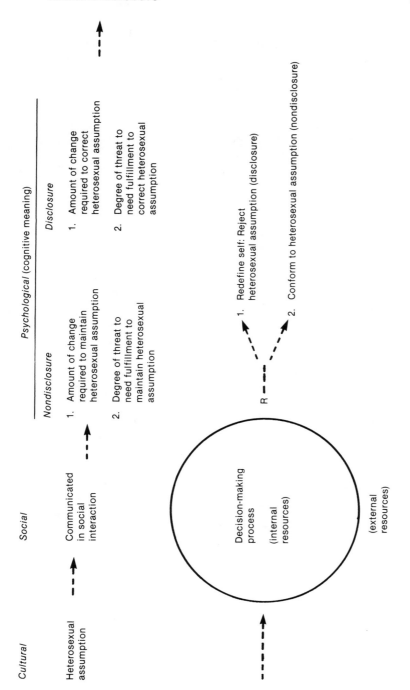

Figure 10-2. Disclosure/Nondisclosure Stress Model for Gay Individual

disclosure in this situation bring me more pleasure than pain, or more pain than pleasure?'' Society in general rewards gay people for remaining invisible and punishes them for being visible. Thus, a gay person who decides to be visible must trade some extrinsic rewards for the intrinsic reward of feeling authentic and self-congruent.

The gay individual's response to the "heterosexual assumption" (end of figure 10-2 sequence) feeds back to the heterosexual person as new input. By nondisclosure, the heterosexual assumption is continued, and the gay person must make adjustments that maintain that assumption. By disclosure, however, the heterosexual person must make adjustments to accommodate the altered perception; adjustment or change is thus shifted from the gay person to the heterosexual person. Figure 10-3 indicates how these interactional sequences might occur.

The interactional sequence of disclosure, then, indicates that stress (change) remains with the heterosexual individual who cannot or will not adjust to the gay person's redefinition of self, but not with the gay individual. On the other hand, when the redefinition is accepted by the heterosexual person, stress is eliminated from their interaction, and the opportunity for authentic communication continues.

As discussed in chapter 6, stress was highest among respondents who thought almost all heterosexual others could discern their gay orientation, less high for those who thought practically no heterosexual others could discern their orientation, and least high for those who thought only other gay people would know that they were gay. These findings underscore the role of fear and anxiety in producing states of stress. In contrast, decreased stress was found to relate to high disclosure ($p < .0001$), disclosure representing a self-determined option that means affirming one's gay identity to others. The evidence from my research, then, supports the view that choosing to disclose one's lesbian identity is interrelated with the attainment of high self-esteem.

Initially, disclosure decisions appear to represent a choice between continuation of external reinforcement (for remaining invisible), accompanied by internal chaos resulting from the necessity to maintain behaviors that are consistent with the heterosexual assumption of others, and losing external reinforcement (by becoming visible) while gaining internal positive self-regard and the ability to act according to one's inner dictates. To what extent the loss of external reinforcement becomes a social reality may vary considerably according to specific person-situation variables, and some of these variables are discussed in the next section. The ability to cope effectively with the stressor of social disclosure, however, appears to depend most importantly on an individual's internal resources.

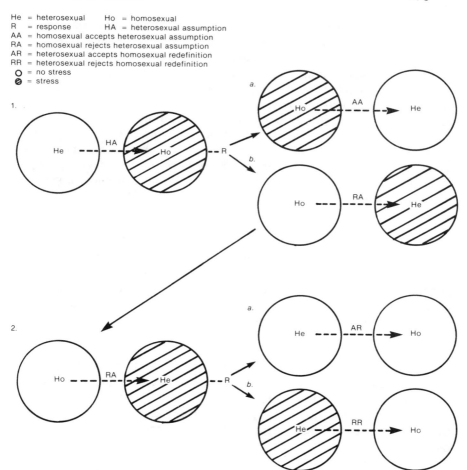

He = heterosexual   Ho = homosexual
R   = response   HA = heterosexual assumption
AA = homosexual accepts heterosexual assumption
RA = homosexual rejects heterosexual assumption
AR = heterosexual accepts homosexual redefinition
RR = heterosexual rejects homosexual redefinition
O   = no stress
◐   = stress

Figure 10-3. Disclosure/Nondisclosure Stress: Interactional Model

Variables in Disclosure Decisions

The best predictors of a gay person's ability to cope effectively with the potential consequences of disclosure appear to be the same as those which predict successful coping with any stressor—level of self-esteem and availability of an intrinsic reward system (internal resources). As Coopersmith (1967) stated, the prevailing level of self-esteem appears to be a key determinant in how well one defends oneself against devaluation.

Thus, a gay person with low self-esteem would be expected to experience a sense of helplessness when confronted with devaluation or adverse events; one with positive self-attitudes would be expected to have the ability to resist or reject devaluating stimuli and to deal with adversity.

An interrelated but conceptually separate variable is the person's degree of dependence on extrinsic rewards. It is reasonable to postulate that the achievement of high self-esteem by a minority-status individual is indicative of a well-developed intrinsic reward system, based on the assumption that negative feedback from sociocultural sources is experienced more frequently by a minority person than by a majority person and that the process of maintaining self-esteem for a minority person may promote a greater reliance on self-evaluation, as opposed to reliance on "others'" evaluations.

The nexus of coping effectively with gay identity, then, is the self-referential meaning of that identity to an individual. Chapters 8 and 9 focused on common areas that often obstruct the achievement of a positive gay identity, and cognitive restructuring in these areas may be necessary preparation for coping with potential outcomes of disclosure. The high level of self-esteem and the availability of an intrinsic reward system necessary to effective coping with disclosure must be based on affirmation and integration of one's sociosexual identity, for these provide the key psychological buffer against external devaluation.

In relation to external resources, evidence from my research indicates that positive identification with other lesbian women also provides a major buffer against external devaluation. One's self-concept as a lesbian woman is integrally linked to one's perception of other lesbian women, and when these perceptions are largely positive, disclosure decisions are facilitated in outer arenas. The availability of a lesbian social group also serves as a major social buffer against isolation that otherwise might result from disclosure is, of course, one's base of economic support, that is, one's oc- that occupies the innermost circles of one's interpersonal milieu (example in figure 10-1) would facilitate disclosure in the outermost circles. That is, support from "significant others" such as family members and close friends provides an emotional buffer against devaluation from more distant groups. An overall high level of self-esteem, the primacy of an intrinsic reward system, and the acceptance and support of individuals who occupy the innermost circles of interpersonal affiliation may be seen as the optimal psychosocial conditions that limit risk factors in broader disclosure of one's sociosexual identity.

The other external resource that may be the most critically impacted by disclosure is, of course, one's base of economic support, that is, one's occupational resources. Again, a gay person must ask, "In this environment, which produces the most stress for me—maintaining nondisclosure behaviors or the potential consequences of disclosure?" Further questions that may require consideration include: Does nondisclosure require constant preoccupation or anxiety? Is upward mobility affected by an employer's belief that marriage and children are the destiny of all female employees? What is the worst possible consequence of disclosure? If it is termination of employment, what are other occupational options? How could one manage economically in the interim? If termination were not the consequence, what other negative consequences could be anticipated as a result of disclosure? Would disclosure affect attitude shifts in subordinates or superordinates? How long would the effects of disclosure in this environment affect me? Could the amount of change that may be necessary as a result of disclosure be handled?

The regional variable is obviously of major importance in occupational disclosure, as indicated by my research. Of respondents from northern California 51 percent could answer affirmatively that their employment would not be jeopardized by disclosure, as compared to only 30 to 33 percent from the other subsamples (described in Appendix A). Since the potential ramifications of disclosure may vary from region to region, the long-range effects of occupational disclosure in relation to the possibility of relocation must be considered also. The number of cities or states with antidiscrimination laws protecting the rights of gay people is still relatively small, but occupational disclosure decisions would benefit from an awareness of which regions or cities would be more or less hospitable than the gay person's current location.

In theory, some occupations would appear to provide a more hospitable environment for gay people than others. For example, it seems reasonable to assume that professions requiring advanced degrees would be more hospitable than occupations requiring less education, based on the evidence (for example, Bettelheim and Janowitz 1964) that prejudice decreases as education level increases. However, unaccounted for in this assumption is the increasing amount of influence an individual acquires in moving up the socioeconomic ladder. Liberal attitudes toward diversity or "difference" are much more easily held toward persons who are perceived to occupy lower status and who are not directly competing for social and economic rewards. "Tokenism" is made tolerable by the belief that the token's sphere of influence will remain less than that of majority individuals and that the token will conform to status-quo ideologies in order to maintain his or her position. If, on the other hand, the token minority individual begins to exceed majority persons in the same occupational setting in relation to achievements (competing for social and economic rewards) and in scope of influence, then institutional and interpersonal sanctions more than likely will be imposed in an attempt to reinstate the token person's culturally ascribed inferior status. Disclosure decisions, then, must weigh the price of occupational disclosure in relation to aspirations and economic goals. Conversely, one must weigh the price of "living a life that can be collapsed at any moment" (Goffman 1963, p. 87).

Factors in individual disclosure decisions, then, would include an appraisal of one's internal resources (level of self-esteem, availability of an intrinsic reward system) and one's external resources (affiliative and economic). Finally, the political meaning of one's decision to disclose or to remain undisclosed must be evaluated.

Disclosure: The Personal becomes Political

These latter considerations of potential economic costs and loss of equal career opportunities may well be the most dehumanizing form of oppression experienced by the gay minority. The structural constraints imposed on the gay minority make a mockery of the notion of upward mobility based on merit—that is, the notion that every citizen in a democratic society is rewarded according to effort and ability (merit) and the corollary notion that these rewards are not contingent on race, sex, or other minority statuses such as sociosexual orientation.

As stated earlier, stratification by sociosexual orientation serves as an effective means for reducing competition for social and economic rewards. The game plan, however, requires compliance by the gay minority: if you remain invisible, you will be rewarded; if you do not remain invisible, you will be punished. So far, the stress of nondisclosure or disclosure has been addressed largely in the individual and social domains. In the progression of minority response patterns discussed in chapter 7, these foci correspond, respectively, to the first phase of self-redefinition and the second phase of establishing and maintaining a positive minority-group identification. The ability of the gay minority to change the game plan of the heterosexual majority will depend in large part on the movement of a majority of gay people into phases 3 and 4, the ability to join in collective efforts with others of one's minority group, and finally the desire to achieve cultural pluralism that requires equality—including equality of lifestyle—for all minorities.

The irrevocable reality for all members of a minority group and minority groups in general is their interdependence of fate. Thus, for any gay person, a cost/benefit analysis of disclosure or nondisclosure that examines only her or his own individual and social situation is incomplete. The cultural stress that impinges on the lives of all gay people, now and in the future, also must be entered into the equation. Each individual may formulate a system of buffer zones that protects against the daily litany of stressful events and may behave as the perennial head-in-sand ostrich in relation to what happens to other gay people. It seems inevitable, however, that the unchallenged cultural barriers will ultimately impinge on the lives of all gay people.

The illusion that often maintains nondisclosing behavior, in addition to the inability to risk the loss of external reinforcement from the patriarchal reward system, is that the absence of cultural and institutional buffers will not affect one's own life. The evidence is clear that nondisclosure or fear of visibility is affecting lives of gay peple today. In some instances, the consequences are displayed in dysfunctional behaviors such as alcoholism, drug abuse, psychological impairment, and suicidal predispositions. In others, this stress takes its toll in hypertension, ulcers, obesity, or other indexes of biophysical malfunction. For others, the stress of nondisclosure is constant in their work or social environments and may take its toll in a low frustration tolerance for other stresses or in mild depressive states. Still others find themselves in a downwardly mobile spiral, irrespective of talent and ability, having forgone earlier aspirations and goals because of their sense of futility in relation to structural constraints. Few (if any) nondisclosed gay people will escape some negative consequences from the incongruence of self felt in relation to the external world.

The tradeoff, then, is actually one of external reinforcement predicated on self-negation, for reinforcement—both internal and external—based on self-congruence and social authenticity. By becoming visible as a gay person, those relationships that do remain and new ones which are formed are built on authentic self-representation. Disclosure in one's work environment eliminates the waiting-for-the-other-shoe-to-fall tension and eliminates the doubts about how disclosure will affect one's status—for better or worse. In strategic terms, it means taking one's losses in front, so that subsequent moves are more or less predictable.

The discussion of individual responses and minority-group patterns in chapter 7 is highly applicable to the issue of disclosure. As stated previously, minority-group patterns are essentially a composite of individual responses to the minority condition, and to speak of a pattern, a notable proportion of a given minority group must exhibit a relatively common response. Most negative consequences of disclosure are related to the fact that the majority of the gay population is undisclosed. The fewer the number of disclosed gay persons in any given milieu, the more xenophobic reactions will occur toward those who are disclosed. As a result, the disclosed person's sociosexual identity typically becomes her "master status" to which all other identities and statuses are subsumed. If the prevalent minority-group pattern of gay people were open disclosure, incrementalism and tokenism as approaches to social reform on behalf of the gay population would be rendered ineffective.

Aronson (1972) discusses the "psychology of inevitability" in the context of the impact of legislation on interracial relations. He argues that "stateways can change folkways" because, in general, people tend to make the best of something that they know is bound to occur. Citing a number of studies that support this premise, Aronson (1972, p. 201) states that "The best way to produce eventual interracial harmony would be to launch into behavioral change. Moreover, and most important, the sooner the individuals are made to realize that integration is inevitable, the sooner their prejudiced attitudes will begin to change." Aronson believes that diverse groups can be brought together under conditions of equal status. In sum, institutional behavioral change (nondiscriminatory laws protecting the equal rights of gay people) can affect individual changes in attitudes, because of the psychology of inevitability.

Political realities make clear that no reforms are initiated on behalf of an invisible constituency. The interdependence of fate of the gay minority, then, means that what each gay person decides to do in relation to social disclosure affects every other gay person. Nonetheless, the model of minority stress and coping utilized in this book emphasizes that mastery of minority stress proceeds through a number of stages, and disclosure is viewed as a process that emerges behaviorally following mastery of the first two stages. Thus, resolution of the disclosure decision does not infer the surcease of minority stress; it *does* infer transformation of personal conflict into collective social action. Self-redefinition and self-acceptance imply a mastery of stress at the psychological level, positive minority-group identification indicates effective coping at the social level, joining collective efforts toward equality merges the social and cultural, and seeking equality for all minorities (that is, having pluralistic goals) demonstrates stress-management ability at the cultural level.

Premises regarding the minority-stress model presented in chapter 7 bear repeating in this context. Change invariably requires a temporary increase in stress in order to attain an overall reduction of stress. Integration at one level allows for movement to the next. Movement from one level to the next signifies a reduction in stress associated with the previous level and an increase in stress associated with the present level. Movement through the progression provides a net increase of stress-mediating resources, both internal and external.

The ideal collective minority response of widespread disclosure would deliver feedback at the cultural level—from the minority culture to the majority culture (see figure 7-7), which by the sheer force of numbers would defeat the present game plan—one which makes social and economic rewards contingent on compliance to the heterosexual assumption. At this juncture, the polarization of the issue would be at its most intense, but also resolution of the issue would be nearest at hand. Presently it appears that this will not occur until patriarchal institutions are tottering on the brink of dissolution.

The attainment of social justice and civil rights cannot be forever withheld from an estimated 20 percent of the adult population, who control an estimated one-fifth of national income, who are disproportionately represented in the professions and affluent strata (however silently), and, most importantly, whose collective psychological well-being will no longer permit submission to heterosexual oppression.

Just as personal conflicts in regard to disclosure must eventually give way to their political meaning, the denial of civil rights to minority groups eventually must be recognized as the fatal weak link in democratic societies. As Sussman (1965, p. vii) observed:

> The social problem of minority group relations is our society's most press-ing problem today. Its lack of resolution germinates the seeds of destruc-tion of a free democratic society and prepares the ideological foundation for seizure of power within and for supportive action by the Communist world without.

> . . . The simple question is—How does this nation which has attained the highest standard of living for the largest number of people in the history of mankind, handle the problems of its minority groups and abolish the bar-riers against individual's achieving the *largesse* of that society because of membership in a particular cultural or racial group? The world watches, waits, and will decide. On this decision rides the ultimate resolution of the question of whether our society can maintain over time its system of action in consonance with its value system.

The role of gay citizens in their struggle for equality under the law and for cultural equality of lifestyle is, then, in the final analysis, an effort to make our society's system of action consonant with its democratic value system. For those willing to fight tyranny in all its forms, no words seem more appropriate than those of John F. Kennedy, delivered in his Inaugural Address of 1961:

> . . . The torch has been passed to a new generation of Americans. . . . In your hands, my fellow citizens, more than in mine, will rest the final suc-cess or failure of our course.

> . . . The trumpet summons us again—not as a call to bear arms, though arms we need; not as a call to battle, though embattled we are; but a call to bear the burden of a long twilight struggle, year in, and year out, "rejoicing in hope, patient in tribulation."

References

Aronson, E. *The Social Animal.* San Francisco: W.H. Freeman, 1972.

Bettelheim, B., and Janowitz, M. *Social Change and Prejudice.* New York: Free Press, 1964.

Coopersmith, S. *The Antecedents of Self-Esteem.* San Francisco: W.H. Freeman, 1967.

Derlega, V.J., and Chaikin, A.L. *Sharing Intimacy: What We Reveal to Others and Why.* Englewood Cliffs, N.J.: Prentice-Hall, 1975.

Goffman, E. *Stigma: Notes on the Management of Spoiled Identity.* Englewood Cliffs, N.J.: Prentice-Hall, 1963.

Jourard, S.M. *Self-Disclosure: An Experimental Analysis of the Transparent Self.* New York: Wiley-Interscience, 1971.

Sussman, M.B. Editor's introduction. In J.M. Yinger, *A Minority Group in American Society.* New York: McGraw-Hill, 1965.

Appendix A:
Methodology

This appendix presents a brief overview of the data-collection instrument, a description of major variables and indexes constructed with these variables, and an account of sample sources and methods of data analysis.

Questionnaire Design

A seven-page questionnaire was used to collect data (see Appendix C). Most items related to one of the following categories: demographic information, histories of stress-related dysfunction, degree of "visibility," disclosure, exposure to feminist ideology, interpersonal affiliations, sex-role perceptions and behaviors, and attitudes or values. Two items were derived from other research: Kinsey, Pomeroy, and Martin's (1948) heterosexual-homosexual rating scale (question 20) and a list of childhood activity preferences (question 33) derived from three sources (Gundlach and Riess 1968; Kaye et al. 1967; Poole 1972).

Variables and Indexes

The hypotheses of my research related to the dependent variables of stress-related dysfunction, deviance, and decreased stress. Independent variables relating to hypotheses included socioeconomic status, visibility, disclosure, feminist exposure, and positive minority-group identity. Other indexes not related to the hypotheses that are described here include the value index, childhood role-play scale, and adult role functions (androgyny).

Life-Stress Scores (Stress Index)

Three indicators of stress were combined to formulate a stress index: hospitalization for "mental illness" (question 36), drug addiction (question 41), and attempted suicides (question 44). Question 41 inquired about the degree of drug use in the past. Seven categories of drugs and four degrees of use were employed, ranging from "never used" to dependence (addiction). Question 36 investigated possible hospitalization for psychiatric disorders; and question 44, possible suicide attempts. Responses to these questions were converted from their initial coding to the following codes for index construction:

Question 41 (Past Drug Use):

	Never	Occasional	Frequent	Dependent
Initial	1	2	3	4
Converted	0	0	2	3

Question 36 (Hospitalization):

	No	Yes
Initial	0	4
Converted	0	3

Question 44 (Suicide):

	Never	Felt, no attempt	Attempt, no medical	Attempt, medical
Initial	1	2	3	4
Converted	0	2	3	3

Range: 0-9
Low stress: 0-2   Moderate stress: 3-5   High stress: 6-9

Thus, the *low-stress* profile represents no hospitalization, never or occasional drug use, and "never felt suicidal," but may also include either "felt suicidal, no attempt," *or* frequent drug use. The *moderate-stress* profile represents no hospitalization, *both* frequent drug use and "felt suicidal;" or any one of the following—hospitalization, drug addiction, or attempted suicide; or either frequent drug use *or* "felt suicidal" *and* one of the three—hospitalization, drug addiction, or attempted suicide. The *high-stress* profile represents two of the three (hospitalization, drug addiction, attempted suicide); or, one of these three plus *both* frequent drug use and "felt suicidal"; or two of these three plus either frequent drug use *or* "felt suicidal"; or, all these—hospitalization, drug addiction, and attempted suicide.

For purposes of this research, all drug-use responses that indicated "dependence" were coded as 3s, irrespective of the drug to which it applied. The salient factor here was the respondent's self-report of drug dependence, viewed as a dysfunctional response to stress. Whether certain drugs are physically addictive or psychologically habituating or whether dependence on one drug is of the same order as dependence on another drug is of medical importance, but the focus here was the admittance of drug dependence.

Decreased Stress

Question 42 asked about degree of present drug use. Initial coding of present drug use was the same as question 41 on past drug use, with a range of 1 to 4. A drug-change score was derived by subtracting present scores from past scores. The possible outcomes are shown in the following grid:

	4	−3	−2	−1	0
Past	3	−2	−1	0	+1
	2	−1	0	+1	+2
	1	0	+1	+2	+3
		1	2	3	4

Present

Inclusion in the decreased drug-use group was restricted to only those respondents who had no increased use on any drug. That is, a single respondent may have decreased in use of one or more drugs but increased in use of another drug. With increased use of any drug, however, that case was excluded from decreased-drug-use statistics. A separate variable was created for all cases showing any increase in drug use. In effect, statistics pertaining to decreased stress are based on drug-change scores of 0, +1, +2, or +3 on one or more drugs and exclude cases with any −1, −2, or −3 scores.

Illegitimate Opportunity Structures (Deviance Index)

Two items identified "deviant" activity of respondents: Question 6 ascertained source of income and included the option of "illegal means"; question 45 determined whether respondents had ever engaged in prostitution. The resultant index had three categories: none (0—neither activity), some (1—one or the other), and both (2—both activities).

Socioeconomic Status (SES)

Socioeconomic status was determined by the two-factor index of social position (Hollingshead 1957). Both the factor *occupation* and the factor *education* are rated on a scale of 1 to 7, with 1s representing the highest levels and 7s representing the lowest levels. Each rating is multiplied by a factor weight (occupation, 7; education, 4), and these two products are summed. For example, an attorney who has a graduate professional degree and a housewife with less than seven years of school would have the following scores:

	Factor	Scale Score	Factor Weight	Score × Weight
Attorney	Occupation	1	7	7
	Education	1	4	4
			Index score:	11
Housewife	Occupation	7	7	49
	Education	7	4	28
			Index score:	77

These examples represent the range of possible scores on a continuum from a low of 11 to a high of 77. These scores are then divided into a hierarchy of score groups as follows (see Hollingshead 1957):

Social class	Range of computed scores
I (highest)	11-17
II	18-27
III	28-43
IV	44-60
V (lowest)	61-77

Visibility

Respondents were asked to check one of three options relating to self-perceived "public visibility" as a lesbian woman (question 30). The three possible responses were (1) "only other gay people might think I'm gay" (in-group); (2) "don't think it would occur to anyone that I'm gay" (not visible); and (3) "anyone who looks at me could guess I'm gay" (highly visible). These responses were anticpated to be hierarchical in relation to stress, that is, response 1 indicating the lowest stress-producing situation and response 3 indicating the highest stress-producing situation.

Disclosure

Question 29 provided respondents with eight response options for the purpose of determining their level of disclosure about their lesbian orientation. A respondent could check as many options as appropriate, resulting in a range of disclosure scores that were categorized as "low," "moderate," and "high." The operational definition of these three categories was as follows: The range of a *low* disclosure rating is from those who checked "practically no one I know" through and including those who checked any or all family members and close friends. A *moderate* disclosure rating included anyone who checked "people I work with" either singularly or in combination with any or all family members and close friends. A *high* disclosure rating included anyone who checked "practically everyone I know" either singularly or in combination with any or all the other categories.

Feminist Exposure

This composite measure consisted of two items: question 52, which asked whether respondents had participated in gay or feminist consciousness-raising groups, and question 53, which asked whether respondents had read recent books or literature on lesbian women. The index, as used in data analysis, consisted of three categories: those with no feminist exposure (0); those with some exposure, either books or groups (1); and those with both exposures (2).

Reference Groups

Two reference-group variables were created from single items to analyze the influence of various factors on decreased drug use. The first, lesbian reference group, included those who indicated that most of their close friends were gay females (question 46) and that it would not matter to them to be seen in public with anyone who was obviously gay (question 31). The second reference-group measure, feminist reference group, provided more inclusive criteria. This measure included those who indicated that most of their close friends were female, either heterosexual or lesbian, and who also would not object to being seen in public with anyone who was obviously gay.

Value Index

An index was constructed to explore selected values of respondents. The value index is a composite measure of three items: question 12, which measured attitudes toward legally sanctioned, same-sex marriages (marriage); question 14, which measured attitudes toward child raising (children); and question 27, which measured attitudes toward sexual fidelity in a couple relationship (monogamy).

The options under each item allowed for a classification of value constellations as "traditional" or "nontraditional." The traditional classification represents two or three of the following choices: expects sexual fidelity in a couple relationship, probably would get legally married, and may want to raise a child. The nontraditional classification represents two or three of the following choices: prefers to be free to have affairs, would never want to be legally married, and has no desire to raise a child.

Childhood Role Play

Question 33 listed fourteen childhood activities or characteristics, half of which would be considered typically "feminine" and half of which would be considered typically "masculine." The list was composed of items used in other studies of lesbian women (Gundlach and Riess 1968; Kaye et al. 1967; Poole 1972).

Respondents could check as many options as were appropriate. With seven "masculine" choices and seven "feminine" choices, each final score was computed by subtracting the number of feminine choices from the number of masculine choices. The range was $+7$ to -7, with $+7$ indicating a preference for all seven "masculine" activities and no feminine activities and -7 indicating the reverse. Classifications were made as follows:

$+7, +6, +5, +4$	High masculine
$+3, +2, +1$	Moderate masculine
0	Equally masculine and feminine
$-1, -2, -3$	Moderate feminine
$-4, -5, -6, -7$	High feminine

For example, if a respondent checked five of seven "masculine" preferences and also three of seven "feminine" preferences, the score would be

$$\begin{array}{ll} 5 & \text{masculine} \\ \underline{3} & \text{feminine} \\ 2 & = \text{moderate masculine} \end{array}$$

If a respondent checked five "masculine" and five "feminine" items, the resultant score would be zero, or equally masculine and feminine.

Adult Role Functions: Androgyny Scores

Question 35 listed fourteen adult role functions, half of which would be considered traditionally "masculine" and half of which would be considered traditionally "feminine." Respondents indicated which parent was primarily responsible for each of the fourteen functions or if both were equally responsible. (Respondents whose family structure was not comprised of two parents were coded on this question as "missing data" and thus, were not included in subsequent data analysis of androgyny scores). Then they indicated who they would prefer to take responsibility for each function in a couple relationship of their own, themselves, their partner, or "both equally."

The fourteen adult role functions were coded as separate variables in both the parent and respondents' sections. Frequency distributions were computed for each of the twenty-eight variables, which indicated the percentage of respondents that checked each of the three possible options in each section (parent section: mother, father, both about equally; respondents; section: self, partner, "both equally"). The percentages of "both about equally" responses in the parent section were summed and divided by 14 to yield the parents' androgyny score; the percentages of "both equally" responses in the respondents' section were summed and divided by 14 to yield the respondents' androgyny score.

Sample

The initial distribution of 2,000 questionnaires and the second distribution of 200 questionnaires occurred between April 1975 and August 1975. The method of distribution falls into four categories. First, I left questionnaires at various establishments with the permission and cooperation of employees or management. These establishments included women's centers, women's coffeehouses, women's restaurants, gay service centers, and lesbian bars. Some questionnaires were distributed directly to some of my friends. Numerous requests for additional copies, once the questionnaire began to circulate, provided a third source. These were received by mail, and as many requests were honored as the supply allowed. Last, assistance was received from Amazon Art Works, whose owners contacted me and offered to distribute the questionnaire along with the book *Loving Women* as it was mailed or sold to customers. Their efforts made the questionnaire available to various conferences,including a conference of the National Organization for Women and an American Library Association conference, both held in San Francisco. The summary of distribution by region (table A-1) does *not* include the 400 questionnaires distributed by Amazon Art Works since it is not possible to determine their dispersion by region.

Of the total distribution, then, 35.7 percent were mailed by request, 34.8 percent were dispersed at women's establishments, 15.9 percent at lesbian bars, 6.8 percent at gay service centers, and 6.5 percent to friends.

Table A-1
Summary of Questionnaire Distribution

Area	City/County	Place	Number Left/ Mailed	Returns/ Percentage
San Francisco Bay area	San Francisco	Bars	275	Total northern California: 517
		Women's coffeehouse	100	
		Friends	10	
	Berkeley	Bar	75	Total returns: 243
		Friends	10	
	Marin County	Friends	22	Percentage: 47%
	Sonoma County	Friends	25	
Los Angeles area	Los Angeles	Women's building	100	Total Los Angeles area: 345
	Santa Monica	Women's center	175	
	Los Angeles	Friends	5	
	Riverside[a]	Women's center	15	Total return: 129
	Los Angeles[a]	Gay center	50	Percentage: 37%
Orange County	Orange County	Friends	45	Total Orange County: 155
	Orange County[a]	Individual	100	
	Orange County	Feminist store	100	Total return: 31
				Percentage: 20%
San Diego	San Diego	Gay Center	100	Total San Diego: 400
	San Diego	Women's Center	100	
	San Diego	Women's restaurant	175	Total return: 128
	San Diego	Friends	25	Percentage: 32%
				Total southern California: 900 Total return: 288 Percentage: 32%
Other states and Canada	Phoenix[a]		25	
	Minneapolis[a]		50	
	Portland[a]		70	Total out-of-California: 375
	Tempe, Ariz.[a]		20	Total return: 131
	Salt Lake City[a]		20	
	Atlanta[a]		50	
	New York City[a]		50	Percentage: 35%
	Adirondacks, N.Y.[a]		10	
	Toronto, Ontario[a]		25	
	Victoria, B.C.[a]		2	
	Dallas[a]		30	
	Houston[a]		25	
	San Antonio[a, b]		5	

[a]By request.
[b]More copies were photocopied; number unknown.

The five areas were further condensed into three subsamples to facilitate comparative data analysis: (1) northern California, represented by the San Francisco Bay area; (2) southern California, including the Los Angeles area, Orange County, and San Diego; and (3) other, which includes all returns not from California. Additionally, there were twelve returns from other towns in California and one which did not specify residence. The discrepancies in number of returns by region and the actual number included in the statistical subsamples is due to the inclusion of a fourth subsample, separated for purposes of data analysis, consisting of eighty-nine bisexual women (1 to 3 on the Kinsey scale), who, as can be seen in table A-2, were included in the regional breakdown of distribution. Thus, 80.6 percent of the total sample resided in California (36.1 percent Bay area; 44.5 percent southern California), and 19.4 percent resided out of California.

The overall rate of return was 31 percent. Evaluating the rate of return on questionnaire surveys as high or low is generally a subjective judgment. Survey questionnaires differ in length and complexity, target populations vary in accessibility, and respondents may or may not be remunerated.

Methods of distribution in researching lesbian populations have ranged from a person-to-person selection of respondents (Hedblom 1972; Oberstone 1974; Poole 1972; Thompson, McCandless, and Strickland 1971; Wilson and Greene 1971) to solicitation of participants from members of homophile organizations (Armon 1960; Bene 1965; Freedman 1967; Gundlach and Riess 1968; Hopkins 1969; Kenyon 1968; Siegelman 1972) or lesbian organizations and periodicals (Brown 1975). Of the remaining five studies listed in table 2-1, two samples consisted of psychiatric patients (Kaye et al. 1967; Swanson et al. 1972), one sample was from varied sources (Saghir and Robins 1969), one consisted of "rap group" participants (Raphael 1974), and the source of the sample was not stated in information available on Liddicoat (1957).

Table A-2
Regional Returns and Subsample Size

	Total Return	Subsample Number
Bay area	243	216
Southern California	288	245
Other	131	125
Other California	12	
Bisexual		89
Missing data	1	
	675	675

Of these eighteen studies, only one reported the number of question-naires mailed (to Daughters of Bilitis members) in relation to number returned (Siegelman 1972). In the Siegelman study, seventy-five question-naires were mailed, and forty-six were returned (61 percent). In contrast, a questionnaire survey of women's sexual behavior (Hite 1976, p. 23) reported that "one hundred thousand questionnaires were distributed, and slightly over three thousand [were] returned," which represents a 3 percent return. There is, then, considerable variation in return rates, and there is no uniform standard by which to evaluate differing rates.

Because of a printer's error, the first distribution of 2,000 included only 1,000 self-addressed return envelopes, so that many respondents, notably in the Los Angeles area and Orange County, were not provided return envelopes. Further, for the most part, questionnaires were delivered in bulk to the various outlets and left unattended for consideration of patrons. Although subjective, a return of 31 percent, given these factors, seems highly favorable compared to prior research.

Last, 36 percent of the distribution was in response to requests for copies. Requests, in fact, exceeded supply, and if the work had been conducted with financial support, an even larger sample might have been obtained. That the contents of the questionnaire were generally viewed as relevant and uncharacteristically nonoffensive by those who returned ques-tionnaires is also suggested by the write-in comments as well as the 100-plus letters received from respondents.

This sample, although drawn from more varied sources than any prior research on lesbian women, nonetheless represents to some extent a self-selected group. Thus it is not possible to estimate the parameters of the population from which the sample is drawn.

Data Analysis

The Statistical Package for the Social Sciences (SPSS), a system of com-puter programs, and the computer facilities at the University of California, Berkeley, were utilized for data analysis. Pearson product-moment correla-tion coefficients and partial correlations were computed for variables which by either transformation to indexes or their already existing structure could be considered interval-level data. Contingency tables and nonparametric tests of significance and measures of association (chi square and gamma) were computed for other variables, as well as for interval-level variables to obtain joint-frequency distributions. Since the hypotheses were directional, one-tailed tests of significance were computed, and the .05 level of significance was accepted as the basis for rejecting or accepting hypotheses. The statistical results reported in percentages, unless otherwise indicated, represent adjusted frequencies.

References

Armon, V. "Some personality variables in overt female homosexuality." *Journal of Projective Techniques* 24 (1960):292-309.

Bene, E. "On the genesis of female homosexuality." *British Journal of Psychiatry* 111 (1965):815-821.

Brown, L. "Investigating the sterotypic picture of lesbians in the clinical literature." Paper presented at the 83 Annual Convention of the American Psychological Association in Chicago, 1975.

Freedman, J.J. "Homosexuality among women and psychological adjustment." Doctoral dissertaton, Case Western Reserve University, 1967. *Dissertation Abstracts* 28/10-B (1967):4294 (University Microfilms No. 68-03308).

Gundlach, R.H., and Riess, B.F. "Self and sexual identity in the female: A study of female homosexuals." In *New Directions in Mental Health,* vol. 1, edited by B.F. Riess. New York: Grune & Stratton, 1968.

Hedblom, J.H. "Social, sexual, and occupational lives of homosexual women." *Sexual Behavior* 2 (1972):33-37.

Hite, S. *The Hite Report: A Nationwide Study of Female Sexuality.* New York: Dell, 1976.

Hollingshead, A. *Two-Factor Index of Social Position.* New Haven, Conn.: privately printed, 1957.

Hopkins, J.H. "The lesbian personality." *British Journal of Psychiatry* 115 (1969):1433-1436.

Kaye, H.; Berl, S.; Clare, J.; Eleston, M.; Gershwin, B.; Gershwin, P.; Kogan, L.; Torda, C.; and Wilbur, C. "Homosexuality in women." *Archives of General Psychiatry* 17 (1967):626-634.

Kenyon, F.E. "Studies in female homosexuality, 4 and 5." *British Journal of Psychiatry* 114 (1968): 1337-1350.

Kinsey, A.C.; Pomeroy, W.B.; and Martin, C.E. *Sexual Behavior in the Human Male.* Philadelphia: Saunders, 1948.

Kohout, F.J. *Statistics for Social Scientists: A Coordinated Learning System.* New York: Wiley, 1974.

Liddicoat,, R. Letter to the editor. *British Medical Journal* 2 (1957):1110-1111. (Summary of author's doctoral dissertation at the University of Witwatersrand," *Homosexuality: Results of a Survey as Related to Various Theories.".*)

Oberstone, A.K. "Dimensions of psychological adjustment and style of life in single lesbians and single heterosexual women." Doctoral dissertation, California School of Professional Psychology, 1974. *Dissertation Abstracts* 35/10-B (1974):5088 (University Microfilms, No. 75-8510).

Poole, K. "The etiology of gender identity and the lesbian." *The Journal of Social Psychology* 87 (1972):51-57.

Raphael, S.M. " 'Coming out': The emergence of the movement Lesbian." Doctoral dissertation, Case Western Reserve, 1974. *Dissertation Abstracts* 35/08-A (1974):5536 (University Microfilms No. 75-5084).

Saghir, M., and Robins, E. "Homosexuality. I. Sexual behavior of the female homosexual." *Archives of General Psychiatry* 20 (1969): 192-201.

Siegelman, M. "Adjustment of homosexual and heterosexual women." *British Journal of Psychiatry* 120 (1972):477-481.

SPS: Statistical Package for the Social Sciences, 2d ed. New York: McGraw-Hill, 1975.

Swanson, D.; Loomis, S.; Lukesh, R.; Cronin, R.; and Smith, J. "Clinical features of the female homosexual patient: A comparison with the heterosexual patient." *Journal of Nervous and Mental Disease* 155 (1972):119-124.

Thompson, N.L.; McCandles, B.R.; and Strickland, B.R. "Personal adjustment of male and female homosexuals and heterosexuals." *Journal of Abnormal Psychology* 78 (1971):237-240.

Wilson, M.L., and Greene, R.L. "Personality characteristics of female homosexuals." *Psychological Reports* 28 (1971):407-412.

Appendix B: Demographic Description of Sample

The modal pattern of the total sample could be described as follows: 30 years of age or under, white, never married, no children, highly educated, middle-class, self-supported, not members of homophile organizations, and not indigenous to California. A summary of demographic data providing absolute numbers and actual percentages is presented in table B-1.

The following adds a brief discussion of some of these items.

Age. The median age of the sample was 27.9, and over two-thirds of respondents were 30 years of age or under (68.4 percent).

Race. Respondents were predominantly white (88.9 percent), with 9.7 percent representation of racial or ethnic minorities.

Marital Status. This question addressed the legal marital status of respondents and provided six response options (see Appendix C, question 11). More than seven out of ten respondents were never married (71.9 percent); 3.7 percent reported that they are married in name only; 9.2 percent were married but divorced or separated before an interest in a female relationship; 8.4 percent were married but divorced or separated for a female relationship; 3.1 percent reported that they were presently married and live with their husbands; and 3.4 percent checked "other." In absolute numbers, then, only 21 respondents out of 675 report a current, cohabitive marriage (3.1 percent), although 24.4 percent have at one time or another tried marriage. This percentage is surprisingly consistent with the findings of the Gundlach and Riess study (1968) in which it was reported that 29 percent had tried marriage.

Children. Approximately one-sixth of the sample have had children (16.5 percent), a finding which is also similar to the Gundlach and Riess figure of one-fifth, or 20 percent. In my research only 2.8 percent had more than two children.

Among those respondents who have had children (111), 31.5 percent do not live with their children, 48.6 percent do live with their children, 8 percent live with their children part-time, and 9 percent have children who are older and on their own. In absolute numbers, 35 of the 111 lesbian mothers in the sample are completely separated from their children, or approximately one-third.

Table B-1
Summary of Demographic Data

Variable	Category Label	Frequency	Percentage
Age	Under 21	56	8.3
(question 1)	21-25	203	30.1
	26-30	203	30.1
	31-35	110	16.3
	36-40	45	6.7
	41-50	45	6.7
	51 and over	13	1.9
Race	White	600	88.9
(question 2)	Black	13	1.9
	Spanish-speaking	35	5.2
	Asian	3	0.4
	Other	15	2.2
Legal marital	Never married	485	71.9
status	Married in name only	25	3.7
(question 11)	Divorced/separated		
	before female interest	62	9.2
	Divorced/separated		
	for female interest	57	8.4
	Married, with husband	21	3.1
	Other	23	3.4
Number of	0	561	83.1
children	1	55	8.1
(question 13)	2	38	5.6
	3	9	1.3
	4	5	0.7
	5	3	0.4
Habitation of	Not applicable	561	83.1
children	Do not live w/mother	35	5.2
(question 14)	Do live w/mother	54	8.0
	Part-time w/mother	9	1.3
	Older, away from home	10	1.5
Single or	Single	314	46.5
coupled status	Coupled	343	50.8
(question 26)			
Living	By myself	196	29.0
arrangement	with parents or relatives	41	6.1
(question 15)	Lesbian couple	245	36.3
	Female friend	134	19.9
	Husband	23	3.4
	Gay male	10	1.5
	Straight male	14	2.1
Kinsey scale	0	10	1.5
(question 20)	1	9	1.3
	2	17	2.5
	3	43	6.4

Table B-1 *(continued)*

Variable	Category Label	Frequency	Percentage
	4	243	36.0
	5	217	32.1
	6	128	19.0
	X	4	0.6
Organizational membership (question 19)	DOB member	9	1.3
	Not a member	620	93.2
	No response	37	5.5
Original residence (question 17)	Native Californian	240	35.6
	Not native	432	64.0
Religion (question 9)	Protestant	61	9.0
	Catholic	49	7.3
	Jewish	31	4.6
	None	175	25.9
	Other	41	6.1
	Spiritual beliefs	313	46.4
Might attend church if (question 10)	Gay people accepted	160	23.7
	For gay people only	32	4.7
	For women only	132	19.6
	None of above	351	52.0

(Hollingshead scale)

Variable	Category Label	Frequency	Percentage
Fathers' occupations (question 4)	1	138	20.4
	2	114	16.9
	3	121	17.9
	4	34	5.0
	5	108	16.0
	6	40	5.9
	7	28	4.1
Economic status: Family of origin (question 5)	Poor	74	11.0
	Lower-middle-income	300	44.4
	Upper-middle-income	269	39.9
	Wealthy	23	3.4
Education (question 3)	Didn't finish H.S.	18	2.7
	High-school grad.	70	10.4
	1-2 years college	161	23.9
	3-4 years college	127	18.8
	College graduate	106	15.7
	Postgraduate work	89	13.2
	Professional degree	102	15.1

(Hollingshead scale)

Variable	Category Label	Frequency	Percentage
Respondents' occupations (question 4)	1	41	6.1
	2	110	16.3
	3	113	16.7
	4	92	13.6
	5	32	4.7

Table B-1 *(continued)*

Variable	Category Label	Frequency	Percentage
	6	40	5.9
	7	73	10.8
	(Hollingshead scale)		
Socioeconomic	I	36	5.3
status	II	131	19.4
(question 3)	III	313	46.4
	IV	91	13.5
	V	55	8.1
Income	Under $3,000	246	36.4
(question 7)	$ 3,000- 4,999	105	15.6
	$ 5,000- 7,999	103	15.3
	$ 8,000-11,999	110	16.3
	$12,000-15,999	48	7.1
	Over $16,000	44	6.5
Source of	Salary	363	53.8
income	Own business, craft	63	9.3
(question 6)	Inheritance, trust	13	1.9
	Parents	48	7.1
	Students' funds	46	6.8
	Social security, welfare,		
	unemployment	83	12.3
	Mate supports	29	4.3
	Illegal means	30	4.4

Single or Coupled, and Living Arrangements. Slightly over half of the sample reported being coupled (50.8 percent), and slightly under half reported being single (46.5 percent). Of those who were coupled, 71.4 percent lived together, and although 47 percent reported being single, only 29 percent reported living alone. From another perspective, a little less than one-third of the respondents lived alone, and a little more than one-third lived as a couple. The other 34.7 percent lived with a female friend (19.9 percent), with their parents or other relatives (6.1 percent), or with a male (7.0 percent).

Religion. Previous studies providing information about the religious affiliation of lesbian women, and using the conventional categories of Protestant, Catholic, Jewish, other, and none, have reported the following percentages responding to the "none" category: Kenyon (1968), 22 percent; Thompson, McCandless, and Strickland (1971), 29.7 percent; Oberstone (1974), 44 percent; and Freedman (1967), 51.6 percent. Kenyon appears to be the only one of this group who specifically asked whether his subjects actually practiced a religion. He found that 72.4 percent did not, so that although about one-fourth to one-half of other samples have reported no religion, the Kenyon study indicated that about three-fourths did not participate in religious activities.

This research provided a sixth option to the conventional religious categories which said, "I have spiritual beliefs that do not fit a formal religion." Nearly one-half of the total sample checked this response (46.4 percent), while another 27 percent ascribed to one of the institutionalized religions. Thus, a total of 73.4 percent indicated a belief in a spiritual philosophy of some nature, and 25.9 percent reported none. The reformulation of the question, then, produced almost a reversal of the Kenyon findings.

Respondents were also asked under what conditions they might attend religious services, given the following options: (1) where gay people were genuinely accepted; (2) for gay people only; and (3) for women only. The first was chosen by 23.7 percent; the second, by 4.7 percent, the third, by 19.6 percent; combinations of these, by 2.5 percent; and half of the sample (49.5 percent) either did not respond or wrote in comments indicating "none of the above."

Fathers' Occupations and Family's Economic Status. Both these items on the questionnaire sought to ascertain the respondents' socioeconomic status prior to adulthood. Fathers' occupations were coded by the Hollingshead (1957) 7-point occupational scale. The second question (question 5) simply asked the respondents to indicate their family's economic status when they were growing up, given the options of wealthy, upper middle-income, lower middle-income, and poor. The correspondence between the results of these two approaches is shown in table B-2.

These results suggest that when only a broad classification is necessary, self-report on economic status of family of origin may be as reliable an indicator as a complete status-rating scheme which involves a very time-consuming process. In this research, the self-report item also yielded a higher percentage of responses.

Table B-2
Comparison of Results from Fathers' Occupational Ratings and Self-Report on Family of Origin's Economic Status

Father's Occupation		Difference	Percentage Family's Economic Status	
Level 1 or 2	37.3	6.0	43.3	Wealthy or upper middle
Levels 3 to 7	48.9	6.5	55.4	Lower-middle or poor
Reported	86.2		98.7	Reported
Missing data	13.8		1.3	Missing data

Respondents were also asked to indicate their mothers' occupations. Since currently no scales are available for ascertaining socioeconomic status with formulas that take into consideration the effect of two working parents, the Hollingshead (1957) 7-point occupational scale was used here only in reference to fathers' and respondents' occupational classifications. Mothers' occupations were not coded for data analysis, but a hand counting of responses indicated that approximately 40 percent were reported to be housewives, and data were missing for about 15 percent. Thus, it is estimated that approximately 45 percent of respondents' mothers were employed, a similar figure to that reported by Van Dusen and Sheldon (1976) that 45 percent of married women in the United States are working.

Education. More than twice as many respondents have completed four years of college as in the general white female population (15.7 versus 7.0 percent), and more than nine times as many respondents have five or more years of college (28.3 versus 3.0 percent) (Bureau of the Census 1975). In sum, 44 percent of the sample have a college degree or more, compared to 10 percent of the general white female population. This finding is similar to that reported by Henry (1955) who, in reference to homosexual men, found that there were nearly four times as many college graduates among homosexual men as in the general census group (42 versus 11.7 percent). Other studies (Kenyon 1968; Wilson and Greene 1971) have also found lesbian women to have higher educational levels than nonlesbian women.

Additionally, 19 percent of the sample reported their current occupation as student, or almost one in five. Thus, of the total sample, about three out of five already have or are working toward a college degree (63 percent).

Occupation. Also by using the Hollingshead (1957) 7-point occupational scale, respondents' occupations were found to be fairly evenly distributed between upper- and lower-status occupations (39.1 percent in upper three levels; 35 percent in lower four levels; remaining 19 percent, students).

Socioeconomic Status (SES). About one-fourth of the sample were in classes I and II, and 21.6 percent were in classes IV and V, a fairly even distribution above and below class III. By a selected coding convention, the student population was entered in class III, thus inflating this figure by 19 percent. Class III without the student population would nonetheless still be the mode of the distribution with 27.4 percent of the sample. Data were not available on 7.2 percent of the sample.

Income. The mean income of the sample was $4,739, which is slightly above the general census figure for all white females (mean = $4,328) and considerably below the mean income of white males with a seventh-grade education or less ($5,874) (Bureau of the Census 1975). Notably, almost one in seven had a professional degree while about one in fifteen had an income over $16,000.

Source of Income. About 63 percent of the respondents were self-supported, while about 37 percent received some other form of support. It should be noted, however, that 19 percent of the sample were students and that a high unemployment rate existed in California at the time of this study. (For example, the Bay area rate of unemployment in July 1975 was 10.6 percent.)

Kinsey Scale (1948). Of respondents 87 percent indicated a largely homosexual history, 5.3 percent indicated a largely heterosexual history, 6.4 percent indicated an equal homosexual-heterosexual history. Nineteen percent rated themselves exclusively homosexual; thus, 81 percent of respondents have had some heterosexual experience. This figure is slightly higher than comparable figures from other studies: Daughters of Bilitis (1959), 62 percent; Gundlach and Riess (1968), 75 percent; Kenyon (1968), 62.6 percent; and Saghir and Robins (1969), 79 percent.

Homophile Organizations. Since much of the previous research on lesbian women has utilized the membership of the Daughters of Bilitis as their sample source, it was a matter of interest to determine how many respondents in this sample were of this membership. It was found that 93.2 percent were not, 1.3 percent were, and 5.5 percent did not respond. Respondents were also asked if they belonged to any other homophile organizations. The results showed that 75.1 percent did not and 17.6 percent did. Judging from the write-ins on this question, respondents who did belong to another organization were typically referring to more recently created groups such as the Lesbian Feminists and groups formed at gay and women's centers, rather than the other older, established organizations.

Original Residence. It was found that 35.6 percent of the total sample were native Californians, so that about 64 percent were from other places. These other places included forty states and twelve other countries. Thus, while 80 percent of the sample currently resided in California, only 36 percent were indigenous.

References

Bureau of the Census. In *The World Almanac*. New York: Newspaper Enterprise Association, 1975.

Daughters of Bilitis, Editorial staff. "Some comparisons about lesbians." *The Ladder* 3 (September 1959):4-26.

Freedman, M.J. "Homosexuality among women and psychological adjustment." Doctoral dissertation, Case Western Reserve University, 1967. *Dissertation Abstracts* 28/10-B (1967):4294 (University Microfilms No. 68-03308).

Gundlach, R.H., and Riess, B.F. "Self and sexual identity in the female: A study of female homosexuals." In *New Directions in Mental Health*, vol. 1, edited by B.F. Riess. New York: Grune & Stratton, 1968.

Henry, G. *All the Sexes: A Study of Masculinity and Feminity*. New York: Rinehart, 1955.

Hollingshead, A. *Two-Factor Index of Social Position*. New Haven, Conn.: privately printed, 1957.

Kenyon, F.E. "Studies in female homosexuality, 4 and 5." *British Journal of Psychiatry* 114 (1968):1337-1350.

Oberstone, A.K. "Dimensions of psychological adjustment and style of life in single lesbians and single heterosexual women." Doctoral dissertation, California School of Professional Psychology, 1974. *Dissertation Abstracts* 35/10-B (1974):5088 (University Microfilms No. 75-8510).

Saghir, M., and Robins, E. "Homosexuality. I. Sexual behavior of the female homosexual." *Archives of General Psychiatry* 20 (1969):192-201.

Thompson, N.L.; McCandless, B.R.; and Strickland, B.R. "Personal adjustment of male and female homosexuals and heterosexuals." *Journal of Abnormal Psychology* 78 (1971):237-240.

Van Dusen, R., and Sheldon, E. "The changing status of American women: A life cycle perspective." *American Psychologist* 31 (1976):106-116.

Wilson, M.L., and Greene, R.L. "Personality characteristics of female homosexuals." *Psychological Reports* 28 (1971):407-412.

Appendix C: Questionnaire

1. Age:
   ____ Under 21
   ____ 21-25
   ____ 26-30
   ____ 31-35
   ____ 36-40
   ____ 41-50
   ____ 51 and over

2. Race:
   ____ White
   ____ Black
   ____ Spanish-speaking
   ____ Asian
   ____ Other

3. Education:
   ____ Did not finish high school
   ____ High school graduate (or passed GED)
   ____ 1-2 years college or business-trade school
   ____ 3-4 years college
   ____ College graduate
   ____ Postgraduate work
   ____ Professional degree (M.A., Ph.D., M.D., LL.B., etc.)

4. *a.* Father's occupation: _____
   b. Mother's occupation: _____
   c. Your occupation: _____

5. My family's economic status when I was growing up could best be described as:
   ____ Wealthy
   ____ Upper middle income
   ____ Lower middle income
   ____ Poor

6. Indicate your usual regular source of income:
   ____ Salaried job
   ____ Own business, craft
   ____ Inheritance, trust fund
   ____ Parent(s)
   ____ Student loan, grant, etc.
   ____ Social security, welfare, unemployment
   ____ Mate supports me
   ____ Illegal means

7. About how much was your gross income last year?

     ____ Under $3,000
     ____ 3,000- 4,999
     ____ 5,000- 7,999
     ____ 8,000-11,999
     ____ 12,000-15,999
     ____ Over 16,000

8. Parents' religion:

     ____ Protestant
     ____ Catholic
     ____ Jewish
     ____ None
     ____ Other

9. Your religion:

     ____ Protestant
     ____ Catholic
     ____ Jewish
     ____ None
     ____ Other
     ____ I have spiritual beliefs that do not fit a formal religion

10. *a.* (Circle one) I do/do not attend religious services now.

    b. I might attend religious service (check one)

        ____ Where gay people were genuinely accepted
        ____ For gay people only
        ____ For women only

11. Check one of the following which best describes your legal marital status:

     ____ Never married
     ____ Married now in name only (e.g., to a gay male, for U.S. citizenship, or other circumstances requiring a "paper" marriage)
     ____ Was married; divorced or separated before interest in female relationship
     ____ Was married; divorced or separated for female relationship
     ____ Married now and live with husband
     ____ Other (please specify) _____

12. If same-sex marriages were legally and socially sanctioned,

_____ I probably would have married at some time in the past, but no longer think I would.

_____ I probably would get married now or at some time in the future.

_____ I would never want to be legally married.

13. Have you had any children? (circle one)

None   1   2   3   4   5 or more

14. *a.* If so, they_____ do not live with me

_____ live with me

_____ live with me part-time

_____ are older and on their own

b. If not, check whichever of the following best describes your feelings:

_____ I have no desire to have a child.

_____ At some time in the past, I wanted to have or adopt a child, but no longer think about it.

_____ At some time in the future, I may want to have or adopt a child.

_____ I would like to help raise a child of my partner's.

15. What is your present living arrangement?

_____ Live by myself

_____ With one or both parents or other relatives

_____ Lesbian couple

_____ With one or more female friends

_____ With husband

_____ With one or more gay males

_____ With one or more straight males

16. In what city or area do you live now? _____

17. Where were you primarily brought up?

a. State or region _____
Country (if not U.S.) _____

b. (Check one)

_____ City

_____ Suburb

_____ Rural

18. *a.* Father's birthdate or astrological sign _____
    b. Mother's birthdate or astrological sign _____
    c. Your birthdate or astrological sign _____

19. *a.* I am a member of the Daughters of Bilitis: ____ Yes
                                                     ____ No

    b. Of another homophile organization? ____ Yes
                                             ____ No

    c. I am not a member of any, but I know women who are:
          ____ Yes
          ____ No

20. Please rate yourself on the Kinsey scale: (Circle one)

    0   1   2   3   4   5   6   X

    0 = entirely heterosexual
    1 = largely heterosexual but with incidental homosexual history
    2 = largely heterosexual but with a distinct homosexual history
    3 = equally heterosexual and homosexual
    4 = largely homosexual but with a distinct heterosexual history
    5 = largely homosexual but with incidental heterosexual history
    6 = entirely homosexual
    X = without either

21. I would rate my sex drive in respect to that of other women as:

    _____ Excessively high
    _____ Above average
    _____ Average
    _____ Below average

22. I am ____ never   sexually attracted to men
         ____ rarely
         ____ occasionally
         ____ equally
         ____ more

23. Unless your response to the last was "never," please answer the
    following:

    When I do find a man sexually attractive, he is generally, in com-
    parison to other men,

                          ____ more masculine ____
    a. physically   ____ not distinctive ____   *b.* psychologically
                          ____ more feminine ____

24. *a.* I consider myself to be:

_____ More masculine than feminine
_____ More feminine than masculine
_____ Equally masculine and feminine

    b. I prefer a mate who is:

_____ More masculine than feminine
_____ More feminine than masculine
_____ Equally masculine and feminine

25. Check the one which suits you best:

_____ I prefer my partner to initiate love-making.
_____ I prefer to initiate love-making.
_____ Doesn't make any difference.

26. I am presently _____ Single
                                _____ Coupled

27 In a relationship with another woman, I would: (check one)

_____ Expect sexual fidelity
_____ Want both of us to be free to have affairs

28. Check one of the following which best expresses your viewpoint:

_____ I believe lasting relationships are possible and desirable.
_____ I believe relationships can be good for awhile, but don't expect them to last.
_____ I prefer not to get involved with only one person so I'm free to do whatever I choose.

29. Indicate with a checkmark those persons who know that you are gay: (if deceased, check if they did know)

_____ Mother   _____ Close friends
_____ Father   _____ People I work with
_____ Sisters/brothers   _____ Practically everyone I know
_____ Other relatives   _____ Practically no one I know

30. (Check one) When out in public,

_____ I feel like anyone who looks at me could guess I'm gay.
_____ I feel like only other gay people might think I'm gay.
_____ I don't think it would occur to anyone that I'm gay.

31. (Check one) When out in public,

_____ I would rather not be seen with anyone who was obviously gay.
_____ It wouldn't matter.

32. Would your job or business be in jeopardy if your homosexuality were known?

_____ Definitely yes
_____ Probably
_____ Don't know
_____ No

33. Indicate with a checkmark the following statements which apply to your childhood: "As a child, I . . ."

_____ Had physical fights
_____ Played "house" with myself as mother
_____ Played with guns
_____ Played "mother with dolls"
_____ Excelled in athletics
_____ Played "getting married"
_____ Disliked dolls
_____ Played "having a baby"
_____ Preferred boys' games
_____ Played "grown-up lady"
_____ Played mostly with boys
_____ Played mostly with girls
_____ Was regarded as a "tomboy"
_____ Was regarded as a "little lady"

34. If your mother worked outside the home, indicate at what age period:

_____ Did not work
_____ Always worked
_____ Infancy
_____ Childhood
_____ Adolescence

35. *a.* In your family, which parent was primarily responsible for the following: (In the left-hand column, indicate F for father, M for mother, and B for both about equally.)

    b. In a couple relationship, I would prefer the following to be a responsibility of: (In the right-hand column, indicate M for mine, P for partner's and B for both of us about equally.)

a.   *b.*

____   Deciding where we lived   ____
____   Cooking   ____
____   Mowing yard, gardening, etc.   ____
____   Housecleaning   ____
____   Handling the finances   ____
____   Laundry   ____
____   Car repairs   ____
____   Arranging social activities   ____
____   Driving the car   ____
____   Caring for pets or children   ____
____   Household repairs   ____
____   Buying groceries   ____
____   Earning the income   ____
____   Choosing friends   ____

36. (Circle one) I have/have not been hospitalized for "mental illness."

37 Are you now, or have you ever been, in individual or group psychotherapy?

____ Yes
____ No (skip 38 and 39)

38. *a.* It is/was ____ not at all helpful.
                    ____ fairly
                    ____ very
      b. It is/was destructive ____.

39. Therapist is/was (*a*) male   ____   (*b*) straight   ____
                          female ____   gay   ____
                                                      don't know ____

40. If I ever felt the need for professional counseling, I would prefer to see a (Rank in order of preference, 1 through 4):

a. ____ Straight male   *b.* ____ Wouldn't matter
      ____ Gay male
      ____ Straight female
      ____ Gay female

41. Regarding your use of drugs *in the past*, check the appropriate column for each of the following:

Never used or only once/twice	Occasionally used	Frequently used	Was dependent on	
				Alcohol
				Marijuana/hash
				Psychedelics
				Cocaine
				Amphetamines
				Barbiturates
				Heroin

42. Regarding your use of drugs *in the present*, check the appropriate column for each of the following:

Never use	occasionally use	Frequently use	Am dependent on	
				Alcohol
				Marijuana/hash
				Psychedelics
				Cocaine
				Amphetamines
				Barbiturates
				Heroin

43. If there has been a significant change in your use of drugs from past to present, please indicate the most important reason under (*a*) or (*b*), whichever is appropriate:

  a. *Less use* (Check one)
      ____ Bad trips
      ____ More health-conscious
      ____ Spiritual beliefs
      ____ Too expensive
      ____ Psychiatric/medical intervention
      ____ Got busted
      ____ Other (please specify:) _____

  b. *More use* (Check one)
      ____ Pleasure
      ____ Addiction
      ____ More available
      ____ Under more stress
      ____ Other (please specify:) _____

44. Check whichever of the following is applicable to you:

_____ Never felt suicidal
_____ Felt suicidal but no attempt made   Number of times:
_____ Attempted suicide; no medical atten-
       tion required   _____
_____ Attempted suicide; medical attention
       required   _____

45. *a.* Have you ever provided sexual services for money?

        _____ Yes
        _____ No

    b. If yes, indicate frequency:

        _____ Regularly
        _____ Occasionally
        _____ Only a few times
        _____ One person only

46. Most of my close friends are:

    a. _____ Male
        _____ Female
        _____ Equally male and female

    b. _____ Gay
        _____ Straight
        _____ Equally gay and straight

47. I have the most difficulty relating to (rank 1 = most difficult and 2 = second most difficult):

_____ Straight men
_____ Gay men
_____ Straight women
_____ Gay women

48. To me, the most unattractive aspects of heterosexual relationships are (Please rank 1 through 4):

_____ Society's assumption of male dominance and superiority
_____ Birth control, abortion, pregnancy concerns
_____ Intercourse
_____ Women's role expectations
_____ Lack of emotional involvement
_____ Lack of knowledge of female sexuality

49. Check one of the following that comes closest to expressing your viewpoint:

_____ Capitalism is the best system, and it works pretty well for most everyone.

_____ Capitalism may be the best system, but so far it doesn't seem to work very well for some.

_____ The present power structure must be radically changed before capitalism can work for most everyone.

_____ The means of producing and distributing goods and services must be radically changed before any system can work for everyone.

_____ All formal governments are corrupt; all of them should be eliminated.

50. If you belong to more than one oppressed group, please rank "1" that which you feel has caused the most stress in your life, "2" second most stressful:

_____ Being female
_____ Being gay
_____ Race or ethnicity
_____ Other (specify: _____)
_____ Have never felt oppressed

51. The following are goals in life with varying importance to different people. Please rank them (1 through 6) in importance to you:

_____ Financial security
_____ Notable achievement or a sense of satisfaction in my work
_____ A stable love relationship
_____ Spiritual growth
_____ A few dependable, trustworthy friends
_____ Good sexual relations

52. (Circle one) I have/have not participated in gay or feminist consciousness-raising groups.

53. (Circle one) I have/have not read recent books or literature on lesbian women.

Index

Index

Abortions, 19, 139
Achievement motivation, 23
Affiliative resources, 117-120
Age: and attitude toward child-rearing, 59-61; and income, 101; and attitude toward monogamy, 58-59, 61; and socialization, 29; and socioeconomic status, 101, 160; and stress, 97, 98, 101, 103
Aggression, 23, 25, 26
Aid to Families with Dependent Children program, 141
Alcoholism, 57, 91, 115, 177
Alienation, 83
Allen, D., 39
Allport, G.W., 8, 55, 78-79, 97, 109, 117-118, 123, 124, 143, 145-147, 153, 160-161
Androgens, 12, 13
Androgyny, 7, 17, 39-48, 135, 155; and self-esteem, 112-113
Animals, homosexuality in, 14-15
Anomie, 86
Anti-Semitism, 79
Anti-shame exercise, 148
Antonovsky, A., 161
Anxiety, 43
Armed Forces, women in, 54
Armon, V., 42-43
Aronson, E., 177-178
Assertiveness, 41-42
Assertive training, 147
Assimilation, 123
Authoritarian personality, 157

Baer, J., 147
Bars and clubs, 137, 153, 154, 156, 157-159
Beck, A., 144
Belief systems. See Value system
Bell, A., 142
Bem, D., 39, 41-42
Bene, E., 17
Bernard, J., 43

Bettleheim, B., 160-161
Biophysical characteristics; and causes of lesbianism, 11-17, 54, 80; and coping with stress, 111, 112, 113
Birth control, 19, 139
Bisexuality, 17, 28, 48
Blacks, 79, 83-84, 157
Blaming the victim. See Individual-deficiency model
Bloom, B.S., 26
Broverman, I.K., 40, 42, 45
Brown, G.W., 72-73

California, 5
Cancer, cervical, 19, 142
Cannon, M., 44
Caste, women as, 54
Castration complex, 18
Catatonia, 115
Causal theories of lesbianism, 6-7, 11-32; biophysical, 11-17, 54, 80; psychological, 6, 15-16, 17-22, 42-46, 54, 57, 133-134; sociological, 22-32, 54, 56-57
Cervix, 12; cancer of, 19, 142
Chafetz, J., 31, 62-63, 155
Chester, P., 57
Child abuse, 140
Childhood: and coping, 108-109; and sociosexual orientation, 6-7, 11, 17-18, 22-32, 133-134
Child-rearing, attitude toward, 59-61
Chinese immigrants and stress, 76
Chromosomes, 11-13
Civil Service, women in, 54
Class: and lesbian women, 155-159; and sex role development, 25. See also Socioeconomic status
Cloward, R., 86-87
Cognitive-developmental model, 23, 24, 26, 112
Cognitive dissonance, 83, 143, 145, 148, 154

213

Kardiner, A., 79
Kasl, S., 84
Kaye, H., 17, 21
Keller, S., 41, 45, 142
Kennedy, John F., 179
Kenyon, F.E., 18, 21
Kinsey, W.C., 8, 14, 21
Kinsey scale, 17, 28

Lawyers, women as, 54
Lesbian, 8
Lesbian women: and age, 58-61, 97,
98, 101; and androgyny, 7, 39-48,
135, 155; causal theories of, 6-7,
11-32, 54, 57, 80, 133-134; and
child-rearing, 59-61; and class,
155-159; courting behavior of, 137;
and deviant activity, 91, 93-94, 96,
98, 99, 100-101, 102, 155, 157, 158,
177; and disclosure, 63-64, 95-96,
98, 100-101, 102-103, 137, 167-172;
and drug use, 91, 93, 94, 102, 155,
157, 158, 177; and economic stress,
7, 62-65, 96, 101, 137, 170, 174-175;
educational levels of, 45, 62, 160;
and attitudes toward family, 7,
58-61; femininity, 46-48; and
feminist movement, 97-98, 101-102,
103; health of, 19, 142; heterosexual
histories, 8, 19-20, 21-22, 29, 61;
hospitalization for mental illness,
93; identity conflicts, 136-149; illegal activities of, 93-94, 96, 98, 99,
101; income, 64, 101; life goals of,
61, 62; males, attitudes toward,
19-20, 47; and marriage experience,
61; masculinity, 46-48, 135, 155;
and mobility, 159-162, 176; and attitude toward monogamy, 58-59, 60,
61; as mothers, 60; number of, 5;
organizations for, 15; and parents,
17-18, 21, 24, 134; partners, 47;
political orientation, 58-59, 60, 64,
157; and politics, 29, 30, 162-164,
176-179; and prostitution, 93-94, 99,
101; self-destructive behavior, 144;
and self-esteem, 135-136, 147, 148-
149, 161, 173-174; and sex roles, 9,

23-32, 134, 155-156; social life,
137-138; socioeconomic status,
59-60, 95, 99-100, 101, 103,
159-160; stress response, 91-104;
studies of deficiencies in, 15-17; and
suicide, 91, 93, 144, 177; and
therapy, 144-145; and visibility, 95,
96, 98, 99-100, 155
Lieberman, M.A., 73, 108, 116, 117
Life goals, 120, 124, 125; of lesbian
women, 61, 62
Life stages, 26, 29
Lindenthal, J.J., 73
Love, B., 96
Lower class: culture, 154-155; and sex-
role development, 25; and visibility,
100
Lower-middle class, 156-157
Loyalties. See Affiliative resources

Maccoby, E.E., 23, 24, 27
Males: aggressiveness, 25, 26; attractive
characteristics to lesbian women,
47; aversion to, 19-20; crimes by,
141; dominance by, 29-30, 31-32;
earnings of, 54; femininity of, 47;
homosexual, 62; homosexual experiences, 8; and marriage, 44, 140;
and mental-health criteria, 40-41;
reward systems of, 47-48; satiation
with, 18, 20; sex-role development
of, 23-24, 25-27; and sexual fidelity,
59; sexuality of, 141; venereal
disease rate of, 19, 142
Male-supremacy system. See Patriarchal system
Mander, A., 104
Marriage: declining rate of, 62, 140;
and lesbian women, 61; psychological adjustment by women,
15-17, 41-44; same-sex, 58, 59, 61
Martin, C.E., 8, 14
Masculine characteristics, 6; biological,
11-13; and lesbian women, 46-48,
135, 155; psychological, 17-22; and
self-concept, 39-40, 135; and socialization, 23-24, 25-27. See also Males
Maslow, A.H., 29-30, 136

About the Author

Virginia R. Brooks is currently a professor of graduate social work at the University of Houston. She received the D.S.W. from the University of California at Berkeley in 1977. She has taught in graduate schools of social work for nine years and, before that, worked for many years in public welfare. She is currently working on a second book, *Human Behavior: A Systems Approach to Stress*, and has published articles in *Sex Roles* and *Clinical Social Work*.